Growing Intellectually, Spiritually and Prophetically in the Hebrew Israelite Culture and Faith

Growing Intellectually, Spiritually and Prophetically in the Hebrew Israelite Culture and Faith

A Guide for African Edenic Hebrews, Jews and Gentiles searching the Israelite Scriptures for Truth!

Rabbi Shalomim Halevi Ph.D
Leader of the
Israelite Torah Covenant Community Inc

Writers Club Press
San Jose New York Lincoln Shanghai

Growing Intellectually, Spiritually and Prophetically in the Hebrew
Israelite Culture and Faith
A Guide for African Edenic Hebrews, Jews and Gentiles searching the
Israelite Scriptures for Truth!

Writers Club Press
an imprint of iUniverse.com, Inc.

For information address:
iUniverse.com, Inc.
5220 S 16th, Ste. 200
Lincoln, NE 68512
www.iuniverse.com

Author has taken the liberty to retranslate or Transliterate verses and names
where it was felt necessary to clarify more accuratley the passage(s), locations
or names of characters in the Scriptures. In Keeping with the modern move to
restore the Divine name, Author has taken Liberty to replaced the pagan words
LORD found in modern scripture with the proper Hebrew name of the Eternal
Creator as ,Yahweh, Yah or the tetragrammaton YHWH; *Lord* with Adonai,
and the title *God* with Almighty, mightyone(s) or Elohim.

ISBN: 0-595-17699-2

Printed in the United States of America

This book is Dedicated to my Three Sons of Light, HaNasi Mashiakh-Kohane(3), Meshakh Yahqim-Shalom(1) and Yishai HaRukhammah-Ammi(10mths); The Two royal Israelite Ishahim who birth, raise and nurture them in the Spirit of Yah according to his Torah... and my long time friend, Minister Michael Albertie Jr., In whom I pray Yah will fully ingraft into the Israelite Community and Eternal Kindom very soon!!

"For it is time, oh Yahweh, to Work; for they have made void thy TORAH(LAW)" **Tehillah(Psalms) 119:126**

"To the Torah and to the Witness, If they speak not according to this Word; it is because there is NO Light in them" **Yeshiyah(Isaiah 8:20)**

Contents

Introduction xi

Chapter 1 1
Section 1 [Definition of YAHUDAISM] 1
Section 2 [YHWH, the forgotten father and creator] 13
Section 3 Unity Of Yahweh 38

Chapter 2 44
Section 1 Torah   Covenant   CommunityDevelopmental   Covenant
        Theology 44
Section 2 Covenant of Provision-The Torah Community 84
Section 3 Torah, Yishra'ala culture, the way of life for the Hebrew
        Community 103

Chapter 3 111
Section 1 111
Section 2 Origins of the Renewed Covenant Movement in 1st Century
        Israel 118
Section 3 Messiah(s) Concept and the Son of Yahweh 125

Chapter 4 139
Section 1 PaRDes The Four Levels of Biblical Interpretation &
        Understanding 139

Chapter 5 144
Section 1 144
Section 2 Biblical HolyDays or Festivals of Yah (the Witnessess) 165
Section 3 S'mikhah The Practice of Laying on of Hands 185

Section 4 Torah Instructions on Dietary and Healithness and Briefing of other Customs and Practices 188

About the Author 209
Appendix 211
Statement of Faith for Israelite Torah Covenant Community 211
Guiding Principles for "Israelite Torah Covenant Community" 213

Introduction

This is the season and time that Yahweh (Ya-u-ah) the True Eternal Creator of the heavens and earth, the heavenly Father and author of the Hebrew Israelites, his Chosen, is once again restoring his people to his Universal Laws that are relative to the establishing a Kingdom and World where Truth, greatness, prosperity and purpose reign. These universal Principles are set in motion waiting to be tapped into and activated by the Men, women and children who has inherited the Yah mind, to create a renewed World void of sickness, disease, war, pestilence, immorality, and all of the destructive abominations that Euro-gentile man has created to annihalate his environment, himself, and those around him.

In the great awakening of the ancient Hebrew Israelite movement from the four corners of the earth, many a leaders both Cushite(African) and European, writers, singers and artistic have arisen and have found the lost history of the so-called Black America. The History, artafacts, and African presence of the Scriptures has been felt, with both warm reception and controversy. We have been told who we are, where we came from and who we should worship. The dry bones have been spoken to, but now we are in need of fixing those bones and giving form and growth to the body in whose bones have arisen. This Body is the African Edenic people of Yishra'ala..

Now that we have returned to Yah and are seeking his Torah, we must began our journey in growing Intellectually, Spiritually and Prophetically in his Purpose and calling for our very lives. We must take the necessary steps from being Babys In Yah to becoming Spiritual adults who bare the fruits of Righteousness and wisdom in Yah's Kingdom.

We must die to the Spirit, mind, mentality, Religions and ways of our Euro-gentile oppressors in which we have lived for 500 plus years, and learn to live, with a renewed mind, in the culture and lifestyle of the Yah Kingdom, the Israelite Torah Covenant Community. We must take heed and build off of where we came from originally(Eden) so that we can take our own destiny and determine where we are going, purposefully.

Yahweh has/is raising up Anointed Hebrew Messiah(s) and Leaders to teach, guide and Spiritually prepare Yishra'ala for the Great and Awesome day in which Yah will return and Set the Messianic Kingdom in full motion through-out the Earth. Yisrael must be prepared for it is through them(us) as a nation that Yah will return to bring redemption and salvation to all.

This book is such a book to help in the Spiritual preparation of Yishra'ala, along with other leaders such as Ben Ammi ben Yishra'ala in Dimona, Yishra'ala, Kohane Micheal Ben Levi and many other great spiritual Hebrew Messiahs(anointed ones).

We as African Edenic Israelites, the fullness of the Adahmic Lineage must take hold of the keys to obtaining truth and use them effectively in opening up the Windows of Yah to reinforce his promise of redemption for all. This book is just one approach and view to obtaining such keys.

Chapter 1

The Elementary "principles" the Hebrew Faith

Section 1-[Definition of YAHUDAISM]

We can define YAHUDAISM as *"the biblical faith and religious culture and Traditions of the descendants of* **Yishra'ala** *(Ya'akob)."* It is the Faith of the Hebrew (YaHudim) and Hebrew Believers (YaHudaim proselytes). YAHUDAISM is and will always be the **Faith, culture** and **practice** that the Eternal Creator, **YHWH,** introduced to humankind, through Abraham, and Fully Established as a religious community/Nation, through Moshe.

Bereshit (Genesis) 12:1-3, "Now YHWH had said to Abram, 'Get out of your country, from your kindred and from your father's house to a land that I will show you. I will make you a great nation; I will bless you and make your name great: and you shall be a blessing. I will bless those who bless you and curse those who curse you and in you all the families of the earth shall be blessed.'"

*Bereshit 17:27, "I will establish my **B'rith** (covenant) between me and you and I will make you exceedingly numerous. As for me, this is the B'rith with you: you shall be a **father** of a multitude of nations*

*I will maintain my B'rith (covenant) between me and you and your off-spring to come, as an **everlasting B'rith** throughout the ages, to be father and supporter to you and your offspring to come."*

YAHUDAISM is the everlasting contract/covenant between the children of Yishra'ala (Hebrews) and **YHWH** the one true Creator of the universe. Everlasting means, *"forever."* This denotes that this B'rith cannot and will not be changed. If any changes do seem to occur as in to alter or change the original B'rith, it was because humankind tampered with the B'rith not **YHWH***(i.e., Exodus 6:6-8).*

YAHUDAISM was actually given as the name for the Way the Hebrew Yishra'alites lived after the Nation split into a southern nation, Yahudah, and a northern nation, Yishra'ala. The Yishra'alites tribes that dwelled in Yahudah followed the traditional path and customs of their forefathers and they Worshiped YHWH as their sole Creator, while Yishra'ala, the northern nation, went astray of the Traditions of our forefathers, Abraham, Yitzkak, Ya'akob and Moshe. They incorporated pagan sacrifice, both human and animal, and they also worshiped pagan deities'. Their chief deity was Allah'im. Those Hebrew Yishra'alites who lived in Yahudah(later known as Judea) became known as YaHudaim(Yahudiys) and YAHUDAISM was used to identify their African Edenic Hebrew culture and faith. Today when I reference that we are Hebrew YaHudaim, I am speaking of the Hebrew Yishra'alites that dwelled in Yahudah, after the Kingdom split, and worship YHWH as opposed to Allah'im. Any Hebrew from any of the Twelve tribes of Yishra'ala, or a Torah observant Edomite(European Jews) or Yishra'alite(Arab) can be a Hebrew YaHudaim as far as the Tradition and Yahwistic Faith goes.

[HEBREW DEFINITION]

YAHUDAISM in itself is from the Hebrew word **Yahudah (Judah)** which means, *"praise and worship of YHWH."* As we should understand, *praise and worship* is a spiritual aspect. **YHWH** is *Ruakh (spirit)*, and he desires us to worship him in his Ruakh (spirit). Therefore ordained by the eternal creator, YAHUDAISM is *"the religion and culture of praise and worship of the Eternal Creator of Yishra'ala."* Every teaching, ritual, ceremony and festival of the **Torah** is a witness of a spiritual truth of *praise and worship* of YHWH. This means that a true Hebrew or Hebrew proselyte and adherer to YAHUDAISM must have a measure of praise and worship of YHWH in the fruit of his life and lifestyle(Psalm 33:1-3, Lev. 19:24, Deut. 10:20-21).

YirmeYah(Jeremiah) *13:11, "For as the sash clings to the waist of a man, so have I caused the whole house of Yahudah to cling to me," says* YHWH, ' *that they may become known for* **praise** *and for* **glory.**'"

[Definition of YaHudaim]

YaHudaim(plural) is also derived from the word **Yahudah** which means, *"praise and worship of YHWH."* Yahudah was also the son of Leah born to Ya'akob (Jacob). He is one of the founders of the 12 tribes of Yishra'ala. YaHudaim in the Natural sense are the physical descendants of the tribe of Yahudah (Judah, Duet 29:35). They are 1/12 of the Hebrew Yishra'alites.

YaHudaim can be classified into two categories; 1.*Physical YaHudaim* 2.*Spiritual YaHudaim&/or Hebrew proselytes.* The physical YaHudaim 'only' without YAHUDAISM or worship of **YHWH** is *"a descendant of Yahudah who could be an atheist, pagan or a religious/Cultural apostate* (i.e., Christian/Islamic converts)."

The spiritual YaHudaim/Hebrew is *"one who is either a physical descendant of Yahudah or any of the twelve Tribes or a proselyte gentile(i.e., Israelites)* who adheres to the Hebrew faith according to the Torah of Moshe' and worships YHWH 'only', who is the one true creator and Lord of the universe."

The spiritual YaHudaim/Hebrew and proselyte know YHWH as his Father and provider. He or she worships YHWH with faith and faithful obedience to YHWH's Word (Torah) and will. He or she has a true relationship with the creator, and being in total fellowship with the Ruakh Ha-Kodesh (spirit of the Holy-one), has so much confidence and assurance in his or her faith that he or she will begin to live as a testimony and light of YHWH to others.

[Characteristics]

The characteristics of a Spiritual Hebrew (see def. Of Hebrew) is *praise, worship and the countenance of the Ruakh Ha-Kodesh*(spirit of the Holy-one).

Charter of a Hebrew Sectarian Association(DSS) 4:3-8, "one enlightens a mans mind, making straight before him the paths of true righteousness and causing his heart to fear the Torah of Yah. This Spirit engenders **humility, patience abundant compassion, perpetual goodness, insight, understanding and powerful wisdom** resonating to each of Yah's deeds, sustained by his constant faithfulness. It engenders a spirit knowledgeable in every plan of action, zealous for the Laws of righteousness, holy in its thoughts, and steadfast in purpose. This Spirit encourages plenteous compassion upon all who hold fast to truth, and glorious purity combined with visceral hatred if impurity in its every guise…through a gracious visitation all who walk in this spirit will know healing, long life, and multiple progeny, followed by eternal blessings and perpetual joy through everlasting life…."*

Galatians 5:16-23, "What I am saying is this: run your lives by the Ruakh (Spirit of YHWH). Then you will not do what your old nature(evil impulse) wants. For the evil impulse wants what is contrary to the Ruakh (Spirit), and the Ruakh wants what is contrary to the evil impulse (old nature). These oppose each other."…. "but if you are led by the Ruakh, then you are not in* *subjection to the system that results from perverting the* **Torah** *into legalism (i.e., anti-Torah by Christians, vain Torah observance by many Israelites of rabbinical Judaism; manmade traditions of religion v.s. Torah observance)."...*"*But the fruit of the Ruakh is* **Love, Joy, peace, patience, kindness, goodness, 'faithfulness', humility, self control.** *Nothing in the Torah stands against things."*

Sefre' Deut. 49:85a, "But how is it possible for a man to be called by the name of the Holy One, blessed be he? As the All-present is called Compassionate and gracious, so be you also compassionate and gracious, and offering free gifts to all. As the Holy One, blessed be he is called loving, be you also loving"(Everymans Talmud pg.211, Cohen).

"**Nothing** *in the Torah stands against such things (Gal. 5:23)"*

Even Shaul(Paul) in his deception and apostasy from truth maintained in Galatians some truth of the Renewed Covenant Hebrew peoples of the Dead Sea Scrolls and the Pharisaical Peoples of the Oral Torah concerning the Characteristic of a true Hebrew or gentile. The above passages reveal the fruit of a true Hebrew. This means that this is his or her daily lifestyle both publicly and privately as he is led by YHWH's Ruakh. This is the witness to a Hebrew Israelite being immersed or having a mikveh(immersion) of the Ruakh Ha-Kodesh(Psalm 29:1-2; 30:4; YirmeYah 7:2; YeshiYah 59:21; Yechezki'ala(Ezekiel) 37:14; Yah'ala 2:28-32). The Complete YHWH inspired Hebrew/YaHudaim is the Spiritual YaHudaim.

[Definition of Hebrew]

The name Hebrew is from the Hebraic word *Ibri (Eber).* **Eber** is the grandson of Shem and the ancestor of Terah. Abrahams father (Bereshit/genesis 10:21-11:10-26). He and all his descendants were actually known as Hebrews. *Ibri(Eber)* means to *"cross over or to come from beyond."* It is by no coincidence that Abraham and his descendants (Yishma'ala/Yitzkak) is later referred to as *Hebrews.* This name did not originate with Abraham, but with his ancestor Eber. Think of this as you would think of the descendants of Yishra'ala; they are known as Yishra'alites, or of the different tribes(descendants) of Yishra'ala; they, as a group, are named after the founder of that tribe (i.e., Benyamites are descendants of Benyamin). Hebrew/Christian literature also teaches that the ancient Cana'anites or Palestinians referred to Avrahams and his people as Hebrews because he came from beyond/or crossed the Euphrates. Abraham was from Ur of Chaldee which was a city of Mesopotamia beyond the Euphrates from Cana'an(Bereshit 11:31; 14:13). However it goes, all of Abrahams descendants became known as Hebrews, including the Arabs(Yah'rabbas) and Edomites, who are also Shemites. Their culture & language became known as Hebrew which pre-existed before Abraham. The sacred scriptures that were given to the world, both the Tanakh and B'rith Chadasha(Older/Newer Covenants) were written 'originally' in Hebrew (some Aramaic and Chaldean). **A YaHudaim, Yishra'alites, or Hebrew** can be used to identify the Descendants of Abraham, Yitzkak and Ya'akob (Yishra'ala).

[Definition of Yishra'alites (Israelite)]

Yishra'ala is a Hebrew word that means, "he who prevails/rules with power or strength." Yishra'ala is the name given to Ya'akob by YHWH after Ya'akob wrestled with a Malak (Angel) of YHWH (Bereshit 32:25-31). Ya'akob is the son of Yitzkak who was the son of Abraham (Bereshit 25:19-34). In the biblical since, all of the descendants of Yishra'ala are Yishra'alites; *Simeon, Lehwi, Yahudah, Dan, Naphtali, Gad (God), Asher, Yissachar, Zebulun, Yosef, & Benyamin(Bereshit 29:32-35; 30:1-25; 35:17-18).* However, after the split of the kingdom in 933b.c.e, Yishra'ala(ites) applied only to the ten tribes of the northern kingdom until their destruction in 722b.c.e. The southern kingdom was known as Yahudah and their citizens were the YaHudaim, later to be renamed Judea (Judeans).

After the destruction of the Temple in 70c.e the Hebrews/Judeans were dispersed among the nations(again). Many intermarried with Europeans and Converted them to the Hebrew faith. Most of the Hebrew tribes were lost through time and the Judaism(a form of the Israelite Faith) became a dominant European Religion/Culture. The true Shemite(Negroid) culture was replaced with a Caucasoid Yiddishkite culture.

In 1948 when the Hebrew Yishra'alites homeland was secularly reestablished (although a spiritual event for the Beta Yishra'ala and Hebrew Yishra'alites of Dimona), it was given the name Israel. The citizens are called Israelis as opposed to Yishra'alites, and the religious (not necessarily spiritual) adherents to rabbinical Judaism are called Jews(this is a majority European Yiddish/Gentile Culture not to be confused with the now minority true Hebrew culture and worship of YHWH which is being restored in this time among Black peoples & some Europeans as prophesied).

In a corrective modern biblical since, Yishra'ala is the Homeland (present/future) of the Hebrews who are descendants of Abraham Yitzkak and Yishra'ala(Ya'akob). This fulfills the prophetic utterance of Ya'akob in Bereshit 49:9-10 & Zachariah 8:18-23.

[What is a Jew?]

For hundreds of years people have been tricked into thinking that a Jew is a European descendant of Yishra'ala fourth son Yahudah(Judah). Most people that I have come into contact today who believes that the Euro-Jews are descendants of Judah believe this for various reasons, but in particular because of Linguistic sound. For example *Jew*, sounds like a shortened form of *Judah*. Yet the two words have nothing in common. That's like trying to equate *Jephath* with *Japanese*. Many Jews, that is European Jews argue that Jew is a romanized Latin word for Judah, which was translated into English as Hebrew. How is this so? Judah is not a Hebrew word, it is an English word. Hebrew has no J sound. The correct word would be *Yahudah*..

Jew is synonymous with the German word Yiddish, which is a combination of Slavic German and Hebrew. European Jews are just that, Europeans from different European nations who have converted to a religion called Judaism a form of the Hebrew faith of Yahudah after the split of Yishra'ala.

A Jew is not a race or nationality, as some would have it to be. They are non Shemitic . A Jew is "anyone" who converts and practices the religion of Judaism, regardless of race. Most Jews are Hebrew Speaking Gentiles. They have their own culture(s), their own practices, which at times is the very opposite of Hebrew Teaching in the Torah and they have their own way of Worship.

Modern Euro-Jewish culture is called *Yiddishkite.* That speaks for itself. An Israelite can be a Jew if he converts to the Jewish religion, but a Jew cannot automatically be a Hebrew unless he is a descendant of one of the twelve tribes.

[Jewish Classifications]

European Jews are divided into two classes Ashkenazic and Saphardim. Ashkenazic Jews are descendant from the Yaphetites(Japhetites) traditions and have no Hebrew roots racially whatsoever. The Saphardim are descendants of Israelites and other Eastern cultures such as the Chinese, Indians etc...Many of them are of Shemitic origin or descendants of Esau, Edomites or one of the 10 lost tribes of Yisrael.

The African Hebrew Edomites are said to be the founders of the religion called Judaism, which started after the restoration of the 1st Temple in which many Europeans were converted to(i.e., Khazars). They are the ones who were a mixture of Babylonian, Israelite and Edomites after the people in Babylonian exile returned to the "Land of Judea". They came after the Hebrews, just like Italians came after the Greeks.

A Jew is like a Christian or Muslim, He or she had to be converted. However Euro-Jews claim that to be a born a Jew your mother has to be a

Jew. If this was the case no one should know who is a Jew after several decades. It is a serious contradiction to a person being a Jew through conversion. However anyone who spiritually and faithfully practices Judaism is a Jew which is a Gentile-Hebrew, as opposed to a heathen religion that tries to practice the faith and culture of Yishra'ala. Yet Most Jews main guide is not the Torah, but the writings of ancient Rabbis called the Talmud, an interpretation of the Torah. Any Jew of Shemitic origin is of African Origin.

Jose V. Malcioln in his book *African Origin of Modern Judaism* writes concerning Sergi, "Sergi's findings proved that if someone professes to be a Semitic(or Shemite) Jew or Hebrew, with claims of Legitimacy which do not recognize original Hebrews and Arabs or Palestinians as being of African origin, he or she must surely be a descendant of European converts or an "imposter" as Gamal Abd-an-Nasir called the Zionist."

[False Linguistics of Anti-Semitism]

People who do not identify or are against the Euro-Jewish way of Life are usually labeled *anti-Semites*, which is Pseudo-Linguistic, they are foolish terms and names. According to Jose V. Malcioln, the word "Semitic" comes from Latin; It means *'A Path'.*" This means In other words, Anti-Semites are against the Path and motives of how European Jews try to get over on people for their own gain and power, using deceit, robbery(as in Yishra'ala) and oppression. This has nothing to do with Anti-Shemitism, which includes Blacks, Arabs and other eastern races of non European origin. In this case Those Europeans and Jews, such as Zionist are the actual Anti-Shemites, which is simply racism.

Yet the good Euro-Jews are the ones who are spiritual, knowledgeable of truth and practitioners of Justice and Righteousness.

[Ethnic Origin of the Hebrews]

Most truthful scholars and lay-people with knowledge of biblical/ancient culture will agree and admit that the original Hebrews

Yishra'alites were Shemite-Cushite(Negroid; Black or dark peoples). Avrahams, a descendant of Eber and father of the YaHudaim/Hebrews, name means *father of Ra or Many"*. His name is a Hamitic Combination of *"Av"*, which is Cana'anite for **Father**, *"Ra"*, which is Egyptian after the Deity **RA**, and *"Ham"*, Which means, **many**. His geographical dwellings indicated he lived in a Cushite-Chamite black country Ur of Chaldee in Mesopotamia which was also Shemitic. You could not tell the difference between the two. There was only a distinction in culture.

If one properly studies archaeology and ancient ethnic cultures, one would see that Cham and Shem were a people of color. The Arabs for example are a Shemitic people of color and they were the 1st born of Abraham.

Victor H. Matthews in his book, *Manners and Customs in the Bible* revised addition, has written,

"What did the Patriarchs and their families look like? The Patriarchs and their families were Semites(Shemites), the dominant ethnic group in Mesopotamia and much of Syro-Palestine. Physically, Semites in the ancient Near East had black hair, were short in stature(averaging about 5 feet tall for males), with a swarthy complexion burned even darker by the sun, and a prominent flat nose."

If you study the map of Rabbi Pinchas Winston's book, *Bible Basics*, on pg. 140 (Recommend for biblical study), you will notice that the Shemites and Chamites dwelled together, especially in the land of Ethiopia (Cush)[International Traditions Corp, Boca Raton Florida].

It is by no coincidence that the Midianite, a descendant of Abraham (Bereshit 25:2), who married Moshe was an Ethiopian or Cushite (Numbers 12:1; Exodus 2:16-22), or that one of the sons of Cush was a Benyamite (psalms 7). Shlomo's Descendant Hezekiah (1Chronicles 3:13) was the great great grandfather of Cushi who was the father of the Nabi (prophet) Zephaniyah (Zephaniyah 1), making both Shlomo and his father Ha Malek David Cushite or Negroid (Black). Tradition/History shows that the Ethiopian(Cushite) Hebrews are descendants of Shlomo and the Queen of Sheba (which explains how Cushi pops up in Shlomo's descendants genealogy being the father of Zephaniyah). Zephaniyah the son of Cushi see's the Ethiopians and Yishra'alites as one and the same. This can be seen of his prophetic utterance concerning Ethiopia/Cush his fellow people:

Zephaniyah 3:8-20, "'Therefore wait for me', says Yahweh, 'Until the day I rise up for plunder; my determination is to gather the Nations.......For then I will restore to the peoples a pure language, that they may all call on my name, that they may call on the name of **Yahweh** *to serve him with one accord. From beyond the rivers of Ethiopia (Cush),* **My worshipers, the daughter** *of my dispersed ones shall bring my offering......I will leave in your mist a humble people, and they shall trust in the name of Yahweh.....Sing oh* **Daughter of Zion** *! Shout oh Yishra'ala! Be glad and rejoice with all your heart, oh* **Daughter** *of Yerushalem...... The King of Yishra'ala is in your mist.; you shall see disaster no more....I will gather those who sorrow over the appointed assembly, who are among you, to whom its reproach is a burden. Behold, at that time I will deal with all who afflict you; I will save the lame, and gather those who were driven out; I will appoint them for* **praise** *and fame in every land where they were put to shame. At that time I will bring you back, even at the time I gather you; for I will give you a name and praise among all the peoples of the earth, when I return your captives before your eyes, says Yahweh."*

Notice in this text Ethiopia is called the remnant of Yishra'ala and the Daughter of Zion. YHWH compares Yishra'ala with the Ethiopians/Cush (Amos 3:7). When YHWH speaks to YeshiYah about the restoration of Yishra'ala and gathering the Dispersed people of Yahudah he mentions Egypt and Cush(Nubia/Ethiopia), two black nations (YeshiYah 11), as part of the restoration (which is partially fulfilled in modern times with the Ethiopian Falashas called Beta Yishra'ala/ and other legitimate Hebrew sects.

It is by no coincidence that an Ethiopian(Cushite) Eunuch with a copy of the scroll of YeshiYah went to worship in the Temple in the B'rith Chadasha writings (Acts 8:27-28). Remember during 1st century YAHUDAISM in time of Yahshua of Nazareth there were no printing presses and the only people who had a copy of the Hebrew scrolls were Hebrew scholars, priest and scribes or very learned high-class Hebrews-Selah.

Ethiopian(Cushite) YAHUDAISM was traced all the way up to the slave trade in which the black slaves were cut off from their Hebrew heritage and their Descendants were taught Christianity, Islam or a Form of Rabbinical/Yiddish white-washed Judaism. Modern media Jews who are Caucasian/European are the result of proselytism and heavy intermarriage of Hebrews(i.e Edomites) and Gentiles in earlier times before Slavery of Black Hebrews (the worst holocaust).

[Note]

It should be noted that the use of Cushite, Cush or Ethiopian Jew or Hebrew does not necessarily mean that they are descendants of Chams son Cush. The land of Cush was preexistent before Cham. According to Bereshit 2:13, Cush(Kush) is one of the Oldest cities that ever existed since Creation of Mankind.

Cush means, "burnt or dark". In general all black peoples are Cushite, and since all races came from the Black man, all people in general are Cushite, so to speak. A Cushite Hebrew is an African Edenic Hebrew or original Hebrew Israelite. Remember at one time Cush or Ethiopia and "Eden" referred to the whole land of Africa. Yishra'ala or Palestine is in Northeast Africa.

Section 2 [YHWH, the forgotten father and creator]

In this season and last days, as most people believe, the name of our heavenly father, Yahweh, has been forgotten. I have experienced how people respond to the name of Yahweh. Many times when someone thinks of the name of Yahweh, they think of something negative as if it were a bad name. Many people in religious groups have never even heard of the name Yahweh, nor do they even really want to know who Yahweh is.

When I try to explain that the word LORD in the bible comes from the Hebrew name Yahweh, being ignorant as they are, they say that this is not true and that they don't believe in this. The name of Yahweh being found in the original Hebrew for the Creator is not a matter of faith or belief, it is a matter of *fact*. His name is there, whether you choose to believe it or not.

To say that you don't believe that the name Yahweh is found in the original bible is like saying you don't believe that there is a brain in your skull, which is outright ignorant! When you say you don't believe in Yahweh, you are basically an atheist, rejecting the whole of the scriptures. You cannot believe in, nor follow the Holy-scriptures correctly apart from Yahweh.

When one fails to understand Yahweh and his will, it is because one is lazy and has failed to study to be approved.

2Timothy 2:15, "do all you can to present yourself to Yahweh as someone worthy of his approval, as a worker with no need to be ashamed, because he deals straightforwardly with the **Torah** *of truth."*

YHWH name has always been in the scriptures, yet over the centuries and millennia his name has been totally forgotten. Yahweh himself has been totally forgotten.

YHWH name has been replaced with titles. And because Yahweh and his Torah has been forgotten, this world suffers and aims at the path of global destruction. Why do You think poverty, violence, wars, immorality, genocide, freaks of mother nature, demonizations of Religions and cultures abound in this time like never before? Because of increased distance from Yahweh and his Torah(MattiYah 24:1-12; Yechezki'ala 23:28-35; YirmeYah 23:25-27).

Why is it that even those who practice a form of righteousness or are religious (Christian, Israelites, Muslims etc..) seem to always end up under Satanic attack and affliction? Even those who claim to be "charismatic" and spirit-filled? Or have you ever wondered why after you've been through a serious suffering trial or tribulation and have even been victorious over Ha-Satan in one area of your life, you seem to have to fight and suffer in another area of your life? Even though you may keep winning!

Shouldn't Ha-Satan get the message the 1st time around that you have some kind of Spiritual Authority over him? No! These situations occur and re-occur with people simply because they are apart from Yahweh and his Torah, which is his everlasting covenant. No matter how righteous you think you are, you are out of his will and therefore are not protected by his Word(Torah).

Yahweh specifically gives you a choice of how you can live. And each choice comes with consequences. Every good and evil thing that happens in this world is summed up in *Deuteronomy 28*.

If You are a child of the Torah covenant according to YHWH way, one who obeys the voice of Yahweh and his Torah then you are redeemed from the curses of the Torah found in Deuteronomy 28. Yet this world suffers from the very curses found in chapter 28, when they could be living in the blessings.

No-one has to suffer from poverty, sickness, disease, oppression and catastrophes, especially if they are children of Yahweh, HaGadol Malek ha melekim, Adon ha adonim(the Great King of kings and Lord of lords). Many are Living in misery, fighting amongst one another, destroying each other and dying by the sword of Ha-Satan, every day because they don't know Yahweh!

We must first understand that without proper Hebraic scriptural understanding of the scriptures, many false doctrines and misconceived teachings can arise. If you understand demonology, then you'll know that the slightest open door for the Ha-shatanim will give them entrance into the situation and make things worst and leave a chain-link reaction of deception. This has occurred in many of the religions of the world, especially Christianity and their Cults and Islam and its Cults, because they use the Hebrew scriptures as apart of their own self proclaimed scriptures, yet reject the Hebrewness of the scriptures.

This has resulted in pagan Doctrines and teachings about the Eternal Creator and his Torah and even the Messiah (i.e. blasphemy such as the Trinity, Old testament vs. New testament, Supernatural Christ equal with the Eternal Creator).

[The Many Wrong Names]

The typical Christian, minister or religious leader without knowledge of Hebraic thought, worship and Culture will tell you that "God has many names". Most Christians call him *Jehovah*, *Lord* or *almighty*, and even *Jesus.* The Muslims call him *Allah* and Israelites call him *Hashem, Adonai,* or *Allah'im(elohim).* Almost everybody calls him *God.* Yet you have some who use his name correctly *(Yahweh or YahoWah),* but have distorted the Creators Character and misrepresented him. They either are apart of some Dooms Day sect or believe that some man is Yahweh (as in the House of Yahweh in Texas or Yahweh Ben Yahweh in Florida).

However there are those who are legitimate Yahweh inspired Groups of Israelites and Jewish groups who use the name of Yahweh correctly and worship Yahweh 'only'.

Most Christians believe that Yahweh(Jehovah/Jesus in their case) has multiple names such as "*Yahweh Nissi*; *Yahweh Shalom*; *Yahweh Tzedekinu*; *Yahweh Yirah*; *Yahweh Shammai*; F *Yahshua, Father, Almighty, King of Kings* etc…Yet if one gives proper study, one would clearly see that these so-called names are just characteristics affixed to

YHWH name or are titles(in the true Israelite Faith non of these titles belong to Jesus).

For example; Yahweh Nissi means, *"the Eternal one is the leader or sign(Exodus 17:15)";* Yahweh shalom means, *"the Eternal one is Peace or my completeness(judges 6:24)";* Yahweh Tzedekinu means, *"The Eternal One is righteousness/just";* Yahweh Yirah means, *"The Eternal One will see/provide(Bereshit 22:14)";* Yahweh Rapha means, *"the Eternal One is the healer";* Yahweh Tzava'ot means, *"Eternal One of the Heavenlies";*Yahoshua, Yahshua or Yahwehshua means, *"Yahweh Delivers"etc.*…As you see YHWH Character is always affixed to his name. Many characteristics, but one name, which is properly Yahweh. YHWH Character can be summed up in psalms 23,

Psalms 23, "Because Yahweh is my Shepard, I Have everything I need(**Yirah**)! *He lets me rest in meadow grass and leads me beside the quiet streams. He restores my failing health*(**Rapha**). *He leads me in the paths of Righteousness for his* **names** *sake*(**Yahweh Tzedekinu**). Even when walking through the dark valley of death I will not be afraid; for you are close beside me, guarding me, guiding me all the way(**Yahshua, Nissi, Shalom**). *You prepare a table before me in the presence of my enemies. You anoint my head with oil; my cup runs over. Surely goodness and mercy (*Harachaman*) shall follow me all the day of my life; and I will dwell in the house of Yahweh forever."*

Everything in YHWH character shows who Yahweh is, & what Yahweh does. It shows the plurality of his majesty and ultimately his Father-hood. Everything about his concern for mankind is found in his characteristics. One name, but many characteristics.

[Allah'im, Adonai, Lord, God, Allah]

Allah, Lord and *God* are actually titles. Except for Allah, Lord and God can apply to a deity(s), idols or mankind.

Right now we want to deal with the titles **Allah'im and Adonai**. Allah'im and Adonai are *originally* the names and titles for the Cana'anite gods(even though Adonai can be used towards Yahweh or humans as a form of respect when placed before their names as lord/master/sir). Allah'im actually is not an original Hebrew-Israelite name, yet you will find it in the Late Hebrew manuscripts. It is a Cana'anite Word for Deity's-mighty ones.

Allah'im is found in *Strongs numbering system#430* which is believed to be the plural of *El(ala)* which is *Strongs#410,* which means *strength or mighty*, but is actually the plural of *Elowahh* which is *Strongs#433,* which means *a deity or Mighty-One in general*. It is a Feminine word.

Then you have Adonai which is translated as Lord from Hebrew. Now found in the translations of English bibles (i.e. KJV), you will find: *lord, LORD, God, GOD, god, Lord,* and all of these can be a translation of *Yahweh, Adonai, Allah'im,* or even *Ba'al.* For example: in Bereshit 2:4, **LORD God** is use to replace *Yahweh Allah'im*; in Bereshit 15:2 *Lord GOD* replaces *Adonai Yahweh*; in Exodus 23:17, *LORD GOD* replaces *Yahweh, Yahweh*; now if you go back to Bereshit 18:26, *LORD* replaces *Yahweh*; Yet in Bereshit 18:27 *Lord* replaces *Adonai*; Deuteronomy 9:26, *LORD, Lord GOD* replaces *Yahweh, Adonai Yahweh*; 1Kings 9:9 *LORD, God, gods* replaces *Yahweh, Allah'im, Allah'im*; in Dani'ala 2:18 *God* replacws *Allah*(Chaldean); In Dani'ala 2:47, *"truly your God is the God of gods, the Lord of kings"* is a replacement for *Allah is Allah of Allah, Mare of kings.*

This may seem confusing or mind scratching to some at first sight, but this is how it is found in the earliest manuscripts that we have today(which are actually late).

To the average reader who knows nothing about the Hebrew texts, they will always think that the different Lords and Gods is the same Word or refers to the same subject/character. This pattern goes on from Bereshit to Malachi, and gets even worst in the Greek translation of the biased New Covenant. Even Ba'al which is a Phoenician Deity means *Lord.*

Now if you have been studying the above by this time, you will notice that according to the Hebrew original, the Holy One of Yishra'ala does appear to have many names and titles. This is totally incorrect. Lets study Exodus 20:1-17

"and God spoke all these words saying: 'I am the LORD your God who brought you out of the land of Egypt, out of the House of bondage, you shall have no other gods before me…..You shall not bow down to them or serve(worship) them. For I the LORD your God, am a jealous God…. You shall not take the **name of the LORD** *your God in* **vain….**"

Notice, the words *LORD your God* in the text. *LORD* is from the Hebrew word *Yahweh,* and word translated *God is Allah'im.* A *Yahweh Allah'im* Combination.

Now notice in verse 3, after putting it in proper context, *"you shall have no other Allah'im before me"* the word for *other* should be *"hinder(Hebrew word Acher Strongs #312), "you shall have no hinder(former) Allah'im before(with or by) me."*

Remember in vs. 2, Egypt, during the time of Moshe, was the place where every pagan idol and Allah'im(god(s)) was to be located. Jewish writings says that the Egyptians have a book with all of the pagan Allah'im names, except for the name of Yahweh. It can't be found. As a result of all the Allah'im, Egypt was known as a *house of bondage.*

Now lets look at Deuteronomy 7:1-6; 12:28-32

"When Yahweh your Allah'im brings you into the land which you go to possess, and has cast out many nations before you, the Hittites and the girgashites and the amorite and the **Cana'anite's** *and the perizzities and the hivites and the yebusites, seven nations greater and mightier than you, and when Yahweh your Allah'im delivers them over to you, you shall conquer them and utterly destroy them. You shall make no* **covenant** *with them nor show mercy to them…..For they will turn your sons away from following me, to serve* **hinder**

Allah'im; *so the anger of Yahweh will be aroused against you and destroy you suddenly. But thus shall you deal with them: you shall break down their sacred pillars*(sacrifice alters), *and cut down their Asherim (deities) and burn their carved images with fire....Therefore, know that* **Yahweh** *your* **Allah'im,** *he is* **Allah'im,** *the faithful* **El** *who keeps his covenant(B'rith)...."*

12:28-32, "observe and obey all these words which I command you, that it may go well with you and your children after you forever....when **Yahweh your Allah'im** *cuts off from before you the nations which you go to dispossess, and you displace them and dwell in their land, take heed to yourself that you are not ensnared to follow them, after they are destroyed from before you, and that you do no inquire after* **their Allah'im,** *saying, 'how did these nations serve their Allah'im? I will do likewise'. You shall not worship* **Yahweh your Allah'im** *in that way....whatever I command you,* **you shall not add to it or take away from it"** *!!*

If you are able to discern and use common sense, you would notice that something isn't right about the appearance of the text's. Now Yahweh specifically instructs Yishra'ala not to worship Allah'im or to worship him like an Allah'im. Yet right at the end of YHWH's name is the very name Allah'im! In fact in the text Yahweh is Yishra'ala's Allah'im!!

Allah'im according to Strongs Hebrew Concordance means *mighty-one(deity's)* in the plural. In fact Chapter 1 of the Bereshit account says that Allah'im Created the heaven and the earth. How is this? is Yahweh against Allah'im, or is Yahweh against himself?

If you study Rabbinical Judaism/ history, it will tell you that Allah'im, which is originally a council of Cana'anite deities, was later adopted by the Hebrews to apply to the Plurality of YHWH Majesty and power as in his *strength.* Now this is correct meaning that the Hebrews did use a word to refer to the plurality of YHWH power and strength, but it was not the word Allah'im. How is this ? If one closely studies the word for *God* in the Strongs Hebrew concordance #430 which supposedly is plural of #410 *El,* **El** itself means *strength, power, mighty.* this is a shortened form of Strongs

#352 *ayil or yl* which means, "strength, support, power, or almighty", not God or gods. If *Allah'im* was really the plural of *El,* then Allah'im would then mean *Mighty ones or Great Powers,* Not Gods.

El itself was used as a proper noun for the name of the Chief divinity of the Cana'anite *Allah'im council.* It is also used as an adjective in common usage as anyone who was strong, had power or was a mighty one(i.e Judges 6:12). Allah'im however was put into later manuscripts due to scribal errors either to hide/replace the name of Yahweh or make Yahweh one of the Pagan Allah'im.

[The Many possibilities to Israelite History]

Isaelite history show that YHWH name, due to the superstition of later apostate Hebrews(post exilic) priest, because they were ignorant of YHWH Tanakh (scriptures) that said,

"whosoever calls upon the name of Yahweh shall be delivered(Yah'ala 2:32)",

began to teach that the people should not pronounce the name of Yahweh except on the day of atonement, and even then the name was pronounced so low that one could not hear it.

Eventually the post exilic scribes of this time when recopying the Hebrew texts(as the texts would deteriorate), because they followed the deceptive superstitions, they added Allah'im and took out the name of Yahweh deliberately to keep the people from pronouncing the name in later generations.

Then there is another possibility of what happened; because the scribes went astray of Yahweh and began to worship the Allah'im of the Cana'anites, when they were recopying the scriptures, they made Allah'im the Eternal Creator and totally suppressed YHWH name, and then later on they added Yahweh and Affixed Allah'im's name at the end showing that not only did they supposedly worship Yahweh as an Allah'im, but they also worshiped other Allah'im, therefore being able to totally eliminate Saying, "Yahweh", because when they worshiped and Said, "Allah'im", Yahweh was already included in the deities(this is actually where Christianity later got their trinity concept, using Allah'im in the Genesis account to refer to their three persons in one deity council).

Both possibilities have shown to be interlinked with how Yishra'ala forgot Yahweh for the Allah'im.

[What the Scholars Say?]

It has been pointed out by scholars that the Torah and writings were compiled and edited and combined by scribes from four different sources; the **J or Yahwist** source, the **E or Elohist** source and the **P or Priestly** source(the latest or earliest source) and the **D or Deuteronomic** source.

In *The Book of J(David Rosenberg and Harold Bloom) pp5* in the preface, it has been pointed out that the **J** source is the oldest writings of the Torah composed around the Tenth century B.C.E. The later strands of writings in Genesis, Exodus and Numbers are revisions, editing and censoring of **J** or the Yahwist source in which we get the name **Yahweh**(YHWH). These groups of writers are known as **E** or **Elohist**. They use **Allah'im** as a plural name for Yahweh. It should be noticed that the Yahwist source uses the name Allah'im to refer to pagan gods in general and not as a name of Yahweh.

The Interpreters Dictionary vol 2 gives the Yahwist source as Yahudahite(Judahite) in origin and is an earlier writing(10th-9th century B.C.E.) than the Elohist source(8th century B.C.E.) which is Yishra'alites(Israelite) in Origin(see pp1,94, 777). Yishra'ala and Yahudah split into two separate kingdoms after the death of HaMeleck Shlomo; Yishra'ala being the Northern Kingdom(Samaria was its capitol) and Yahudah was the Southern Kingdom(Yerushalem its capital).

Both Yahwist and Elohist writings stem from a common source before the Kingdom split. The Elohist follows the outline of the Yahwist document, except the Elohist replaces YHWH name while the Yahwist keeps his name which is original(*The Anchor Bible, Proverbs-Ecclesiastes vol. 18 pp xxxi*)

This was a very deceptive thing, which mens they blinded a lot of innocent people and YHWH name was Blocked, Even until today in Yishra'ala.

This Actually therefore means that, before the apostate scribes got a hold of the Hebrew scrolls to recopy them, everywhere you Found the word **El or Allah'im** translated God(s), as in reference to The Eternal Creator (YHWH), should actually be the Name **Yahweh**. As far as who he is, he should be known as the Almighty or *Yahweh Almighty* which is from Ayil **(YL)**, which is translated as**, Power, might, strength or support** as in a Father.

Some believe that although *El(alla)* is proper when using it as an adjective to denote ones might, power or strength, it should not be used when using it as a proper noun for Hebrew names or the name of Yahweh. *Ayil,* in which *El is* derived from, should be used to make a distinction from paganism and the Cana'anite El or Allah'im, because Yahweh is not *El(chief Cana'anite Deity)* or an *Allah'im* and his people should not be called by that name!! But lets search further for a positive resolution.

But remember, Yahweh is not the *Allah'im(God(s))* of Abraham, Yitzkak and Ya'akob, But the *Strength or Almighty One(*as in a father-ala'him) of Abraham Yitzkak and Ya'akob.

Although Allah'im was an error of the scribes in referencing Yahweh, it can be seen through its usage in biblical scripture of what it was many times used as. Whenever referring to Yahweh as the Allah'im, one could see that this referred to the *Transcendental Creator*, who was above his creation at a distance, the *Great almighty* who was mainly concerned with ritual(as in Sacrifice-Selah) as a contrast to when the writer used the name Yahweh itself. In this case it denoted YHWH concern and intimacy with mankind and stressed ethical behavior instead of ritual. Stop and think about this.

Yahweh was(is) a gracious, personal, compassionate and communicable Creator with his creation. Allah'im was the type of figure who would have said, "*I brought you into this world and I'll take you out*".

[Yahweh's Allah'im(Elohim) as opposed to the 'Other' Allah'im]

It should also be noted the Ancient Yishra'alites used Allah'im in a very unique way, of Describing the Heavenly Council of YHWH. As far as legend-history goes, Allah'im was a counsel of Elders, Malakim and Spirit beings with authority over various areas of the earth and the universe and mankinds actions. Yahweh himself being the head and author of the Allah'im. The Malakim in the Scripture are many times when talking with a human being are responded to as if the person was talking directly to Yahweh. The Malak him/herself usually speaks as if Yahweh was speaking directly. This is because Yahweh gave that authority to the Malak to speak for him.

In the creation story, it is said that Allah'im created the heavens and earth. Allah'im are the mighty ones and are seen as the seven Malakim(messengers) of Yahwehs presence.(Bereshit 16:7-11; 22:11-15; Shemot 3:2-4;14:19 18:1-22; 1 Melekim 22:19-23; 2Chronicles 18:18-22; Dani'ala 10:12-13,20)

Although We praise Yahweh for our health, our victory over our enemies, for prosperity and for authority given us, Yahweh most of the time is not directly involved. This is because he has created and given/delegated certain Malakim different callings and functions. For example the Archi-Malak Rapha'ala is Responsible for healing, curing the sick and instilling knowledge of Medical needs and research with scientists and medical doctors. He along with other Malakim with unique functions work together with Counselors and Ministers and those who are called to bring Spiritual, mental, and other healings and rehabilitation within the earth. The Archi-Malak Micha'ala is responsible for establishing and maintaining Yahwehs authority and order within the earth. He is the Chief and head authoritative figure under Yahweh. And it goes on and on.

Why do we give praise to Yahweh for the work of his Messengers and Servants, Because Halelu Yah He is the Author of it all!!!!

If you have studied ancient cultures and their gods that existed before Yishra'ala, you would probably notice that their gods functions were similar to that of Yahweh and His Servants. This is true. Yishra'ala Allah'im is simply a reformed version of other cultures. It could very well be the same gods or mighty ones except in Yishra'ala not all the mighty-ones are worshiped. Instead Yishra'ala Allah'im is consisted on One Divine Eternal Creator of everything and all the rest of the mighty-ones(Allah'im) are his created "servants" designed to execute his will. Meaning, the Allah'im worships YHWH, as opposed to the Cana'anite definition of El being the Chief deity and the rest of the Mighty-ones being worshiped also.

This explains passages such as Psalms 8:1-9. *"Yahweh made man a little lower than the Allah'im."*

How is this? The Allah'im here are the Malakim and spirit beings of the Heavenly host. That is why in most English translations, Allah'im is translated as Angels(Malakim). Or how about psalms 82:6. *"Mankind is Allah'im"*, not as being Yahweh, but as establishing his authority and judgement throughout the earth. In Yahweh we are mighty ones. The only difference between Mankind and Allah'im, the mighty-ones or the Malakim is that Mankind have physical bodies, which makes us lower than the Malakim who are spirit beings. Yet we still have a responsibility in the Plan of Yahweh. See Bereshit 1:26-30. When we die we become as the Malakim, the Angels or spirit beings

Remember Allah'im as a whole is Yahweh plus his servants the Malakim, elders, and Spirit being etc…Yahweh is a singular being, Echad, but functions in a pluralistic way, through his Malakim.

As opposed to the 'other' Allah'im dilemma above, this Yahwistic Allah'im is simply an honest Cultural Derivation and adoption from Previous cultures and Practices in which the Hebrews evolved. Yet when we forget Yahweh and call upon and worship Allah'im without knowing Yahweh, we simply revert ourselves back to the form of pantheon Pagan worship of ancient gods or mighty-ones, which is out of Yahwehs will.

Take notice in the first command of Yahweh in the Ten Teachings, *"Though Shalt have no hinder Allah'im Before or besides me."* Understanding the cultural similarities in the Function of the mighty ones(Allah'im), then we can understand that Yahweh was not making many of the Divine Spirit Beings(mighty-ones-Allah'im) obsolete, he just made it clear that they are not to be worshiped or equaled with him. The Allah'im are beneath and are servants of Yahweh and his people.

Shocking as it is The Gnostic Netzarim book of Revelation found in the Christian bible, testifies of what I'M writing. For example read Revelations 4:1-11. There are elders and spirit beings(known as Seraphim in Hebrew) sitting before and worshiping Yahweh Tzava'ot.

The ancient Hebrew Sanhedrin is also another earthly replica of how the Hebrews viewed the ancient Yahweh Allah'im!!

If one would began to see how the ancient Hebrews saw Yahweh, They would notice that Yahweh was their Creator, shield and just judge, without Yahweh they were weak and helpless against their enemies and were bastards without a father. They had no direction and was void of knowledge and wisdom Yet when they worshiped Yahweh, he became their Shepard, provider, teacher, father and Strength. He became their complete-ness and peace.

[Yishra'ala and the 'other' Allah'im controversy continues]

Notice that most of the Hebrew names have a Cana'anite pre-fix or Suffix of El at the beginning and end. As stated this is simply a cultural derivative, considering Ancient Hebrew, both culture and language is the Phoenician(Cana'anite) culture and language. Yet in many instances the Ancient Yishra'alites would revert back to Heathen worship and affix the Heathen deity being worshiped to their names.

If one Studies the scriptures, one would see that this was not the first time the Yishra'alites fell into deception and error concerning paganism, apart from Yahweh. In You turn to Judges 7:1, you will see the name of Gideon as Yeruba'al; 1Chronicles 8:33;9:39 you will find the name of Yishba'al; 1Chronicles 8:34; 9:40 you will see the name **Mari Ba'al**. This was the result of the Hebrews disobeying YHWH instruction not to tolerate or inquire of the pagan Allah'im and gods:

*Judges 2:1-5, "Then the Malak of Yahweh came up from Gilgal to Bochim, and said: 'I led you up from Egypt and brought you to the land of which I swore to your fathers; and I said, I will never break my B'rith with you. And you shall make no B'rith (covenant) with the inhabitants of this land; you shall tear down the alters. But you have **not obeyed my voice**, why have you done this? There I also said, I will **not** drive then out before you; but they shall be thorns in your side, and their Allah'im shall be a snare to you.' So it was, when the Malak of Yahweh spoke these words to all of the children of Yishra'ala, that the people lifted up their voice and wept…."*

Yahweh says that because the Hebrews disobeyed him, that the pagan Allah'im would become thorns in their side(in this case the Phoenician Allah'im Ba'al was their snare).

When Yahshua ben Nun was living the Hebrews worshiped Yahweh 'only', even though the pagan worshipers were living in the land. Yet after Yahshua died….:

*Judges 2:11-13;18-22, "When all that generation had been gathered to their fathers, another generation arose after them who did not know Yahweh nor the work which he had done for Yishra'ala. Then the children of Yishra'ala did evil in the sight of Yahweh and served the **Ba'als**(Lord); and they forsook Yahweh their Father(strength) of their fathers, who brought them out of the land of Egypt; and they followed other Allah'im from among the Allah'im of the people all around them, and they bowed down to them; and they provoked*

Yahweh to anger. They forsook Yahweh and served Ba'al(Lord) and the Ashtoreth (Cana'anite female Allah'im.).

vs. 18-22, "And when Yahweh raised up Judges for them, Yahweh was with the Judge and delivered them out of the hand of their enemies all the days of the Judge(s); for Yahweh was moved to pity by their groanings because of those who oppressed them and harassed them..."

Take note!!! When the times of revival came and Judges were raised up and repentance toward Yahweh resulted among the Hebrews, not only did they change their ways but they also changed their names. Names that had *El* or Ba'al at the beginning or end, were changed to Bosheth which means shame (i.e. IISHAMU'ALA 11:21-Yeru**ba'al** to Yeru**bosheth**; IIShamu'ala 2:8-Yish**ba'al** **to Yishbosheth**; IISHAMU'ALA 4:4; 9:6,10-Mephi**ba'al** to Mephi**bosheth**). When Yahweh brought revival and the Hebrews realized the wickedness they had done against Yahweh and the lack of leadership they showed as lights unto the nation, they became ashamed of their actions.

vs 19-23,chapter 3:1-4, "and it came to pass, when the Judge w as dead, that they reverted and behaved more corruptly than their fathers, by following more(other) Allah'im, to serve and bow down to them. They did not cease from their own doings nor from their stubborn way. Then the anger of Yahweh was hot against Yishra'ala; and he said, 'because this nation has transgressed my B'rith which I commanded their fathers, and has not heeded my voice, I will no longer drive out before them any of the nations which Yahshua left when **he died.** *So that through them I may test Yishra'ala, whether they will keep the* **ways of Yahweh,** *to walk in them as their fathers kept them, or not...."*

Notice that when the Hebrews sinned deliberately against Yahweh and his Torah again, Yahweh allowed the Satanic paganistic system of the Cana'anites worship of the demon Allah'im to flourish to test Yishra'ala and show whether they would pass Yahweh test or fail to follow his ways. Did the Yishra'alites pass of fail? Lets see.

YirmeYah 23:26-27, "How long will this be in the heart of the prophets who prophesy lies? Indeed they are prophets of the deceit of their own heart, who try to make my people forget **my name** *by their dreams which everyone tells his neighbor as their forefathers forgot my name for Ba'al.*

YirmeYah is prophesying to a later generation of Hebrews who Have forgotten the name of Yahweh and listen to False prophets and wicked priests. This is a continuation of the sins and Yishra'ala failure to follow YHWH Torah and Word from the previous generations. Indeed they forgot Yahweh even generations later.

Deuteronomy 8:19-20; 30:17-20; 31:16-18 "Then it shall be, if you by any means forget Yahweh your Father, and follow hinder Allah'im, and serve them and worship them, I testify against you this day that you shall surely perish. As the nations which Yahweh destroys before you, so shall you perish, because you would not be obedient to the voice of Yahweh your Father…." 30: 17-20, " I call heaven and earth as witnesses today against you, that I have set before you life and death, blessing and cursing; therefore choose life, that you and your descendants may live….".

Notice Heaven and Earth were set before the children of Yishra'ala as Witnesses of their actions toward the Torah. Heaven and earth represents nature, and even today nature is destroying this world like never before, because just about everybody has forgotten the name and Torah of Yahweh. Even the 'majority' of the Jews and Israelites(in which I am), have forgotten Yahweh, and they substitute his name with Allah'im, Adonai, Hashem, God and the LORD!!! They never call YHWH name, namely because of superstition(with the exception of the few Yahweh believing Israelites). Yahweh is not about superstition!!! He's about **restoring his name and true Torah!!!!**

31:16-18 "then my anger will be aroused against them in that day and I will forsake them and hide my face from them and they shall be devoured, and many evils and troubles shall befall them, so that they will say in that day, 'have not these evils come upon us because our Father(Yahweh) is not among us?......

YirmeYah 11:9-10, "and Yahweh said to me, 'a conspiracy has been found among the men of Yahudah and among the inhabitants of Yerushalem. They have turned back to the iniquities of their forefathers who refused to hear my words, and they have gone after hinder Allah'im to serve them; the house of Yishra'ala and the house of Yahudah have broken my B'rith which I made with their fathers."

This is the main problem, even today with the Israelite-Jewish peoples. We bare the iniquities of our Ancient fathers who broke the covenant with Yahweh(that is why its easy for messianic Jews to worship Jesus and a Trinity=other Allah'im, and the Orthodox, Reform and Conservative Jews can't biblically define a True YaHudaim/Hebrew), to worship pagan demons.

YirmeYah testifies that the Scribes later distorted the writings of the Hebrew manuscripts and hindered YHWH name & Changed YHWH Torah (with additions including the Cana'anite sacrificial system):

YirmeYah 8:5-9, "Why then has this people slidden back, Yerushalem, in a perpetual backsliding? They hold fast to deceit, they refuse to return. I listen and heard, but they do not speak aright. No man repented of his wickedness, saying, 'what have I done?' Everyone turned to his own course, as the horse rushes into battle. Even the stork in the heavens knows her appointed times; and the turtledove, the swift, and the swallow observe the time of their coming. But my people do not know the judgement of Yahweh! How can you say, 'We are wise and the Torah(law of Moshe) is with us'? **Look!** *The false pen of the scribe certainly works falsehood(or "your teachers have twisted them up to mean a thing I never said"* **living bible, Tyndale)!!!....so what wisdom do they have?"*

This is the conspiracy of 11:8!! YirmeYah says the scribes have mixed up the writings. Scribes are the ones who recopied the Torah from one manuscript to another, as the manuscripts would deteriorate. They substituted and made the people forget the name of Yahweh and his Torah!!

[Adonai (Lord/master].

Another term and title that was used to substitute and hide YHWH name, *Adonai.* All over the world during prayer and singing, this word is used in place of Yahweh. Even I at one time was carried away by this, because I honestly did not know(this accounts for many other innocent YaHudaim). For example;

"B'ruch atah **Adonai** Eloheinu *Malek ha-olam asher kid'd-shanu b'mitzvotav v'tzi-vanu l'hit-a-tafe ba-tzitzit"*-"Blessed are you oh **Lord our God**, King of the universe, who has sanctified us by thy commandments, and hast commanded us to enwrap ourselves in the fringed garment".

There are two things wrong with this prayer: *Adonai* replaces the name Yahweh and therefore making Eloheinu a reference to a pagan deity, "The text should be read as, " Eternal One **our Strength(Father) or Almighty**". Therefore reading,

"B'ruch atah **Yahweh Allahenu** *Malek ha-olam...."* "*Blessed art thou* **Yahweh Almighty**, *king of the Universe......* "

Using Yahweh assures us of whom we are Worshiping and protects us from Idolatry.
Or how about the saying,

"B'ruch haba beshem **Adonai***" "Blessed is he who comes in the name of* **the Lord***"*

What Lord are we talking about here? Any body can be called Adonai or Lord!!! It should read,

B'ruch haba beshem **Yahweh**" *"Blessed is he who comes in the name of* **Yahweh(the Eternal One)"**

This is how all of the Hebrew prayers and songs should read, using *Yahweh and ALLAHENU* instead of *Adonai and Eloheinu.* I encourage every True Yishra'alites to return and began calling on Hashem Yahweh.

[Pagan usage]

Now even though Adonai was used as a form of respect by the Hebrews, it was many times used as a title or name of Allah'im and other Pagan deities (Originally it was a title of respect towards Elders, kings and wealthy people(Adon) and put in front of Yahweh's name as in *Master Yahweh or King Yahweh[adonai]).*

We are going to do a simple study of 1Kings 22:1-23 and 2Chronicles 18:2-22:

1Kings 22:1-23, "Now three years passed without war between Syria and Yishra'ala. Then it came to pass, in the third year, that Yahshaphat, the king of Yahudah went down to visit the king of Yishra'ala. And the king of Yishra'ala said to his servants, 'do you know that Ramoth in Gilead is ours, but we hesitate to take it our of the hands of the king of Syria?' So he said to Yahshaphat, 'will you go with me to fight at Ramoth Gilead?' And Yahshaphat said to the king of Yishra'ala, 'I am as you are, my people are your people, and my horses are your horses.' and Yahshaphat said to the king of Yishra'ala, 'please inquire for the word of **the LORD** *today." then the king of Yishra'ala gathered the prophets together, about four hundred men, and said to them, 'shall I go to Ramoth Gilead to fight, or shall I refrain?' so they said, 'go up, for* **the Lord** *will deliver it into the hand of the king.' and Yahshaphat said, 'is there still not a prophet of* **the LORD** *here, that we may inquire of him?'".......*

Now notice in the text vs 5-7, that Yahshaphat asked for an inquiry of the **LORD**, and the text says that the prophets gave him the Word of the *Lord*, but Yahshaphat still insists on getting a Word from the **LORD**. How and why is this? Its seems foolish on the surface to ask for the word of the **LORD** and get the word of the *Lord* and then ask for the word of the **LORD**, as if he didn't get it the first time. Actually he didn't get the word of the **LORD** the first time, he got the word of the *Lord* from the prophets. What?!! Lets go back. The word *LORD* and *Lord* are two different Hebrew words. **LORD** is the Hebrew word *Yahweh*, while **Lord** is the Hebrew word *Adonai.* Yahshaphat was wanting to inquire of the word of *Yahweh*, but the prophets gave a word or prophecy of *Adonai.* Therefore Yahshaphat said,

"is there not still a prophet of Yahweh here that we may inquire of him?

In Yahudah the King and people Worshiped Yahweh (and other Allah'im, although Yahweh was the main worship), and in Yishra'ala the King and people worshiped the Adonai Allah'im. Yahshaphat knew the difference between *Adonai's* prophets and *Yahweh* prophets.

If you study 2Chronicles 18:2-22 you will notice in vs 5, that the prophets are to have said, *"go up for* **God** *will deliver it into the kings hand."* The Hebrew word for **God** is *Allah'im.* Remember this is the same story and incident that happened in 1Kings 22, except Allah'im is substituted for Adonai. They are one and the same Pagan deities. The Yishra'alites forsook Yahweh and took the Hebrew title Adonai that was affixed to Yahweh and affixed it to Allah'im(Adonai Allah'im/Lord God).

As you study the rest of the two texts (1Kings 22 and 2Chronicles 18) for your-self you will notice that after Yahshaphat rejected the word of Adonai Allah'im and sent for a Prophet of Yahweh, that the False prophets of Allah'im began to give false prophecies in YHWH name to try to get the king to listen to them instead of MichaYahu, in which the king of Yishra'ala hated. The messenger who goes to get MichaYahu tries to convince him to prophesy like the rest of the Elohist prophets, but MichaYahu says in vs 13,

"As Yahweh lives, whatever my Almighty says, that I will speak".

[GOD, G-d, Gad, Gud, good]

The name/Title GOD is transliterated from Hebrew letters of Gamel(G) and Dalet(D), G-D.

In the Hebrew scriptures there are several reference found that refers to G-D: A) GAD(pronounced in Hebrew as Gawd(God)) is one of the Twelve Sons of Yishra'ala.(Bereshit/Genesis 30:11; 49:19). This is equivalent to Dr. Strongs Hebrew Concordance *#1410,* which means *"a Fortune or Troop."* B) G-D(GoD) is also a name of an Israelite Prophet that lived during the time of Malek(King) Davyid(1Samuel 22:5; ; 2Samuel 24:11)…(Remember there are no vowels in Hebrew. Vowel pronunciation was passed on Orally) C)G-D is a Babylonian/Phonecian Deity of Good Fortune also known as "that Troop", as the Prophet YeshiYah(Isaiah) 65:11 Condemns Yishra'ala for worshiping instead of YHWH. (Strong Hebrew #1408-1409).

"And you are they who forsake YHWH, who forget my mountain of Holiness; who line up a table for GOD; and who fulfill the cocktails to fate:…"

The Only match in the Hebrew Scriptures for the English Deity GOD is The Phonecian-Babylonian Deity GOD which is used in English Bibles to Deceive millions of people into Forsaking YHWH for GOD!!!

So how did we come to use the term God as a proper noun? No doubt, the Judeans and Hebrews who returned from the Babylonian Exile was exposed to the Name of GOD and names of other pagan deities and Euro-Judaism is very much responsible for spreading the name to the European Nations such as Germany, England and America as they were influenced a great bit by Babylon as seen in their formation of the Babylonian Talmud which superceded the Palestinian Talmud, and their use of such

Babylonian terms as, *"Gud Shabbos",* and the common dual usage of "Good Luck/fortune" literally *"God(Fortunate/Lucky) Shabbath"*

In Smiths Bible Dictionary, Nelson, pp220, the definition of *"God"* is immediately followed by *"Good"* is parenthesis.

God is also found in Gesenius Hebrew Chaldee Lexicon of the Old Testament, Baker pp157, #1408,

"Fortune; with art., specially the divinity of fortune, worshiped by the Babylonians and by the ISRAELITES exiled among them; else where called Ba'al, i.e the planet Jupiter, regarded in all the east as the river of good fortune"

Now concerning Jupiter, a deity adopted from the ammonites, with the connection to God, we find in Roman Mythology that Jupiter is Zeus, the Roman Olympian heralded as the Morning Star who usurped his fathers throne to become the King of Kings and Lord of Lords and Savior of the world. Then we have the Jesus in English which is originally Iseous(ee-Zooose-HeyZoose in Spanish) who is heralded by the Euro-Gentile Roman Catholic and Protestant Churches as the Savior of the World and King of Kings and Lord of Lords in place of Yahweh, which comes from the Greek name of Jesus associated with Zeus. It comes out to be the same name from the same origin, culture and language, ROME!!!

Then we look at American government and see their role in the whole GOD scheme. The White house and every chief city building in each state is known as the *Capitol Hill* or *State Capitol.* But Why not *Capital* Hill and State *Capital?*

The American Heritage Dictionary, third Edition defines **Capital** as, *"A town or city that is the official seat of government in a political entity"*

Usage: *the term for a town or city that serves as a seat of government is Capital. The term for the **building** in which legislative assembly meets is **Capitol***

Yet we find in the definition of **Capitol**, *"[<Latin. Capitolium,* ***JUPITERS TEMPLE IN ROME!!!***

So we have the Babylonians exiling the Israelites and introducing them to the Babylonian Deity of Fortune named God and God later becomes the Roman Jupiter who in turns becomes the Mighty Zeus who becomes the

Savior of Roman Christianity, who in turn establishes the United states of America on Roman principles and their State and National Buildings become their Capitol Buildings, which are the Temple of Zeus/Jupiter/Jesus and the American peoples Moto becomes, IN GOD WE TRUST, established on Christian Roman Principles!!!! And Now all Religions, Judaism, Christianity, Islam and the like, in English worship GOD!!!

Come out of Babylon my people!!!!

[Modern Islamic Allah as opposed to Ancient Allah(El, Eloah)]

Now we are back to the name Allah(elah), a Chaldean/ or Arabic word. *Allah* is Strongs Hebrew #424. Allah is actually the feminine of Ayil #352, *"strength/support"*. *Allah* is the name of the modern deity of the Islamic Culture.

Islam was founded by Ali Mohammad, a Cushite(Ethiopian)Hebrew Arab, son of Ibn-al-Mutabib, of the Kuraish tribe of western Arabia.

Jose' V. Malcioln in his book, *The African Origins of modern Judaism* has written:

before the Proclamation, Ali Mohammad had been a Student of Hebrew Rabbis at Mecca. His Prophetic Characteristics are said to have been 'similar to those of the Hebrew Prophets some twelve hundred years before him.' at that time Mecca was the center of the pagan cult that had great fame throughout the Arab communities. The cult was built around the worshiping of a well - revered stone called EL Ka'aba. This stone was a fallen meteorite and was worshiped alone with a Goddess named Allat. The Prophet envisioned Allat, El Ka'aba and Mecca, the center of the pagan cult, becoming interconnected. The female goddess became a male named Allah, the stone became a relic to be visited, and a God like the Hebrew Yahweh or the Christian Jesus evolved."

Allat as we see was an ancient feminine deity that was converted to a male deity by Mohammad. Noticed that *Allah, Elowahh(Alowah) El(Al) Allah'im(Allah'im)* are all feminine and all derive from the same root word that means, *mighty!*

Although Islam claims to be Monotheistic, Islam in its formation of the modern deity *Allah* is a foreign deity to the Hebrew faith and is not the same deity as YHWH Allahenu as many have erroneously believed and taught, according to the *"God"* theory; *"regardless of what we call him by, we all worship the same god."*

I assure you, we all don't worship the same deity!!!

[in Conclusion]

In conclusion, the view of the Eternal Creator in the Hebrew scriptures and Israelite Torah Covenant Community is monotheism to the strictest degree. Yahweh was, is and always will be, "Asher haya w'howe w'yawo". He is 'not' and never was a human being nor the son of a human being (Numbers 23:19). The Torah echoes the **Shema** in Deuteronomy 6:4, *"Shema Yishra'ala, Yahweh Yloheinu, Yahweh Yachad"*, "Hear oh Yishra'ala, The Eternal One Your Almighty, is **One Yahweh**." Before Yahweh there is no other and after him there is no other to be compared to him! The 1st of the Ten commandments in the Torah say's, *"I am Yahweh your Almighty, you shall have no hinder Allah'im Before/with me(Exodus 20)"*. Yahweh **alone** is the King, Redeemer and Savior of Yishra'ala and the World. **There is no other!**

YeshiYah 44:6-8, "thus says Yahweh, the king and redeemer of Yishra'ala, Yahweh Tzava'ot. 'I am the first and I am the last; besides me there is no other strength(Father).....is there a power besides me? Indeed there is no other Rock; I know not one."

YeshiYah 45:4-25, "For Ya'akov my' servant's' sake, and Yishra'ala my elect, I have even called you by your name; I have named you, though you have not known me. I am Yahweh and there is no other; there is no strength(Divine) besides me...I am Yahweh and there is no other...there is no other Strength besides me; a just father and **savior;** there is none besides me. Look to me, and **be Saved** *all you ends of the earth! For I am Yahweh, and there is no other...that to me(Yahweh Only!)* **Every knee shall bow, and every tongue shall take an oath(confess),** *he shall say, 'surely in* **Yahweh** *I have righteousness and strength'. To him(Yahweh) men shall come, and* **all shall be ashamed who are incensed against him.** *In Yahweh all the descendants of Yishra'ala shall be justified and shall glory."*

Section 3 Unity Of Yahweh

The biblical Conception of Yahweh is total one-ness or Unity, meaning that Yahweh is not composed of parts, deities or personalities. He is **alone***(All One)*. Yahweh alone is responsible for everything that exists. Nothing can be compared to him; no dignitary (divine being), prophet, man or teacher, or idol can compare to him for it is he alone who created them. No one can compare YHWH love, Compassion and power to another(YeshiYah 42:8; 43:11; 45:21-22)!!

Pesachim, 50a "The Rabbis ask: "'and now is not YHWH One? What mean the Words: 'In that day YHWH shall be One and his Name shall be One'?" The answer is : 'Now YHWH is ONE, but his names are many. Everyone conceives Him according to his own vision. But in the World that is to be-in that glorious future that is yet to come-not only will YHWH be One; His name too, will then be One"

"I am YHWH: that is My Name: and I neither give My honor/glory to another, nor My praise to scuptiles..."

[Yahweh is Spirit/incorporeal]

To be incorporeal means that Yahweh is without measure in form, shape, size, dimension or substance. A pious Torah observant Hebrew named Yahshua, in teaching the worship of the Father who is Yahweh said,
Yahchonan 4:24, "Yahweh is Spirit, and those who worship him must worship him in Spirit(as in by his spirit) and in truth(by his Torah)

The implication that Yahweh is Spirit (plurality) means that *a* spirit being (singular) cannot exist without Yahweh and neither can a natural or material existing be. To clarify: water in itself is plural, it has no shape, form, dimension or size. But a glass of water is singular, it has a definite shape, dimension form of size(depending on the glass). There could be no glass of water without there being water; human beings are spirits beings with material shapes(Bodies), sizes and forms. Malak(angels) and other spirit beings have no material existence but have shapes, sizes and dimensions. Humans and Spirit beings are singular. They exist at one place at one time.

Berachoth 10a, "As the Holy One, blessed be he, fills the whole world, so also the soul fills the whole body. As the Holy One, blessed be he, sees but cannot be seen, so also the soul sees but cannot be seen. As the holy One nourishes the whole world, so also the soul nourishes the whole body. As the Holy One, blessed, be he, is pure, so also the soul is pure. As the Holy One, blessed be he, dwells in the inmost part of the Universe, so also the soul dwells in the inmost part of the body."

Also because YHWH is incorporeal, natural attributes given to YHWH also known as anthropomorphism is not to be taken literally. For example the last verses of Deuteronomy speaks of Moshe seeing YHWH face to face. This is not meant to be taken literally that Moshe actually saw YHWH's face. In Hebraic thought, to see YHWH's face is to be in his presence, that is his Shekinah Manifest. "Face to face" implies physical intimacy and direct communication.

Although YHWH presence is everywhere all at once, everyone does not experience that presence, YHWH must manifest himself to us and we must be Spiritually sensitive to YHWH's Presence. When YHWH does manifest himself to us he is Showing forth his Face.

[Omnipresence]

The divine beings exist in a definite remote place at a time. They have shape and form, But Yahweh is every-where at on time and the same time. His presence is everywhere although it may not manifest everywhere or may manifest at one time or another.

Yahshua 2:11b, "For Yahweh your Father, he is Yahweh in heaven above and earth beneath."

The whole earth is full YHWH Glory!

Psalms 139:8-9, "If I ascend into heaven, you are there; if I make my bed in Shoel, behold you are there. If I take the wings of the morning and dwell in the uttermost parts of the sea, even there your hand shall lead me."

Genesis. Rabbah. LXIII.9, " The Holy One, blessed be he,, is the place of his universe, but his universe is not his place"

Shemot Rabbah on verse 3,3, "YHWH appeared to Moshe in a despised thron-bush, not in a carob tree, which men value, in order to teach that there is no place on earth void of the Divine Presense"

My example: Make a ruler which is a foot long(12inch) and hold it. Imagine that this ruler represents all time and space, meaning that nothing outside this rulers measure (1mm-12inch) is time or space(non-existence). Everything that ever existed or ever will exist in time or space is in this ruler. 1mm is the beginning of creation and time and 12inches in the end. Imagine you are Yahweh. You see you operate outside of time. You are eternal(in this example), forever. You are and see the beginning and the end. You hold time up, time doesn't hold you up. So is it with Yahweh the Eternal Creator.

[Yahweh is all knowing/omniscient]

Yahweh is the one true Creator who knows everything about everything from the beginning to the end. There is nothing that can be hidden from him. Yahweh knows our deepest inner-most thoughts(whether righteous or wicked). He knows when we are going and coming.

Psalms 44:20-21, "If we had forgotten the name of Yahweh, or stretched out our hands to Allah'im, would not Yahweh search this out?"

YirmeYah 17:10, "I Yahweh search the heart, I test the mind, even to give every man according to his ways, and according to the fruit of his doings

Only Yahweh truly knows the heart of man. Even when a prophet or prophetic Hebrew Maggid or Spirit-led Hebrew believer in Yahweh perceives anything, whether past, present or future, it is because Yahweh's Spirit has revealed it to them.

Psalms 139:1-6, "Oh Yahweh, you have searched me and known me. You know my sitting down and my rising up; you understand my thoughts afar off. You comprehend my path and lying down and are acquainted with all my ways. For there is not a word on my tongue, but behold Oh Yahweh, you know it altogether."

Psalms 14:1, " the fool has said in his heart, there is no Divine Power(Yahweh)"

The above passage indicates that a fool-a wicked person not only denies the omni-presence of Yahweh, but he also denies the omniscience of Yahweh. This is mostly done by ones life of living according to the evil impulses desire and acting unjustly. He who acts wickedly in secret is the same as one who acts wickedly and unjustly in the light!

Do not ever think that just because some-one broke the Torah commands and was disobedient to Yahweh and got away with it because "no man" knew it, that Yahweh doesn't know it either. He does!! Anyone who fails to recognize this has already like the fool and atheist denied the existence of Yahweh. They have taken Yahweh, his Torah, and his presence in vain.

For example, you are a minister or a religious leader and you are stealing money from your religious organization or is practicing sexual infidelity/immorality in secret, yet you appear to be holy, anointed and righteous in public before man to win his approval. You are psychologically/spiritually sick, because you fail to realize that you fooled man, but you did your sins in the very presence of the throne of Yahweh. You respect men, but you outright disrespect Yahweh in his face!! This includes any unrighteousness against YHWH Torah. Mankind knows nothing apart from Yahweh. Yahweh knows everything. Humble Repentance is the key.

Yahweh also knows all of our cares, sufferings and worries. He knows our going in and going out. He knows our needs and wants. Just as a True Father, because he knows,he is always there by our side to lead us and guide us through this worldly life. When we yet think that no-one else cares or knows our problems and challenges, Yahweh is there to care. He feels our pains, he understands our feelings. And no matter what or who you are. No matter where you've been or where you're going, Yahweh is there to lift you up when you feel down. He is there to listen when you're ready to talk. And when you're ready to do what is right in your life to reach your dreams and goals and fulfill your destined purpose, he is there ready to help you. He is the all knowing compassionate Creator of this World.

Pesikta, Buber, 139a, "YHWH has compassion like a Father, and comforts like a Mother"

[Yahweh is Eternal]

Webster dictionary defines *eternal* as, *"existing without beginning or end"*. Yahweh, the Father of Yishra'ala, the One true Creator of everything is, *"asher hayah, W'howe, w'yawo"*. He *was* and *is* and *is to come*. The tetra-grammaton YHWH, pronounced Yahweh, who is the Father of Yishra'ala, name, in itself means, *"self existent"* or *"Eternal One/Creator"*.

Psalms 102:27, "But you are the same, and your years will have no end."

Yahweh alone is the creator of time and everything that exists in time. Yahweh is the essence of life, for in him there is no death. He lives forever.

Malachi 3:6, "For I am Yahweh, I do not change."

Nothing about Yahweh changes. The Torah is his written Word and the Oral Torah is his spoken Word (accompanied by his Ruakh /bath Kol or divine voice) and it will not change. His covenant with Abraham and the Hebrews will not change. YHWH prophetic voice, his prophets (Nabi'im) are not done away with nor are his prophetic administrations. Yahweh never said they were done away with. Man said they were, because they are not being led by the Spirit of Yahweh.

In these days, by YHWH authority, Spiritual manifestations, healings, miracles, prophetic utterances in the name of Yahweh 'only', and signs in the heavens are manifesting to prove and testify of YHWH Torah and will(against the counterfeit non Hebrew mystical/charismatic movements and the new-age movements).

Most of all, YHWH Love, kindness and everlasting mercy for mankind endures forever(2Chronicles 7:3).

Chapter 2

Section1 Torah Covenant CommunityDevelopmental Covenant Theology

In this section will be an in-depth study of the Torah and its development, YHWH official covenant with Abraham, the established Torah observant community by Moshe, and the not so New Covenant that was said to be established by Yahshua ben Yosef. We will first start with the background of the man Abraham Ben Adamah and the Abrahamic Community among the ancient Cana'anite and other pagan peoples.

It should also be noted that Torah has two meanings in this section; first it means the first five books of the Hebrew bible accredited to Moshe; Bereshit(Genesis), Shemot(Exodus), Leviticus (Wayyicra), umbers(Barmidbar), Deuteronomy (D'bar).

Second the specific Laws and statutes given by Yahweh to Moshe to the Children of Yishra'ala to make up the everlasting Torah Covenant Community. In this latter sence the book of Bereshit is not the Torah and there was no established Torah community before Moshe; only a community developed off of faith in a promise in a pagan land.

Bereshit therefore is the Historical background of the development of YHWH Eternal Covenant with the people of Yishra'ala

[The Adamahic Lineage]

According to Archaeologist/science pre-historic man existed some 21/2 millions years ago, while the Genesis story relates that man(Adm) existed or came into being some 6,000 years ago.

Further more it is implied in science that the earth existed some sixteen million years (see members.xoom.com/torahscience/bigbang1.htm)

So therefore the question arises, "what is the relationship of the Archaeology/science to the Genesis story of only some 6000years ago?" and if it is true and factual that there were people here on earth before Adamah, then what was/ is the need of Adamah being here.

Looking on the surface at the translation of the Bereshit Story of Creation, we all get the impression that Allah'im,(many times wrongly translated as god) created the Whole Heaven and Earth at this particular time. We get the impression that the Genesis Story is a telling or explanation of how the world came into existence and how the whole world fell due to Adamah and chawwahs transgressions.

However, studying deep into the text of the Hebrew and understanding the stories and motives and background of the Genesis creation, there comes a totally different story to be told, and totally different motive.

This different understanding altogether answers many of the long awaited questions of the disciples of the Torah and bible such as,

1. If Adamah, Chawwah, Abel and Cain were the only people on the earth, then where did their sister come into play and who were these people who could possibly kill Cain?

2. Where did Cains great great grandson Lamech get his two wives from

3.What men invoke or called upon YHWH by name(gen 4:26)

4. Who were these Sons of Allah'im that had sexual relations with the daughter of men

a. Bereshit 1:1 " *In the Beginning*" (Bereshit) according to Gesenius Hebrew-Chaldee Lexicon and Strongs Exhaustive Hebrew Concordance it can mean, " *head, chief. A beginning or first of it kind, with regard to time, ORDER or rank, such as first fruits*(i.e proverbs 8:22).

With an understanding of verse 2 and so on and what the Creator(s) were aiming to accomplish in the Bereshit story and what it meant concerning the order of the earth, then it comes clear that this beginning is a beginning of Order as in the Order or the first fruits of YHWH divine plan for an already existing inhibited world.

b. *"Allah'im creates the heavens and the Earth".*

In the creation story, it is said that Allah'im created the heavens and earth. Allah'im are the mighty ones, and are seen as the seven Malakim(messengers) of Yahwehs presence.(Bereshit 16:7-11; 22:11-15; Shemot 3:2-4;14:19 18:1-22; 1 Melekim 22:19-23; 2Chronicles 18:18-22; Dani'ala 10:12-13,20). Refer to the previous section of this book concerning Allah'im.

Now these Malakim(Mighty-ones) under the command and authority of YHWH are said to have created the *heavens* and the *Earth.*

"Create" is written in the present tense. It is from the Hebrew word, *"Bara",* which could mean, *"to cut, to carve out, to form by cutting."* as in a building contractor takes a uninhibited peace of land, from an already inhibited surrounding and creates or makes it to be inhabitable, apart/separate from the others. Compare to YeshiYah 43:1.

"Heavens" is from the Hebrew word, *Shamayim(*plural) which means " *to be lofty or the sky"* In Hebrew Literature it is also a direct reference to Gan-Eden(Garden of Eden-i.e Heaven on earth) inferring the creation of a specific atmosphere or culture apart from others.

"Earth" is from the Hebrew word, *"Eretz",* which means, "country, land, field, ground(earth)."

For example, Eretz Yisrael, "the Land of Yishra'ala".(see Gen 13;6; YeshiYah 9:18-19). In this case it would a specific geographical location that Allah'im creates for the Gan-Eden.

It should be noted that Eretz is the same word used in the flood story of Noach.

c. verse 2, *"The earth being waste and void with darkness upon the face of the deep"*

"Waste" is in the present tense as if it is happening now, *"the earth being Wasted"*. This is from the Hebrew word, "Hayah tahoo", which means, Destroying(i.e YeshiYah 24:10, desolating, becoming vain or nothing"(i.e YeshiYah 41:29)

"Void" is the Hebrew word, *"Bohuw"*, which means, emptiness or ruined. Used several times in scripture with the Word Tahoo(YirmeYah 4:23; YeshiYah 34:11)

"Darkness" is from the Hebrew word, *Khoshek*, which could mean, "to withhold light(as in truth), wickedness, misery, ignorance, death, sorrow, night"

"Face of the Deep" is from the Hebrew word, *"al(above, over, against), paneh(to turn or appear) tehom,*(a great quantity of waters; ocean or sea; gulf i.e Duet 8:7; 7:11; Job 38:16;38:30,) hence we get the Mediterranean sea or perhaps the Persian gulf more likely

And the Spirit(Or Wind as in a current of air) Allah'im broods on the face of the waters (Persian gulf more likely)

d. verse 3, *"and Allah'im says, Light be-and light becomes"*

"Light" is from the Hebrew word, *"are(Ore')"*, which could mean, *"illumination(in every sense including happiness), cheerfulness, bright, clear, day, morning, sun, Truth."*

1. Light is also used in the sense of furnishing an image of good fortune or prosperity, but Especially Truth/righteousness in YHWH and his Word/Torah as opposed to Sin/ darkness: i.e Iyob(job) 22:28; 30:26; YeshiYah 2:5; 9:2; 10:17; 60:1, 3; 49:6; 51:4; Psalm 97:11; proverbs 6:23;

e. *"And Allah'im see's the light is good: and Allah'im separates between the light and between the darkness. And Allah'im calls the light day and he calls the darkness Night."*

1. *"good"* is from the Hebrew word, *"Towb"*, which could mean, *"Kind, upright, Just, pure, cheerful/merry, right, pleasant, great, excelling, best, well favored"*(compare to: YeshiYah 5:20; 37:3; Ecclesiastes 7:20; 8:12,13; 9:7;

Lamentation 3:25; Proverbs 18:5; 20:23; D'barim 6:24; 10:13; YirmeYah 32:39; 1 Kings 8:66

"Day" is from the Hebrew word, *"Yom"(as in Yom Kippur)*, which could mean, "to be hot(as in the heat of the day), season, day(as in the Day of a festival, 7days of the week or even in such events as the ***DAY of Yahweh, Day of Judgement, Day of Salvation***), time period(without reference to days)(See: Yah'ala 1:15; Ezeki'ala 13:5; YeshiYah 2:12; Iyob 24:1)

2. Understanding "Day" in the context of the meaning of light as presented in this text, it should be clear that light(truth/righteousness) being brought forth in the midst of an already existing world would be called Day as in the beginning Days of Yahweh/ Truth /redemption for the lost wicked world of Darkness.

3. Night is from the Hebrew word, "Lilah", which is related to Layil which means night, yet Lilah means, To twist, or fold back away from light(as in an adversity. LILAH is also known as the female demoness of the night as found in Ancient Hebrew Writings and legends, also known as Lilith(She was/is known to be responsible for sudden infant death syndrome and seducing men in their dreams)

With understanding the above analysis and translations, it should be concluded that the Genesis story is not about the Creation of the World, but the Beginning and origins of the Redeeming/ Messianic Adamahic family and lineage taking on fullness of form in the Nation of Yishra'ala.

The Bereshit accounts traces it genealogy from Adamah to Noach, from Noach to Cham, Shem and Yapeth, with Shem taking on Adopted Messianic calling spiritually but not necessarily exclusively physically. From Shem to Abraham, from Abraham to Yitzkak and from Yitzkak to Ya'akov and From Ya'akov to the full embodiment of the 12 tribes of Yishra'ala. These along take on the Name and title Ben Adamah, mostly translated as *Son of Man* or *Humanity*, but means *Son of Adamah*.

This therefore means that not everyone/live being/human/person on earth is a physical descendant of Adamah, considering Pre-historic humans(Neanderthals etc..) existed before Adamah. This does not mean that Non-Adamahic Peoples cannot be spiritually adopted into the Adamahic family(taking on the term, spiritual seed of Abraham), but it does show that the Adamahic family's specific purpose in this whole world was to bring Salvation and redemption by Spreading the Truth and Light of the Dominion and authority of Yah to those who had fallen and become Sons of Darkness.

Non ben Adamahic peoples who are not redeemed through the Redemption message of YHWH are fallen Sons of Darkness(physically and spiritually)

With this understanding, it should be understood also that the Noach flood story and the replenishing of the Land is not about repopulation of the whole world but the repopulation of the Sons of Adamah. Cham, Shem, and Yapeth are all African Edenic Sons of Adamah and does not in any way convey the thought that they are three races of the world with, Cham being black/African, Shem being Asian like and Yapeth being White/European. They were all of the same Adamahic Lineage with the same Father and Mother, therefore they are all entitled to be called the Ben Adamah.

It is the same for the flood story. The whole earth and all people were not necessarily destroyed. The term used for the destruction of the Earth or world is the Hebrew word, *Eretz,* which could refer to a specific location or region. That is why there are other cultures and nations who have writings of the flood story. And while YHWH destroyed many non-Adamahic peoples with this flood, he also destroyed all but eight of the Ben Adamahic Family for their wickedness. What was this wickedness?

Bereshit 6:1-2, " and so be it, humanity begins to abound by myriads on the face of the soil; and they birth daughters: and the SONS OF ALLAH'IM see that the daughters of humanity are goodly; and they take women of all they choose."

Humanity is the Hebrew Word "HaAdamah", which are descendants of Adamah but a specific faction. Considering that there is another group called the BenayElohim or Sons of Yah.

The sons of Yah commit an evil by intermingling with the daughters of the other descendants of Adamah. (Notice that HaAdamah does not say BenAdamah). Why was it a sin? BenayElohim and HaAdamah are both physically descendants of Adamah, but split off into two different seeds afterwards. One seed is the Seed of Cain who intermingles with the Pre-historic Non-Adamahic mortals as evidenced in

Bereshit 4:14-17, "behold, you expel me(for the 1ˢᵗ Adamahic murder) this day from the face of the soil; and from your face I am hid; and I become a waverer and wanderer in the earth; and so be it, EVERYONE who finds me slaughters me…….and Qayin goes from the face of YHWH and settles in the Land of NOD(an already existing land somewhere in modern Iran), on the east of Eden: and Qayin knows his woman(perhaps a non-Adamahic woman or his sister) and she conceives and births Hanoch….(read the rest of his genealogy and the second murder vs18-24)"

The other seed who retains the title *Sons of Yah* are through the seed of Sheth, Adamahs second son to replace Abel,

Bereshit 4:25, And Adamah knows his woman again; and she births a son anc calls his name Sheth: for Allah'im has set me another seed instead of Abel-whom Qayin slaughtered. And Sheth, he also births a son; and he calls his name Enos: THEN BEGINS THE CALLING ON THE NAME OF YHWH….(Then read the genealogies up to Noach).

Thus we have a fallen Adamahic Lineage who intermingles with Non-Adamahic peoples or Sons of Darkness and we have a BenayElohim Lineage. The BenayElohim Lineage then begins to ruin because they in turn intermingle with the Fallen Sons of Adamah. This fallen stage is not because of Physical Lineage only but because they intermingles with Son/Daughters who were of Darkness and wickedness, an Anti-Yah race and culture thus making them Satanic.

Bereshit 6:3,11-13, "and YHWH says, 'My Spirit pleads not eternally with humanity(Adamah) for he is erring inadvertently, he is flesh(not of the Spirit)......and the earth is ruined at the face of Allah'im and the earth is filled with violence: and Allah'im sees the earth and behold, it is ruined; for all FLESH(Adamahic and Non-Adamahic)" on the earth had ruined his way.....And Allah'im says to Noach, the end of all FLESH Comes at my face;....."(Notice it says all flesh, as referenced to the fallen Adamahic peoples, and not all Humankind; this was the region of modern day turkey)

[Adamah the Original Messiah and Son of Yah.]

The Title Son(s) of Yah did not in any way begin with Non-Adamahic Jesus of Christianity. In fact Christianity and its Jesus is just a Mere Imitation/counterfeit of the Original. This is the Motive and the essence of the Satanic Anti-Yahweh system who seeks to destroy and hinder the Truth and light of the Sons of Adamah, the Son of Yah. The anti-Yah Adversary can only imitate truth only "after" Truth has been set in motion and not before.

Thus we get pagan-Christianity teaching Jesus is the Son of God, born by immaculate conception, is the Savior and redeemer of all the World and is the Light unto the nations, is the divine word incarnate...Yet all of this is just a imitation of Truth

If Anything, Adamah was the one who had the 1st and real immaculate conception considering he is made in the very image and likeness of Yahweh. In essence he is the seed not of the flesh or of man but of the Spirit of Holiness of Yah. In fact his only mother is the Shekinah of the Eternal Creator.

When Yahweh created Adamah he placed his Holy Word in him and gave him his mind, the mind of Yah by breathing into him the Wind of Life. Thus Adamah became the incarnate image of Yahweh, bearing the Eternal seed of the truth of his Word implanted within him by Yahweh, to be a Divine bearer of Redemption and Salvation for an already fallen world; bringing the Light of life to the fallen peoples of Darkness.

Hence we get Yahweh's first only begotten Son and Messiah, Adamah. Thus the Adamahic Creation becomes the standard and preferred order of communication between Yahweh and the human peoples. Thus we get that when Adamah fell, Yahs message was descendent through Adamah's elect seed to Yishra'ala. In its full embodiment through the Covenant and Torah of Yisrael, It is the way to attain redemption, Eternal Life and the fullness of Yahweh and all that he is to us.

Thus Yahweh calls Yishra'ala his firstborn after the likeness of Adamah and vows an Eternal Covenant. And How do we distinguish and discern the Sons of Darkness, the Non-Adamahic family? By Their attempts to oppress and replace the Adamahic Family through Yishra'ala with a counterfeit that practices and teaches Anti-Yah doctrines and culture. And by their fulfilling and practicing the very abhorrences as they did when Yahweh decided to flood the Earth.

Bereshit 6:3,11-13, "and YHWH says, 'My Spirit pleads not eternally with humanity(Adamah) for he is erring inadvertently, he is flesh(not of the Spirit)......and the earth is ruined at the face of Allah'im and the earth is filled with violence: and Allah'im sees the earth and behold, it is ruined; for all FLESH(Adamahic and Non-Adamahic)" on the earth had ruined his way.....And Allah'im says to Noach, the end of all FLESH Comes at my face;....."

These are the same Sons of Darkness that has caused many of the BenAdamahic Family to stumble, fall and err in their ways from Yahweh and his Torah as in the beginning with the fall of the Adamahic family in Gan-Eden.

[How did the Adamahic family fall in Gan-Eden?]

Bereshit 2:8-9, "And Yahweh Allah'im plants a garden eastward in Eden; and there puts Adam whom "he" formed: and from the soil Yahweh sprouts every tree desirable in visage and good for food. The Tree of Life also in the midst of the garden. And the Tree of knowledge of good and evil"

Now notice that it speaks of putting Adamah in the garden and giving him food to eat from various trees. Yet it never says that YHWH planted the Tree of life or the Tree of knowledge of good and evil like the other trees. It says also in the midst of the garden were these two types of trees or characters/beings.

Now in verse 15-17, we see Yahweh giving Adamah His life sustaining Word and Commandments. YHWH here is instructing Adamah on how to live eternally on this earth by obeying his Words and following his design and path for the Adamahic Family.

"Of every tree of the garden(in which YHWH planted), in eating eat: and of the tree of the knowledge of good and evil(which was also in the midst of the garden) eat not: for in the day that "you" eat thereof, in dying you die."

Now in understanding that ancient Yishra'ala had its history, its wisdom and its Teachings, It also had its legends and many stories are mixed with myth, yet the point is always to reveal a higher truth. We should understand that the Genesis story is like a parable that reveals truth. We know that behind the tree's for food there was more to the incident in the garden.

The Tree of Life represented the Messengers of Yah sent to be a guiding light to Adamahic family for their survival. In essence the Word or Torah of Yah all through out the scriptures are compared to food and life which are good for us both mentally, physically and spiritually.

The Tree of the Knowledge of Good and Evil represented the Anti-Yah messengers and representatives of the Sons of Darkness in the midst of Truth. They represent the essence of double standards and instability and irresponsibility. For when Light(good) and darkness(evil) is mixed together, it only produces a more destructive evil. In the fullness of the Adamahic purpose, as revealed through the Torah, teaches us to discern and distinguish between clean and unclean, life and death, good and evil.

Yet in order to be able to distinguish or discern between the two, one must first know and follow the good, the Yah way, the Truth before evil can be detected and they must understand the consequences of falling from that Truth; Death and Destruction! This is the case with Adamah.

How do we know that these trees symbolized Messengers? When Adamah and Chawwah disobey the word of Yahweh and compromised the Spirit of truth with the Spirit of err by falling through temptation, their eyes were opened to a double standard, their understanding and comprehension were subjugated to following evil. Therefore they were Stripped of their innocense and the Spiritual anointing and became aware of their nakedness, that is to say, their default in their natural purpose and design in Yahweh and became ashamed and vulnerable to destruction and darkness because of their compromise of the Word of Yahweh. And then Yahweh asks,

Bereshit 3:11, "who told you, that you were naked? Ate of the tree whereof I misvahed you not to eat?"

Trees don't talk, messengers do. Words were exchanged and learning was processed. They were being fed/educated/indoctrinated, except by the messengers of darkness and death.

Their Messengers of Truth were sent to teach them their way of life in Yahweh; how to eat properly, how to care for and take care of the earth and keep it from pollution and waste, how to establish productive and healthy communities and towns, how treat your fellow-man, how to think like, walk like and manifest the presence of Yah in the world; how to establish universal principles of life that will help all humanity to live Eternally, and how to manifest the Light of Yahweh to the Sons of Darkness.

They were designed and sent to foster a complete positive and enlightening environment for the Adamahic family to grow spiritually and healthy in Yahweh. And when Adamah fell, Yahweh passed on the Messianic purpose in its fullness to the Sons of Yisrael, the Seed of Abraham, the seed of Noach, the seed of Adamah. And Yahwehs plan of Salvation for the world is once again being established through the Adamahic lineage in the fullness of his Torah!

Let the Sons Of Light Discern who this group, culture and people are and let the Fallen Sons of Adamah(Cham, Shem and Yapeth non-Israelite descendants) repent and return and restore themselves to the Truth!!!

Psalms1:1-3 "Blessed is HaAdamah who neither walks in the counsel of the wicked, nor stands in the way of sinners, not settles in the settlement of the scornful. But his delight is in the Torah of Yahweh; and in his Torah he meditates day and night; And being as a **TREE transplanted by the rivulets of water, giving his FRUIT in his time: his leaf withers not; and whatever he works prospers"**

Psalms 37:35(ISR), I saw the **Wicked Tyrant** *stripped Naked as a green native* **TREE;** *yet he passes away; and behold he is not...."*

Psalm 52:8, "But **I** *am like a* **green olive Tree** *in the House of Allah'im..."*

Psalm 92:12, "the **Righteous One** *flourishes like a* **Palm Tree"**

Mishle(proverbs) 11:30, "the **fruit of the Righteous** *is a Tree of Life*

Proverbs 15:4, "a **healing/wholesome tongue** *(word/doctrine)is a Tree of Life*

Selah!!!

Now we will continue to study and understand the development of the Torah Covenant Community Through Abraham and Moshe

[Abram in Ur of Chaldee]

Bereshit 11:26-31(JPS), "When Terah Had lived 70 years, he begot Abram, Nahor and Haran. Now this is the line of Terah; Terah Begot Abram, Nahor and Haran; Haran begot lot. Haran died in the lifetime of his father Terah, in his native land, Ur of the Chaldeans.... Terah took his son Abram, his grandson Lot the son of Haran and his daughter in law Sarai, the wife of Abram and they set out together from Ur of the Chaldeans for the land of Cana'an; but when they had come as far as Haran, they settled there."

Most biblical readers studying the bible are ignorant of the background and cultures of its characters and figures and even their ancestral beliefs and practices. Abraham and his family is one main subject. Biblical history records Abraham and his family as being a native of Ur of the Chaldeans. Ur of the Chaldeans was a flourishing city-state of Mesopotamia(apart of Modern day Iraq), the other two city-states being Kish and Susa. Mesopotamia was like an East and West/ north and South kingdom(s). Assyria was the northern kingdom and Babylonia was the southern kingdom. The southern kingdom of Babylonia was also divided in half. The northern part is the ancient kingdom of Akkad and the lower part is Sumeria(*Israelites, God and History, Maxi Dimont*).

Around the 3rd millennium, the Shemitic Akkad King Sargon I conquered Sumeria and formed a kingdom mixed with Sumerian and Akkadian Culture. This kingdom was highly advanced in science, law, and social institutions as well as agriculture.(in which Abraham took part in). Their commerce and industry were very flourishing. This is the civilization that developed Cuneiform writing, using wedges and characters. Around 2100b.c.e., the great lawgiver and king Hammurabi united all the city-states in this area into one great empire known as Babylonia(Moshe gave the Hebrew Torah one Millennia later).

The Chaldeans in Ur were mostly Negroid\Chamitic and Arabian-like(dark-skinned Shemitic). They had various **Religious Temples** for the worship of their pantheons, Idols and Allah'im, such as their moon-God Temple, and a Temple dedicated to Nin-gal, goddess of the moon and wife of Nanner.

They also practiced the **Cult of Sacrifice** of animals in their Temples. Besides their sacred and ritual obligations in their Temples, the priest had many other things to do. They collected **Tithes(10%)** and taxes. When a person paid their dues they were given ancient receipts on clay tablets. A record of the tithes and taxes were kept on a weekly, monthly and Annual basis.

When I say they paid their tithes and taxes, I don't mean just a form of money or currency, but in fruits and vegetables, wool, oil, cereals, wheat, cattle and livestock etc.

The temple priest also ran and owned factories which manufactured goods. As far as living arraignment, most people in Ur of the Chaldeans lived in large two-story villas. Some of these homes are said to have had as many as fifteen rooms. The upper rooms where made of mud bricks and the lower rooms were made of burnt bricks. They decorated their walls with ornaments and pictures. In their architectures, they used mathematics and addition sums to formulate the measure of square and cubic roots.

Yet despite all of the advancement and technology of their civilization(as ours is today), there were still those who kept with their traditions of their fore-fathers as sheep-herders, nomads and agriculture. This is the civilization and culture in which Abraham and his family lived.

Extra-biblical Israelite sources even records Abraham and his family not only being agriculturalist in Ur, but also ran a family business of idol making and marketing, which was common in the Babylonian empire..

Around the year 2000b.c.e Shemitic tribes like the Assyrians and other nomadic peoples from the Arabian desert began to reek-havoc and challenge the Babylonian empire, therefore causing a potential threat to the existence of the civilization. As a result, the man Terah took his Son Abram(Abraham), his grandson Lot and his daughter-in-law Sarai(and their house-hold) and left to take refuge in Cana'an, but only went halfway and settled in Haran(about 600miles northwest of Ur, modern-day Turkey), possibly because their Father Terah became sick and was dying of old age.

[Abraham in Haran-B'rith Proposal]

Bereshit 11:31b-32, "but when they had come as far as Haran, they settled there. The days of Terah came to 205 years; and Terah died in Haran"

Biblical record shows Abraham as being settled in Haran after leaving Ur of Chaldee due to a sudden crisis of wars and invasion. His father Terah now dies at 205 years old in Haran. Haran means, *"cross road or highway"*. This city was located northwest of Ur of Chaldee. Many highways leading to different cities crossed here. As for the religious aspect, Harans worship was centered around the moon-god *Sin*. Abraham and his household was very familiar with the pagan and idol worship of the cultures of Mesopotamia (Ur and Haran). In fact Abraham and his household was well respected among "his people".

[Spiritual Encounter]

As Abraham continued his daily life in sheep-herding, cattle ranching, and idol worship in Haran, something strange happened, at least something that had not happened since the time of Noach. A Bath Kol or divine voice called to Abraham:

Bereshit 12:1-3, "Yahweh said to Abram, "Go forth from your native land and from your fathers house to the land that I will show you. I will make you a great nation, and I will make your name great and you shall be a blessing. I will bless those who bless you and curse those who curse you; and all the families of the earth shall bless themselves by you."

Abraham, being humble and religious as I suppose, meets a divine being(who later reveals himself to Moshe' as Yahweh or Self existence) and on listening to this bath Kol, [probably first in fear and astonishment because he had never heard a god speak or feel the all-powerful presence of a god(properly a divine being)], he is commanded to "go forth".

After the command this divine being makes a *proposal to a promise* . It is here that the beginning of an *eternal Covenant* is being established through an introduction or proposal. The Eternal One first reveals himself as the Eternal Yachad and one with authority, as seen in his command, and then later as one with the power to establish or bring into existence; his existence, his oneness, his incorporeality(Abraham heard but did not see) his omnipotence and omnipresence and omniscience(The Eternal One knew Abraham was a pagan before he revealed himself to Abraham) were all revealed. Yet this promise proposal would only truly began when Abraham obeyed the first command, "go Forth".

[Obedience through faith-B'rith acceptance]

Bereshit 12:4,5, "Abram went forth as Yahweh had commanded him...."

Even though Abram didn't really know the Eternal divine Being, nor his name(or at least his Character), nor had he ever encountered him before, he put his hope in him that he (Yahweh) would do what he had said. As a result of Avrahams faith and hope in Yahweh, the divine being to him, he went on his way in obedience.

A Netzarim Hebraic commentary on the scriptures defined Faith as,

Hebrews 11:1,8, "Trusting(faith), is being confident of what we hope for, convinced about things we do not see....by trusting Abraham obeyed, after being called to go out to a place that Yahweh would give him as a possession; indeed, he went out without knowing where he was going."

Abrams **Obedience** was the act that accepted the covenant proposal. This is the picture of the first spiritual shiddkhan and engagement; when Yahweh selects Abraham and makes a B'rith and Abram accepts it through faith and obedience(a foreshadow of Torah/Oral Torah obedience), yet the actual B'rith is not ratified until later.

[Abraham in Cana'an-B'rith Ratification]

Bereshit 12:5b-10;13:1,12 "when they arrived in Cana'an, Abram passed through the land as far as the site of Shechem, at the terebinth of Moreh…from there he moved on to the hill country east of bethel and pitched his tent, with Bethel on the west and Ai on the east….there was a famine in the land and Abram went down to Egypt to sojourn there..from Egypt Abram went up to Negeb, with his wife and all that he possessed, together with Lot…..Abram remained in Cana'an."

Here Abraham arrived in Cana'an and traveled around a little bit before going to Egypt, due to a famine.

Egypt was a very, "influencing society". They centered their lives around the Nile river. The Nile valley was separated into two parts known as the *river basins/flat alluvial(black soil)* which were rich with life and water fowl. *red desert land* was mostly deserted of life. Egyptians used canals and canal basins to plant crops and vegetable gardens and to water plants.

Agriculture was also apart of Egyptian life. Their diets were some-what kosher consisting of cattle, tree crops, vegetables, fish barley, emmer wheat, beans, chick peas, flax and different types of other vegetables. Oil was their main prize product.

As for the religious practices of Egypt; they had every Allah'im/pagan god that one could imagine. They believed in a *divine ennead,* or the Heliopolitan Origin Myth, which says

"that the world began as a watery chaos called Nun, from which the sun-god Atum emerged on a mond. By his own power he engendered the twin deities Shu(air) and Tefnut(moisture), who in turn bore Geb(earth) and Nut(sky). Geb and Nut finally produce Osiris(Modern day Jesus), Isis, Seth, and Nephthys. The nine gods so created formed the divine ennead which later was known to be regarded as a single divine entity(compare to the pagan Trinity/Tri-Unity)."

Their religious system consisted of a priestly caste made of priest and priestess. Being a priest was more of an every day career helping keep society in order and functioning properly than seeking the divine and trying to understand the minds of the divine. The mystical and religious attributes were considered somewhat secondary(if one really understands Egyptian Religion).

Religion was a way to attain the basic needs of the society, keep society in order, create hierarchy and preserve culture for future generations. priest were either chosen by the king or hereditary means. Priest were more apart of every day life as the people than separated from it. To be a priest was to have a high status.

Egyptians practiced circumcision among males. They believed in the after-life and practiced sacrifice. They practiced purificatory rites in sacred pools. They practiced healings, magical arts, and dream interpretation. They had scribes, who were very cherished among both the pharaoh and priest. They were in charge of writing magical texts, issuing royal decrees, keeping record of funerary rites(book of the dead) etc…they also spent many years working on the crafting of making hieroglyphics.

Egyptians are also the builders of the mysterious, impossible pyramids and other stone/brick wonders of Egypt!! A black-Cushite/Nubian people, the Egyptians were a very intelligent sophisticated people with a very sophisticated military. Much more is to be told of Egypt, time will not permit me to tell.

[Cana'an]

Scriptures then says that eventually Abram came back to Cana'an and dwelled there. This became the permanent home of Abram. Cana'an was also an explicitly Cushite nation founded by *Cana'an* the son of Cham, the great great grand-uncle of Abraham(by blood).

Cana'an was also the home of the **Cana'anites**(Merchants) **Chittites**(either scary people or terrorfiers), **Girgashites**(dwellers in a clayey soil), Amorites(mountaineers), **Perizzites**(people who live in unwalled villages), **Chivites**(people who lived small towns/villages), and **Yebusites**(Inhabitants of ancient Yerushalem/ people defeated/polluted/trodden)[D'bar 7:1], the **Kenites** (business/marketing people; oriental peoples), **Kenizzites**(hunters), **Kadmonites**(an Original Phonecian tribe/ eastern oriental) and **Rephraim**(tall people who were also doctors and medical physicians)[Bereshit 15:16-19].

Cana'an (located at the tip of North-East Africa in modern Yishra'ala) was a very powerful country with fortified walls. They had a very sophisticated wealthy society of doctors & business people and priest. They practiced idol worship using fetishes made of wood, stone, silver and gold. Most of their worship Centered around divine beings known as **Allah'im(mighty-ones)**. The Allah'im was a celestial council of various deities who were considered to be *One in nature(see Egypt above)*. They were considered the creators of the heavens and earth and the universe. They were believed to possess magical powers and were considered the Great-gods(mighty-ones), even greater than the idols. The Allah'im could not be seen as the idol gods could, because they dwelled in the heavens as the Cana'anites believed.

The people worshiped yet another god(possibly on the council of Allah'im) named **Molech**(king), who was the chief and national god of the Ammonites and **Ba'al(lord)**, a Phoenician god, to whom they sacrificed both animal and children. They practiced polygamy and even married their own mothers, fathers, grandparents, cousins or any relative.

They worshiped yet another god whose name was **Ashtoreth**, the Phoenician goddess of love and increase, in which they practiced orgies and Temple prostitution(male and female). Unlike today, in ancient times Prostitutes were highly revered and respected as sacred/religious people.

Yet many of the more civilized religious people centered their life around the Allah'im. One of their forms of worship specialties was their Religious Choirs.

When doing business or socializing whether religious or not they drank wine and ate(broke) bread. This was also a form of honor among the Cana'anites. Abraham and his household were well familiar with these practices and were practicing most of these cults themselves(the episode of Yahweh telling Abraham to Sacrifice his son Yitzkak on the alter was an Mirror of Molech Worship).

Abraham himself was very religious through his humble-ness and meekness even before he met Yahweh the Eternal Yachad, yet after his experience with Yahweh he gradually began to change. It is recorded that Abraham began to call or ask Yahweh what his name was(Abraham didn't know the name of "Yahweh"as in YHWH Character).

Bereshit 12:8b, "and he built an alter to Yahweh and invoked him by name"

The above passage gives the impression that Abraham felt left out/void on the plans of Yahweh and wanted to know more about Yahweh. He had many questions on his heart, and he wanted to know the fullness and deepness of Yahweh and Yahweh's purpose for his life. Abraham wanted answers; why, how, when, and where? Abraham was really serious about seeking YHWH Will and Purpose because he invokes Yahweh's name again (Bereshit 13:4).

As Yahweh continued to reveal himself and remind Abraham of the promise Abraham began to realize that Yahweh indeed was the *true* Creator and Divine!! Abraham then begins to share his beliefs and experience with his family and then neighbors. He and his family eventually became a peculiar people of monotheism among the inhabitants of Cana'an. Abraham showed that he believed his true Father and Creator was above all the Allah'im and pagan gods(not saying that the other gods were obsolete at that time). This is revealed in the dialogue between Abraham and the king of Sodom and Melchizedek the king of Salem.

Bereshit 14:17-23, "the king of Sodom came out to meet him(Abraham) in the valley of Shaveh, which is the call valley of the King. And king Melchizedek of Salem brought out bread and wine; he was a priest of God Most High. He blessed him saying, 'Blessed be Abram of God Most high, Creator of Heaven and Earth, and blessed be God Most High, who has delivered your foes into your hand. and Abram gave a tenth of everything(Selah? Ur). But Abram said to the king of Sodom, "I swear to the to the LORD God Most high, Creator of heaven and earth…..."

Now to the untrained eye and one who has failed to analyze the Hebrew words for Lord and God in the scripture(as the writer of the B'rith Chadasha's Hebrews has failed), he/she would come to the conclusion that Melchizedek and Abram spoke of the same Creator and Lord. Not So!!! In verse 18 Melchizedek is said to be a priest of ***God Most high.*** This is Cana'anite/Hebrew word ***El Elyon***(The Chief of Allah'im). Melchizedek was a Cana'anite pagan priest and the king of Salem(pre-Yerushalem), a Cana'anite city. Melchizedek thought that the Cana'anite Chief Allah'im *EL* had delivered Avrams enemies into his hands. After all, to the Cana'anites, the Allah'im(plural of Elowahh=female mighty one) were supernatural and powerful.

Melchizedek   honored   and   believed   Abram   was   an anointed(Mashiakh)/ chosen one of the Allah'im. That's why he says, *"Abram of El Elyon"*, when he blesses him(Bereshit 14:18-20). Yet when Abram does not accept the king of Sodoms offer, he puts both men in check about the real Creator.

v.s. 22, "I swear to the LORD, God Most High, Creator of heaven and Earth"

The word for *LORD* is **Yahweh** and *God Most High is* **El Elyon** (mighty from/on High), which should properly read,

"I swear to 'Yahweh', Almighty most High.."

Abraham although not fully aware of the Character of Yahweh, knows that Yahweh is the True Almighty most high. Abraham experienced the victory over his enemies by the Power of Yahweh. Yahweh name is his character. He expressed his Character traits to Abraham but he revealed the revelation of his Character to Moshe. Therefore although Abraham and his descendant before Moshe had the name of Yahweh literally, they didn't know the true essence of it. Abram did use the title *Adonai(sir/lord/master)* at times, which was a common cultural word used as a title of respect(including towards pagan deities)[Bereshit 18:27,30-32; 24: 9-65; 43:20 etc).. How-ever, because of the lack of understanding the fullness of Yahweh, He(they) continued to use different titles with his name such as El, Elyon, El Shaddai. Many times they didn't use Yahweh at all. But they knew within themselves which Deity they did worship which was not the norm of paganism.

It should be noted that El was also a common Shemitic term for any deity in general, just as the term god today is a common term for deity's..

[B'rith of 'the Promise']

Bereshit 15:1, "Sometimes later the word of Yahweh came to Abram in a vision...."

Study verse 1-19 for yourself and Selah.... In this prophetic vision YHWH begins to reveal himself as a Father to Abram. He consoles Abram and assures him that he will be his protector and provider(vs.1), his strength. This probably stems out of Abram's then having controversy and conflict with many of his neighbors(and perhaps some family members) about Yahweh the "One" true Creator, A belief that was foreign to

Cana'an, which in turn probably caused persecution and resentment towards Abram causing doubt, pessimism and discouragement in Abram.

There is a rabbinic story of Abraham being refuted for denouncing idolatry and believing in an Ultimate Creator while his father was alive, even before he encountered Yahweh,

Every Mans Talmud(Gen.R. XXXVIII.13) pg1-2, "when he(Abraham) revolted against idolatry, his father took him before King Nimrod, who demanded that since he would not worship images he should worship fire. Abraham replied to him, "We should rather worship water which extinguishes fire." Nimrod said to him: "then worship water." Abraham retorted: "if so, we should worship the cloud which carries water!" Nimrod said: "then worship the cloud." Abraham retorted: "if so, we should worship the wind which disperses the cloud!" Nimrod said: "then worship the wind." Abraham retorted: "rather should we worship the human being who carries the wind!"

This could be the sole reason why Yahweh revealed himself to Abraham in the first place. However Abrahams discouragement and mental frustration is something we all go through regardless of our faith and walk with Yahweh, especially when we began to practice and worship a way that is not considered the norm to those around you. This insecurity can be found in verse 2-3,

"but Abram said, oh Adonai(master) Yahweh(here rendered as GOD) what can you give me, seeing that I shall die childless…since you have granted me no offspring, my steward will be my heir."

For those who are in tune with life, put yourself in Avrahams shoes. Has Yahweh ever showed you or promised you something great, and you were excited about it until you told someone who doubts everything and is always pessimistic in thinking? They laugh at you and say negative things to discourage you or try to make you think that its all apart of your imagination. Or that you are too zealous and presumptuous. They say things like...

"who made you chief and ruler over us? (Exodus 2:14)" or "do you still hold to your integrity? Curse Yahweh and die!(Iyob 2:9)." or "now that I am withered, am I to have enjoyment-with my husband so old(Bereshit 18:12)." or "where do this mans wisdom and miracles come from? Isn't he the Carpenters son? Isn't his mother called Miriam? And his brothers Ya'akov, Yosef, Shim'on and Yahudah? And his sisters, aren't they with us? So where does he get all this(MattiYah 13:54-56)." or "Your doctor, teacher, mother said...."

Faithless people who are not of Yahweh can be discouraging to you when you've put your trust in Yahweh. Especially when you are trusting for things that seem impossible, or other people don't believe in Yahweh.

I Believe this is truly the case with Abraham and his faith in the promise of Yahweh. His doubt caused him to try to pervert the promise by insisting that his steward would be his heir instead of his own seed. This is nothing but a trick of the Evil impulse influenced by the Adversary Ha-Satan.

Ha-Satanim from the beginning have tried to pervert the will of Yahweh. Yet they only succeeds when they're able to influence man-kind to substitute YHWH will for an alternative which in turn causes destruction or produces potential problems for future generations(i.e Yitzkak and Yishma'ala controversy). This is not to say that Ha-Satanim has power, because they don't. Yahweh never gave them power nor authority. He gave Adamah authority, responsibility and a will. And according to how we use our will is according to how good and evil will manifest in our lives and the world. The accountability lies back on us.

We are either going to trust Yahweh according to his will or rebel and hand over our authority to the evil one(s) and face potential and ultimate self destruction. This is what happened to Abram, yet YHWH goes on to comfort and assure Abram of his sovereignty to fulfill his promise, vs.6, *"and because he put his trust in Yahweh, he(Yahweh) reckoned it to his merit."*

[Animal sacrifice doesn't bring possession nor moves Yahweh-B'rith preparation]

Bereshit 15:7-8, "Then he(Yahweh) said, 'I am Yahweh who brought you out of Ur of the Chaldeans to assign this land to you as a possession'...and he(Abram) said,'oh Adonai Yahweh, how shall I know that I am to possess it(Cana'an)?'"

This passage is a continuation of verse 1-6 dialogue between Abram and Yahweh. Constantly being in fellowship and communication with Yahweh will build your faith and faithfulness to his Torah and will as you are lead by his Ruakh, because Yahweh will remind you of his Word(Torah) and promises; from prosperity to healing and purpose as we are faithfully obedient to his Torah(D'var 28).

This is the situation here as Yahweh systematically reveals the revelation of his promise . This part of the revelation of the promise revealed is about the possession or *Provision* to build the seed of the promise, the Hebrew-Israelites). Abraham in his faith and security in Yahweh seeks further instruction and direction on a sign or proof of how he will possess the land of Cana'an. Yahweh then proceeds to answer his question, yet in a peculiar way.

Bereshit 15:9-11, "He(Yahweh) answered, 'bring me a three-year old heifer, a three year old she-goat, a three year old ram, a turtledove, and a young bird.' He brought him all these and cut them in two, placing each half opposite the other; but he did not cut up the bird. Birds of prey came down upon the carcass, and Abram drove them away..."

What? this is YHWH answer? It is recorded that all Yahweh said was to bring some animals; a goat, ram, heifer, turtledove and a bird. That's it!!

Abram got them as Yahweh commanded and set them up to Yahweh, as he did traditionally with his native people and the Cana'anites to their deity's. Yet the only thing that happened was that the bird of prey came down upon the carcass and Abram had to drive them away. Yahweh didn't respond anymore, until later during sunset when Abram fell asleep. What kind of answer was that?

Remember! Sacrifice was a custom of the Egyptians, Cana'anites, Babylonians, Phoenician and other Shemitic and Chamitic pagan cults in which Abram was apart before he met Yahweh. When Yahweh revealed himself to Abram, he revealed himself in a redemptive manner, meaning that Yahweh was taking Abram out of one scenario of Worship and Lifestyle, which was pagan, and teaching him and his descendant to live in another scenario of Worship and lifestyle, which was Yahwistic,(monotheism) and Torah observant. As far a culture wise, Abrahams descendants only evolutionized.

Yahweh was saying prophetically, " worshiping and treating Him as you did your Allah'im and other pagan deities and acting like a pagan will get you *no-where*! Especially in His established **Torah-Covenant Community** of the future seed! This is Echoed numerous times in the Torah of Moshe'(D'bar 12:29-32; Chap 13).

Now many of you will say, "well the Law(Torah) given by Moshe' contain instructions for Sacrifice." Yes it does, in the written form we have it today(Our scriptures today are written in Babylonian Hebrew, not ancient Hebrew), but the prophets of the Hebrew scripture continuously speak a different message.

I YeshiYah 1:10-17, "Hear the Word of Yahweh, You Chieftains of Sodom; Give ear to our Fathers Instructions, you folk of Gomorrah!

YeshiYah calls the Hebrews, peoples of Sodom and Gomorrah. Sodom and Gomorrah were two very immoral Cana'anite cities. YeshiYah was making an analogy to their practices,

"'What need have I of all your sacrifices?' says Yahweh.' I am sated(disgusted) with burnt offerings of rams(See Abram above), and suet of fatlings, and blood of bulls; and I have no delight in lambs and he-goats. That you come to appear before me-who asked that of you? Trample my courts no more; bringing oblations is futile, incense is offensive to me. New moons and Shabbat, proclaiming of solemnities, assemblies **with iniquity** *I cannot abide. your new moons and fixed seasons fill me with loathing; they are a burden to me, I cannot endure them."*

Yahweh through first YeshiYah outright condemned sacrifices. He hated them and called them iniquity and burdensome to himself(Yahweh).

Notice that I have **New moons, Shabbat, proclaiming of solemnities, assemblies and fixed seasons** underlined. This is because to the average reader this passage could seem mis-leading and give the impression that they are not to observe these underlined just as they are not to observe sacrifice. Not so! The passage specifically explains that trying to practice the Torah of Yahweh(Shabbat, new moons, festivals etc..) mixed with paganism and iniquity(sacrifice in this case) is just as sinful as practicing paganism apart from Torah or not practicing Torah at all! The above underlined are very much practices of Yahweh.

Second YeshiYah(whoever he is) goes on to say in Chapter 66:9(NKJ)

"He who kills a bull is as if he slays a man; he who sacrifices a lamb, as if he breaks a dogs neck; he who offers a grain offering, as if he offers swines blood; He who burns incense, as if he blesses an idol. Just as they have chosen their own ways, and their soul delights in their abominations, so I will chose their delusions, and bring their fears on them; because, when I called, no one answered, when I spoke they did not hear; but they did evil before my eyes, and chose that in which I did not delight."

Oy vey!! This passage reveals some very horrible abominations and offences against true Torah, because of offerings and Sacrifices of animals. The Hebrew word for *Kill* is **shakat**, which means, "*to slaughter*" as for sacrifice. The Hebrew word *Slays* is **nakah,** which means, "*to murder*". This means that killing an animal for sacrifice(not food) is the same as violating the seventh commandment in Exodus 20:13; D'var 5:17(JPS)

"*You shall not* **murder**"

If you understand Hebrew leader Ya'akob in his letter, chapter 2:10-11,

"*for a person who keeps the whole Torah, yet stumbles at one point, has become guilty of breaking them all. For the one who said, 'don't commit adultery', also said, 'don't* **murder***'. Now if you don't commit adultery but do murder, you have become a transgressor of the Torah*",

then you should understand that if you even mentally believe in animal sacrifice(or human i.e. Jesus blood redeems)which constitutes murder, then you believe in Transgressing All of YHWH Torah. And as we know, people usually act according to how they think. In this case barbaric, cruel and violent, whether physically or psychotically. Selah.

Sacrifice which is a cruel and inhumane practice, in YHWH mind, has no meaning(contrary to eating). Therefore its like killing for fun. The Hebrew scriptures says in Leviticus 17:14 concerning animal blood after hunting for **food,**

"*For the life of* **all** *flesh is its blood. Any-one who partakes of it shall be cut off.*"

Now if the Blood is the "life" of "all" flesh, including humans, then this means that when you use blood as a means of forgiveness or redemption, something(someone) had to be murdered or killed to get the blood, whether animal or human. Yahweh already said that you shall not murder.

Murder is intentionally and pre-meditative, to kill is accidentally or immediately without pre-meditation.

So therefore using or even pleading blood of a murdered animal or human is an abomination and violation of true Torah. When a Christian or Messianic Jew *"Pleads the blood of Jesus/Yeshua"* and teaches blood Atone-ment through Jesus, they are partaking in the murder of the victim Yahshua and Breaking the very Torah of Yahweh(in which Yahshua taught). This is strictly a practice of the worship of Molech(Lev 18:21)!!

Yahweh is against sacrifice, and he would never sacrifice one of his own people or creatures for the sake of getting his/its blood to forgive sins. He alone can Atone for sins through his grace and mercy and power to forgive.

The view of a blood thirsty Deity is the result of peoples with sub-human thoughts and natures that tries to define the Eternal Creator in Animalistic Barbaric terms

This is just a setup by Humanities Evil Impulse itself. Even the Orthodox Jewish community need to Repent for Teaching the validity of sacrifice and preparing priest for a future Temple to sacrifice. It is a ancient custom of the pagans!! It is only a promotion of human irresponsibility and un-accountability. It totally contradicts Yahwehs commands to mankind in the Bereshit chapter 1. We need to stop trying to use scapegoats and become mature enough to standup to and take accountability for our own fallacies and face the consequence ourselves for our own actions.

Until we do that as individuals first and then as a human race, our hope for redemption and deliverance and guidance is hopeless.

Now notice in the same passage of YeshiYah its makes analogies of breaking a dogs neck, offering swines blood(Oy vey!!), and sacrificing to idols. All of this is a picture of murder and Worship of Molech with unkosher animals. Just from a little Sacrifice and offering. Or is it little in YHWH eyes?

Are you getting the picture? Somebody(has) been tampering with YHWH Torah in the past. Adding things and Taking out things!!

YirmeYah 7:21-23, "Thus says Yahweh Tzava'ot, the strength of Yishra'ala: 'Add your burnt offerings to your other sacrifice and eat the meat! For when I freed your fathers from the land of Egypt, I did not speak with them or command them concerning burnt offerings or sacrifice. But this is what I commanded them: do my bidding, that I may be your Strength and you may be my people; walk 'only' in the way that I enjoin upon you, that it may go well with you.'...from the day your fathers left the land of Egypt until today. And though I kept sending all my servants the prophets...they would not listen to me or give ear."

HoshiYah 6:6, "For I (Yahweh) desire goodness, not sacrifice"

Amotz 5:22-25, "I loathe your festivals, I am not appeased by your solemn assemblies(which have been perverted). If you offer me burnt offerings-or your meal offerings-I will not acceptpt them; I will pay no heed to your gift of fatlings.....did you offer sacrifice and oblation to me those forty years in the wilderness, oh house of Yishra'ala?

These three passages are even a more scarier scenario. Yahweh declares that he never mentioned sacrifice to Yishra'ala after they were delivered from Egypt. The answer to Amotz's question is obviously **no**! If the answer is no, and the scripture says that Moshe' gave instruction on how to sacrifice and give offerings according to Yahweh, then who really gave instructions to Yishra'ala and who were they really sacrificing to if not Yahweh? Selah!

Amotz 5:25, "Yes, you bore the Sukkoth/brush arbor of you sovereign and Chiun, the star of your Allah'im, the images you worked yourselves."

Chiun is another name for the god Saturn. Saturn is known as the star of Yishra'ala Allah'im. Who that Allah'im is, is not known in the Hebrew scriptures. Yet it is strange that a New Testament passage quotes Amotz 5:25 in a different way:

(Jewish New Testament) Acts 7:42-43, "So God turned away from them and gave them over to worship the stars-as it is written in the book of the prophets, 'people of Yishra'ala, it was not to me that you offered slaughtered animals and sacrifices for forty years in the wilderness! No, you carried the Tent of Molekh and the star of your god Reifan, idols you made so that you could worship them."

Whether or not this quote is from an oral tradition or not is not known to me at this time. Yet in light of the Sacrificial cult, *Molech* was the God of Sacrifice, both animal and human. In light of the name Reifan, this is an incorrect Greek transliteration of the name *Chiun*. It seems to me that the tent/tabernacle of the congregation, although created for Yahweh, originally was a tabernacle designed for Molech, and was adopted by the Hebrews in the wilderness.

Actually Most of the Hebrews culture and beliefs is a combination of Egyptian, Cana'anite and other Shemitic and Chamitic cultures evolved into one culture, by Divine will(i.e America is a combination of British, Greek, roman, and Hebrew culture). Because the sacrifice rituals were instituted also, they were considered to be worshiping Molech or Allah'im instead of Yahweh. More research needs to be done on this matter as the Prophet Amotz makes a serious, but good accusation.

YirmeYah 8:8(living bible), "How can you say, 'we understand his laws(Torot)', when your teachers(and scribes) have twisted them up to mean a thing I never said?"

Just as the modern translation of the Greek text of the New Testament is nothing but a creatively rewritten, distorted version of the original Hebrew/Aramaic B'rith Chadasha, which has deceived Millions of people and led them away from Yahweh and the Torah, so is the modern translations of the Hebrew Torah(respectively) a distorted and twisted version of the original, which has led people away from Yahweh and true Worship.

But there is a remedy to this. Yahweh will raise up anointed Hebrew scholars who will have deep knowledge of ancient Yishra'ala and the pagan cultures, and will be able to root out and destroy the added pagan practices(such as sacrifice) and restore the true worship of Yahweh in the Hebrew scriptures.

The prophetic writings are our greatest help in understanding this, for it was the prophets that had the actual writings of Torah, which were a different version that what the Apostate Hebrew priests had. These controversies play a major role in the split of the Kingdom into Yahudah and Yishra'ala. Yahudah maintaining the truth.

As I believe, true Torah and faith teaches Moral responsibility and value for human and earthly life and preservation. If it doesn't better your life and how you treat others, then it is of no use and is not true. Yet when it gives us foundation and strengthens us and teaches us to become one with our inner-being and one with the Eternal Creator and guides us to reach and fulfill our destiny and purpose, then and only then is it considered True Torah, and never at the expense of oppression and disrespect for another peoples culture and beliefs

After the destruction and restoration of Yahudah, the scribes edits and formats the Hebrew scriptures by combining several traditions of Torah(Know as the E, J, D and P sources) into one. The Canonization of the Hebrew scriptures then takes place. For more info read the introductions to **The Torah, a Modern Commentary** by Rabbi W. Gunther Plaut.

[back to the anti-sacrifice proofs]

Even HaMeleck Davyid, who was with out the Majority of written Torah during his reign said,

Psalms 40:6-7, "You oh Yahweh my father, have done many things;... You gave me to understand that you do not ask for burnt offerings and sin offering."

Yahshua the Hebrew Teacher of the Essenes (as opposed to Jesus/Yeshu of post135c.e.) was seen as one who was against Temple sacrifice,

Yahchonan 2:13, " it was almost time for the festival of Pesach(pass-over) in Yahudah, so Yahshua went up to Yerushalem. In the Temple grounds he found those who were selling cattle, sheep and pigeons, and others who were sitting at tables exchanging money. He made a whip from cords and drove them all out of the Temple grounds, the sheep and cattle as well. He knocked over the money-changers tables, scattering their coins; and to the pigeon sellers he said, 'get these things out of here! How dare you turn my fathers house into a market?"

The Gospel of the Ebionites 6 records Yahshua as saying,

"I came to do away with sacrificing and if you don't stop sacrificing you won't stop experiencing **wrath**(The Complete Gospels)!!"

You may ask, "well what about the numerous passages citing Yahweh as accepting and approving sacrifice by individuals"? My answer(s) is first read YirmeYah 8:5-9. There has been numerous of tampering with YHWH Torah. Not only by Christians, but by Apostate ancient Hebrew scribes. It takes a lot of study and insight into ancient pagan cultures and what Yahweh really desires of us concerning his Torah and his teachings.

We must began to see what Yahweh originally planned for his creation. Both humans, animals and plants/seeds. Were they originally for sacrifice? Is the smell of sacrifice really a sweet smelling savor to Yahweh? Is Yahweh so powerless that he needs a life for a life? Is living blood really a means to salvation and redemption? Does Yahweh really sacrifice humans(i.e Jesus) so that their blood can satisfy his Judgement against man-kind, even as the pagans do to Molech? Is Yahweh Molech?

If you answered no to at least one the above questions, then all of the above questions are answered NO! If you answered yes to any of the above questions, then maybe you are guilty of Worshiping Molech!!! the most inhumane Allah'im of all the Ha satans!! If this is true and you truly want to be a worshiper of Yahweh and want true spiritual discernment, then know that YHWH grace and kindness is extended to you for you to repent.

I must however point out that it is a big possibility That YHWH allowed the sacrificial system to continue for a season or so until Yishra'ala spiritually Matured. For in truth it would have been almost impossible to keep the Yishra'alites from reverting back to their former ways of life had YHWH just pulled the rug from under their feet. Yishra'ala way of life and culture was rooted in Cana'anite, Phonecian, Babylonian and Egyptian culture before they met YHWH and it would not have been total justice to totally eliminate the way they worshiped and acted culturally.

Although YHWH himself did not want animal and grain sacrifices, he allowed it to be given to him, that way Yishra'ala would not sacrifice to their hinder Allah'im as they saw their fellow neighbors continuing in their worship and lifestyle. It's the same with Entering the Torah Covenant Community with Gentiles of various cultures. They are spiritual babes and they must gradually be weaned from their former ways of life. Even with the person whose lifestyle having been nothing but Drugs. You can't expect him/her to just stop without proper help and not physically cause harm to themselves or have them revert back to drugs.

If a person who has lived in America all their lives decided to move to China, how would they act when they first got there? Like an American! But the longer they live in China and the more they study and hang around Chinese people and experience the culture they will eventually ingraft themselves into that culture and become Chinese. This is the case with Yisrael and the Problem of Sacrifice.

Yet when it came time for Yishra'ala to become Spiritual Adults they wanted to act like heathenish babies and still sacrifice and practice other abominable things(which eventually caused them to revert back to Pagan practices anyway). So YHWH warned them through The Nabi'im's, they wouldn't heed the warnings, so YHWH therefore destroyed both Temples in such a way that we all knew it was *him* who allowed it to happen...on the same Hebrew day of Tish B Av!

Yishra'ala then had no choice but to understand that *It is the Sacrifice of Praise and worship and the fruit of our lives,as we are dedicated to YHWH and his Torah, that YHWH originally wanted.*

YirmeYah 7:3(JPS), "Thus said the LORD(Yahweh) of Hosts, the Almighty of Yishra'ala: Mend your ways and your actions, and I will let you dwell in this place. Don't put your trust in illusions and say, 'the Temple of YHWH, the Temple of YHWH, the Temple of YHWH are these buildings.' No, if you really mend your ways and your actions; if you execute justice between one man and another; if you do not oppress the stranger, the orphan, and the widow; if you do not shed the blood of the innocent in this place; if you do not follow other gods, to your own hurt-then only will I let you dwell in this place, in the land that I gave to your fathers for all times. See, you are relying on illusions that are of no avail. Will you steal and murder and commit adultery and swear falsely, and sacrifice to Ba'al, and follow other gods whom you have not experienced, and then come and stand before me in this House which bears My Name and say, "We are safe"?-Safe to do all these abhorrent things! Do you consider this House, which bears my Name, to be a den of thieves? As for Me, I have been watching-Declares YHWH."

I believe in the prophetic authority of the prophets of the Hebrew scriptures who, by the Ruakh of Yahweh, condemned the sacrificial system and offerings and other heathenish practices. These are the very Prophets whom Yahweh spoke to Moshe about in D'barim 18:18-20. Although in verse 18(JPS) it says

"I will raise up a Prophet...",

in the Hebrew "*a*" is not found. It was added by translators. The rest of the verse up until verse 20 is written in a singular tone, but is speaking of

Prophetic peoples or Prophets in the plural as evidence of the continuation of the conversation in verse 20,

"But any Prophet who presumes to speak in My name....."

Any Prophet here, is any ordained/ appointed Prophet whom Yahweh raises up like or after Moshe. Verse 22 further shows that although written in the Singular, it speaks plural of any Prophet;

"If the Prophet speaks in the name of the LORD(Yahweh)......"

The Hebrew Scriptures many times write in the singular yet is talking about a plural subject or peoples(i.e YeshiYah 41:9b-12)

In my conclusion of the sacrifice proof, Yahweh was teaching Abram and Ultimately setting the example to all to separate himself from paganism and become set-apart(sacred) to Yahweh and worship Yahweh, not according to former paganistic traditions, but according to the way Yahweh desired(Yahchonan 4:23-24). That is with faith and faithful obedience to YHWH Word(Torah) as we are led by the Spirit of Yahweh.

[sign of the B'rith-Covenant Consecration]

Bereshit 17:1, "when Abram was 90 years old, Yahweh appeared to Abram and said, I am Ayil Shaddai. Walk in my ways and be blameless.

Here Yahweh reveals his character as *Ala Shaddai(Ala Shaddai)*. Notice this is not a name of Yahweh, but a characteristic of Yahweh. This word is usually rendered as God Almighty(almighty god), but this is incorrect. **Ala** (from ayil)means, " power, strength supported as in a father". **Shaddai** is from the Hebrew root word *Shaddai* which also means, "Power, but in a plurality since. As in ones power who is spread out all over".

For example, a national dictator of a specific country has power over that nation in which he controls(singular), but the above power, has power over all nations and countries and galaxies etc, all at one time. While a dictator can only be somewhere at one time physically to show his power(without modern invention), the above power can be everywhere at one time to express its power. Without help or assistance! Rendering to be *self sufficient power(omnipotent)*. Therefore it should read, "**Powerful-strength, Almighty power, Powerful supporter, or power-power*ful*"** This is where Yahweh actually reveals the *Plurality of his majesty, greatness and power.* Most Israelites confuse this with the Allah'im concept. Not so!

Yahweh was showing Abram, that he(Yahweh) alone has the all-sufficient power to supply all Avrams needs and desires, thus showing the ultimate characteristic of a Father of fathers, and the true source in which everything that exists has its being. Yahweh showing himself as Alla Shaddai, also shows him as being Yachad(One), yet he is so powerful and awesome in his greatness that he equals all and more of the Pagan Allah'im and Ha satans altogether, and still has infinite power left over!!

D'var 10:17, "For Yahweh your Almighty is Powerful than the Allah'im's, and Lord of lords, mighty and awesome, who shows no partiality nor takes bribes....."

Malek ha melekim, Ayil ha Allah'im, Adon ha adonim, he is Yahweh Allah'im(King of kings, powerful than Allah'im, Lord of lords, he is Yahweh our Strength)!!!

Bereshit 17:3-8, " Abram threw himself on his face and Yahweh Spoke to him Further, 'as for me, this is my **B'rith** *(Covenant) with you: you shall be the FATHER of a multitude of nation's. You shall no longer be called* **Abram(probably my father is exalted)**, *but your name shall be* **ABRA-HAM,** *for I make(present tense) you the father of a multitude of nations.....I* *will maintain my covenant between me and you, and your offspring to come, as an* **everlasting covenant** *throughout the ages, to be a Father(supporter) to you and to your offspring to come."*

Here Yahweh, in his process of consecrating the **Covenant of Promise**, gives Abraham new name. This name given corresponds to Avrahams, personality, character, ethnic background and purpose/calling. In the Biblical Hebrew faith a persons name not only identified him/her, but it determined/affected their personality, actions and ultimately their future and destiny. A name in biblical YaHudaism cohabits the person.*if you understand the make-up of the Torah/Oral Torah instructions, by now you should have realized that YHWH relationship with Abraham is a prophetic shadow of the written Torah that was manifested through Moshe' later. This is a proof of the pre-existence of the Torah(Word) of Yahweh.

The name changing of Abram to Abraham is also a picture of the process of Nissuin(marriage). Yahweh uses Hoshea to symbolize his relationship with the Hebrews as a husband/wife relationship. This is a spiritual Nissuin(marriage) foreshadowed by Yahweh and Abraham(Ultimately Yahweh will be married to the gentiles who choose to enter his Torah covenant).

In a Nissuin, the bride always changes her name to the grooms name. Avrahams name is named after YHWH ultimate character, *"Father"*. This prophetic significance symbolizes Abraham as having been the **revealed** Character of Yahweh. This is the example all of YHWH Hebrew followers should follow. We are to be the expressed character of Yahweh on earth according to his Torah and Ruakh(Spirit);Vessels that Yahweh can use to do his will in our lives and the lives of the people of the earth.

[Nissuin/ ring-Covenant of Circumcision-Mark of Yahweh]

Bereshit 17:9-14, "Yahweh further said to Abraham, 'as for you, you and your offspring to come throughout the ages shall keep my covenant...such shall be the covenant between me and you and your offspring to follow which you shall keep: every male among you shall be circumcised. You shall circumcise the flesh of your foreskin, and **that** *shall be the* **sign of the covenant between me and you. And throughout the generations, every male among you shall be circumcised at the age of 8days...** *Thus shall my Covenant be marked in your flesh as an 'everlasting' pact. And if any male who is uncircumcised fails to circumcise the flesh of his foreskin, that person shall be cut off from his kin; he has broken(divorced-get) my Covenant."*

This Covenant agreement specifically shows that it is an agreement that cannot become old or annulled unless disobedience occurs. The Covenant of Promise is a covenant between Abraham and Abrahams descendants, the Hebrews/Yishra'alites, and Yahweh. It is an everlasting Covenant. If any other doctrine arises teaching that this covenant is old and done away with and that there is a new Covenant, then it is a Hasatanic Lie!

Yahweh has not and will never replace Yishra'ala the YaHudaim/Hebrews, with another peoples. Any one outside of the Covenant of The Hebrews is considered the world, goyish(gentile), respectively.

A born Yishra'alite that does not Worship according to the covenant is just as much a Gentile as the Gentile is a Gentile!

When Abraham Circumcised his house-hold and himself, he showed physically that he entered Spiritually the Fullness of the Covenant of Yahweh, the Covenant of promise. He then had access to all of Yahweh's blessings and prosperity as a Great Father.

The sign of the Covenant is *B'rith Milah (circumcision)* in which regardless of age, all must go through to as a sign that he/she has entered the fullness of the B'rith. This Covenant of Promise is also known as the **Covenant of Circumcision/or Covenant of Redemption.**

Section2-Covenant of Provision-The Torah Community

Exodus(Leviticus, Numbers, Deuteronomy) is the book(s) which speaks of the physical and spiritual birth of Yishra'ala as a Nation...*and Torah Community*. It contains the stories of enslavement and liberation(*salvation*), of revelation and wanderings, of belief and apostasy; it is the repository of fundamental laws and of the rules *and teachings* governing national *and Community* worship [italics by writer]-(The Torah, a modern commentary, Union of Hebrew congregations, New York)

The Covenant of Provision(Deliverance) is the established Community of Hebrews and Hebrew proselytes under Torah teachings that Yahweh manifested through Moshe to the Yishra'alites to be the initial religious community that provides a foundation and protection to maintain YHWH Covenant of Redemption given through Abraham.

Exodus 3:1-6, "Now Moshe, tending the flock of his father-in-law Yethro, the priest of Midian, drove the flock into the wilderness, and came to Horeb, the Mountain of Yahweh. An angel of Yahweh appeared to him in a blazing fire out of the bush. He gazed, and there was a bush all aflame, yet the bush was not consumed....When Yahweh saw that he had turned aside to look, Yahweh called to him out of the bush....'I am', he said, ' the Father(or strength/Creator) of your father, the Father of Abraham, the Father of Yitzkak, and the Father of Ya'akov."

The development of this B'rith begins when Yahweh the Eternal Creator reveals himself to Moshe', the Egyptian Hebrew, through his Malak(Divine messenger) in a burning bush on Mt. Horeb in Midian, a Cushite/Yishma,alite, Cana'anite(Bereshit 37:25-28,36; Numbers 12:1) Hebrew city that worshiped like the Mesopotamians (his father in law Jethro was a Cana'anite priest, possibly after the order of Melchizedek).

In verse 5, YHWH's first command to Moshe' was, *"do not come closer"* and *"take off your sandals"* because Moshe was standing on Holy ground.

This was relating to Moshe that when and where-ever YHWH direct manifested presence is everything around that area is sacred and Holy.

Now Yahweh is omnipresent. His presence is every-where, yet he must manifest himself for one to be mentally, physically or spiritually aware. This episode teaches us that because Yahweh is omnipresent, we as a Hebrew Holy-Nation and Torah community should always be sacred and holding fast to righteousness, Holiness and Justice, both publicly and privately, because YHWH presence is there, whether manifested or not.

Yahweh goes on further to identify himself to Moshe' as the Mighty one or strength of Abraham, Yitzkak and Ya'akov. He identified the three to indicate that throughout the generations of his people and their descendants he **constantly renews his covenant.**

Notice Yahweh says that he 'is' the Mighty-one of Abraham, Yitzkak and Ya'akov in the present tense, as if they were still alive. This is the indication that Yahweh is the father of the Living, meaning that the seed of Abraham is still Abraham, and the seed of Yitzkak is Abraham and Yitzkak, and the Seed of Ya'akov is Abraham, Yitzkak and Ya'akov. They were very much alive in their seed! This also gives us the idea that Abraham Yitzkak and Ya'akov are still alive in the spiritual realm, although dead in the natural, meaning that when a person dies, his spirit-soul lives on. To further clarify: Yahweh is not the Father of the dead, but the father of the living.

When Yahweh declares some-one dead, this means that they are eternally separated from him unto damnation and utter destruction, yet those who live on inherit the olam Haba(the World to Come). Yahweh is indeed the Father of the Living, Abraham, Yitzkak, and Ya'akov.

Abraham, Yitz'kak and Ya'akov are then properly called the Son(s) of Yahweh, since he is their father. This is through the concept of Spiritual adoption. Now even though all peoples are created by Yahweh, does not mean that he is all of our father. He is our bio-spiritual daddy, but for him to be our father, we must submit to his teachings, care and support and let him raise us by his Ruakh.

There is no such thing in heaven as an **only begotten Son**. Yahweh does not have one Son/daughter, he has many sons. First the divine Malakim, then Adamah and Eve, then Abraham being the first to be adopted etc..

To be a Son of Yahweh, one must be living according to YHWH divine decrees. This was in the minds of the original followers of Yahshua the Netzarim Essene before the gentiles rewrote the Gospel accounts and created Jesus. Yahshua the Teacher of the Netzarim YaHudaim was a Torah observant teacher under Hillel who taught and lived like the P'rushim/Essenes according to first century YaHudaism Halacha. He always spoke of Yahweh as his father and taught that anyone who lived according to Torah and worshiped Yahweh was considered Son/Daughter of Yahweh. Anyone who enters the Covenant of Yahweh is a Son/Daughter of Yahweh.

Shaul although a Hebrew Apostate from the tribe of Benyamin, makes some valid points within his writings that was maintained after he fell into deception,

Romans 8:14-15, "All who are led by YHWH Spirit are YHWH Son. For you did not receive a spirit of slavery to bring you back again into fear(see Abraham and Moshe'); *on the contrary you received the Spirit, who makes us Sons and by whose power we cry out "Abba"(this" dear Father!").*

[Yahweh and Moshe']

Now up to this time Yahweh just revealed his Character and features to Moshe, yet later on when Moshe inquires of the Eternal One on what he should tell the people his name was,

Exodus 3:13-15 "...."and Yahweh said to Moshe', 'AhYah-Asher-AhYah'. He continued, 'thus you shall say to the Yishra'alites, AhYah sent me to you.'"

The Eternal One for the first and last time in all biblical record, reveals himself as **AhYah.** AhYah is the first person singular of the word *to be.* It could mean either, *"I am"* or *"I will be".* **Asher** could mean either, *"what"* or *"who".* Therefore the verse could read, *"I am who/what I will be"; "I will be who/what I am"; "I will be who/what I will be"; "I am who/what I am".* What-ever the case Yahweh reveals himself as the Eternal Self-existent. This name actually sets the tone for Yahweh to finally reveal his actual Character/and full name to the Hebrews for the first time. Notice Ah-Yah is the first part of Yah's name.

Exodus 3:15, "…."thus shall you speak to the Yishra'alites: **YAHWEH**(Pronounced Yah-hu-weh or Yah-hu-wah), *the father of your fathers, the father of Abraham, the father of Yitzkak, and the Father of Ya'akov, has sent me to you."*

Even the more, because Yahweh is the source of all things, needs and answers, *ahYah-Asher-ahYah* could indicate that Yahweh is capable of responding to all of man kinds needs; spiritually, physically, financially, mentally, and nationalistically. In YHWH name alone there is power and Authority to live a victorious life from bondage, poverty, sickness and spiritual death.

[Signs and Wonders-the power of YHWH Words]

As you study the Texts for yourself you will notice that Yahweh later shows signs and Wonders, the force of his power among the Egyptians and Children of Yishra'ala. This is to prove the validity of his all-power and Authority and being the One true Creator with the power to bring Salvation to the Children of Yishra'ala from the oppression of the Egyptians. True signs and Wonders back up and testify of the Words and Torah of Yahweh, showing that his Torah whether spoken or written is true. YHWH validated himself by proving his Word to Yishra'ala with his

Power. It is the supernatural manifestations of Yahweh that prove his Word, Existence and actions. Especially to prove that the Hebrews are his chosen people and beloved nation. This is why YHWH spirit has many manifestations for the purpose of leading and guiding us in YHWH Paths of righteousness, and convincing the gentile of YHWH Torah Covenant. Yet if it should occur that miracles do happen and it does not confirm the Torah, then it is false and not of Yahweh, no matter how true it is or how wonderful it feels.

The greatest miracles that can ever occur through Man is the rebuilding of this world, saving the ecological system and getying nature back on balance and establishing righteous productive families and peoples to build the Eternal Kingdom of Yah on this Earth…If we believe and are faithful to Yah

[Torah Covenant proposal]

Exodus 19:3-6, "Thus shall you say to the house of Ya'akov and declare to the Children of Yishra'ala: 'you have seen what I did to the Egyptians, how I bore you on eagles wings and brought you to me. Now then, if you will **obey** *me* **faithfully** *and keep my Covenant, you shall be my treasured possession among all the peoples. Indeed all the earth is mine, but you shall be to me a* **Kingdom** *of priest and a holy nation…."*

D'var 29:8, "Therefore observe faithfully all the terms of this Covenant, that you may succeed in all that you undertake. You stand here today, all of you, before Yahweh your Almighty-your tribal heads, your elders and your officials, all the men of Yishra'ala, your children, your wives, even the stranger(gentile proselyte) within your camps, from woodchopper to water drawer-to enter into the Covenant of Yahweh your father, which Yahweh is concluding with you this day, with its sanctions(punishments and rewards for breaking or keeping the B'rith); to the end that you he may establish you this day as his people and be your Father, as he **promised** *you and as he swore to your fathers, Abraham Yitzkak and Ya'akov. I make this Covenant, with its* *sanctions(see D'var 28), not with you alone, but with those who are standing here with us this day before Yahweh and with those who are not with us here today(future Gentile proselytes)."*

Here Yahweh through Moshe makes a Covenant proposal to the nation of Yishra'ala. This covenant is based off of Faithfulness and obedience, instead of belief/trust alone. As a result of Yishra'ala faithful obedience to the Covenant, they would be the "Chosen People" a "Kingdom of Priest" and a "Holy Nation".

What does this mean? Yishra'ala would be chosen, not because they are a better people than other peoples or nations, but because of YHWH promise to Abraham. That Yishra'ala, the Hebrew people, would be the elect of Yahweh to be bearers of Divine Truth for the sake of being a Light unto the nations aboutf Yahweh the One True Creator(see YeshiYah 41:8-9; 42:1-4; ZachariYah 8:23-this explains the "Kingdom of priest" concept)

[Kingdom of Kohanim-Priests]

In Hebraic thought, a **priest** is the Mashiakh(anointed-one) who was a mediator between the people and Yahweh. He or she is also the Head Leader of Yishra'ala. He acted on behalf of the people before Yahweh, while a prophet acted on behalf of Yahweh before the peoples, and the King(melek; malak; Messenger) was YHWH's anointed over the political aspects of the nation(all three offices constitutes three types of Mashiakh).

Therefore Yahweh Calling The Hebrews as a whole a *Kingdom of Priest* indicates that they(we) are to be the mediators between Yahweh and mankind. They act on behalf of the world before/for Yahweh as they are led by his Ruakh. They(we) are the real Messiahs!

Proverbs 2:1,5, "my son, if you accept my words and treasure up my commandments....then you will understand the fear of Yahweh and attain the wisdom of the father."

The fear of Yahweh has nothing to do with being afraid, but being in total reverence and submission to the one true Creator Yahweh, the Father of the Yishra'ala. This involves accepting the whole of the beliefs and practices of the Hebrew-Israelites, the Torah Community, that Yahweh has commanded and taught his Worshipers.

Rejecting the Hebrews and their Way of Life is rejecting Yahweh, the father of the Hebrew Israelites. This is why the Essenes and Netzarim YaHudaim who followed the teacher Yahshua and Ya'akob HaTzaddik called themselves the 'Way'(Study YeshiYah 62:10; YirmeYah 5:4(KJV); Malachi 3:1; Shaliachs 9:2;18:25-26; 19:9, 23: 22:4; 24:14,22; 2Kefa 2:2,21: MattiYah 3:3;

*DDS Damascus document, Geniza A1: 11-13; 2:6, "so he raised up for them a teacher of righteousness to guide them in the **Way** of his(YHWH) heart. He taught to later generations what Yahweh did to the generations deserving wrath, a company of traitors. They are the ones who depart from the proper **Way**."*

*4Q270 frag. 9 col. 2:17, 14:7 "…..as one lies with a woman, these are the ones who violate the true **Way**….The priest who presides at the head of the general membership must be between thirty and sixty years old, learned in the book of meditation, and in all the regulations of the Law, speaking them in the proper **Way**."*

*Charter of a Israelite Sectarian Association 9:17-21, "for those who have chosen the **Way**, treating each as his spiritual qualities and the precepts of the era require….if then the secret **Way** perfected among the men of the Yahad, each will walk blamelessly with his fellow…. that will be the time of preparing the **Way** in the desert….these are the precepts of the **Way**…."*

Ha Malek Davyid said in Psalms 19:10,

"the fear of Yahweh is pure, abiding forever.; the judgements of Yahweh are true, righteous altogether."

The Israelite faith, the Torah Covenant, is the true Way to Yahweh, through faithful obedience. Yet our Faithful obedience to YHWH Torah, is dependent on our trust and relationship with YHWH(proverbs 9:10; Chabakkuk 2:4).

The Essence of the priests is to teach the people the True Way of Yahweh-Selah. Halacha in YaHudaism and Judaism means, "Path or Way".

[A Holy-Nation]

To be Holy implies the concepts, "to be **whole, unique, separate** and **complete** in ones self". This can only happen when we are in YHWH, who is Holiness. Without Yahweh, no religion, Nation or people is complete or whole. Because Yahweh is the Yachad(One) true living Creator, he is separate and unique and those who imitate his Way and does his will are the same.

Holiness is sacredness. It is "to be set aside to Yahweh from everything else". Holiness is dependant upon obedience to YHWH Torah and Word, which manifests through ones character, fruit and actions in life. As your obedience grows, your deliverance(T'shuva) shows.

If you are not apart of the Way of Yahweh, which is the Torah Community, obeying his Torah, then you are not Holy. Yishra'ala is the Holy religious nation and Culture of Yahweh.

[Yahudaism -the Everlasting Torah Covenant]

When studying the Covenant of Yahweh in the Hebrew scripture, one must began to see the Covenant as Yahweh see's it. Failure to do so leads to heretical doctrines, legalism, adding and subtracting to YHWH Word(i.e replacement covenant theology), man-made religions/Cults, anti-blackness/Shemitism, fundamental ignorance, pseudo-biblical truths. This has been the case with modern day Christianity, Islam, many aspects of Rabbinical Judaism, and other beliefs and Cults, simply because they have failed to study thoroughly the Hebrew scriptures from the Hebraic Point of View in which it was written. They have failed to be doers of their own scripture. Hebrew is the perspective in which Yahweh revealed himself.

One cannot be truly Christian, Islamic, Jewish or Israelite unless he first adheres to the people of the Book(MattiYah 5:17-18; Romans 11:16-18; Ya'akov 1:25)

Koran 3:2,3; 2:136, "Allah! There is no god but he...it is He who sent down to thee(step by step), in truth, the book, confirming what went before it; and he sent down the Torah of Moshe.. Say ye: We believe in Allah, and the revelation given to us, and to Abraham, Isma'il, Isaac, Jacob, and the Tribes, and that given to Moshe and Yahshua, and that given to all the prophets from their Lord. We make no difference between one and another of them: we submit to Allah."

Romans 11:18, "However if you do boast, remember that you are not supporting the root(YaHudaism), the root(YaHudaism) is supporting you!"

Rabbi Tony Mccraw, "Don't deceive yourself into thinking that you are, without YaHudaism and its Torah. You are not. You are without a foundation and like a building built on sand, prepared to sink or be washed away. You are not the life of YaHudaism, YaHudaism the life of You."

Yahweh sees his Covenant with Yishra'ala as a issuin(marriage)[Hoshea 2:4-5,9,18-19]. In a marriage contract, known as a **K'tuba**, both parties of the contract must agree with the terms and conditions in order for the marriage to work. The K'tuba are the teachings and precepts found in the Torah. There are 613 total precepts and teachings, yet we must look to the prophets to determine the ones Yahweh did not add, but were added by scribes(i.e sacrifice, burnt offerings and grain offerings). We must also go to the Synagogue or House of Worship to be taught by our Rabbi's, Kohanim and Teachers, so that we may learn and follow proper practical Halacha of the Torah Teachings.

Obedience to YHWH K'tuba Covenant would create a household or Spiritual Community. All of YHWH teachings are summed up in the basic teachings(Ten Commandments) found in Leviticus 26:1-13; Exodus 20:1-17; 31:18; Duetoronomy 5:6-21

[K'tuba Ring-Sign/Mark of the Covenant]

As with any Marriage, regardless of Culture, there is a sign or proof that the marriage has been established and consummated. Not only is this found in the contract(K'tuba), but there is a physical sign. This is called the *Marriage Ring-Yoke*(Physically it is a necklace).

Exodus 31:12-17, "Nevertheless, you must keep my Sabbaths, for this is a **sign** *between me and you throughout the ages, that you may know that I Yahweh have consecrated you. You shall keep the Sabbath, for it is* **holy** *for you. He who profanes it shall be put to death: whoever does work on it, that person shall be cut off from among his kin. Six days may work be done, but on the seventh day there shall be a Sabbath of complete rest, holy to Yahweh…the Yishra'alites people shall keep the Sabbath, observing the Sabbath throughout the ages as a Covenant of all time(forever): it shall be a* **sign** *for all time(forever) between me and the people of Yishra'ala…."*

The Shabbat, the sign of YHWH Torah covenant is Forever, meaning that Yahweh will never take his off his ring, which then means divorce, and turn away from Yishra'ala for another people. Those who hold to the Covenant and wear YHWH ring will be chosen forever(Sunday Worship is a Divorced Worship).

YirmeYah 31:35-37, "Thus says Yahweh, who establishes the sun for light by day, the laws of the moon and stars for light by night, who stirs up the sea into roaring waves, whose name is Yahweh Tzava'ot: If the laws should ever be annulled by me-only then would the offspring of Yishra'ala cease to be a nation before me for all time(forever). Thus says Yahweh: 'if the heavens above could be measured, and the foundations of the earth below could be fathomed, only then would I reject all the offspring of Yishra'ala for all that they have done-declare Yahweh."

Yahweh hates divorce and broken vows, Therefore he would never divorce or break his Covenant with those in whom he has made-The Hebrews. Yahweh does not have two chosen people(dual covenant theology). Either he's rejected Yishra'ala or 'not'. If there is another Religion or Community claiming to be chosen apart from or superseding the Hebrew Israelite and the Hebrew faith using our Hebrew Scriptures, then this is the result of man influenced by Ha-Satan/deception and not Yahweh.

Psalms 89:31-36, "If his sons forsake my Teaching and do no observe my rules; if they violate my laws(Torah), and do not observe my Commands, I will punish their transgression with the rod, their iniquity with plagues. But I will not take away my steadfast love for him; I will not betray my faithfulness. I will not violate my Covenant, or change what I have uttered."

If you are not originally apart of the Hebrew community, a Gentile, or you have fallen away from the Torah, yet you want to be restored and truly worship Yahweh, then I encourage you to Circumcise your heart with repentance and accept YHWH chosen people and religious Torah Community(discussed further later).

[Covenant Exhortations]

A. Listen to the precepts and teachings of Yahweh
1. Don't add to YHWH Torah and Word or take away from it
2. Don't change the meaning through additions and subtractions of YHWH Torah

B. Be careful to observe all Yahweh commands with faithful obedience
1.This is Wisdom and understanding. Nations shall see your Wisdom

2. YaHudaism has Yahweh so near to her

C. Don't forget YHWH teaching and Words

D. Do not worship any hinder Allah'im or gods besides Yahweh
1. Shema Yishra'ala, Yahweh Yloheinu, Yahweh Yachad. Hear oh Yishra'ala! Yahweh our father, Yahweh is One

F. Teach this Torah Covenant to your Children
1. Make a habit of talking about them and reciting them
2. Write them down, even on your doorpost and gates

G. Fear and love Yahweh, serve him in faithful obedience to his Torah
1. Circumcise the foreskin of your heart, repent when you transgress his Torah

H. Yahweh 'only' is the LORD of lord, KING of kings, and POWER over the gods
1. No other divine or human being has rights to these title

I. YHWH teaching is not a mystery
1. His Word and Torah is in your heart
2. His Torah precepts is your life and lifestyle

J. Yahweh was, is and always will be a loving and merciful Father
1. He forgives Torah transgressors when they repent
2. He loves his people as a Father loves his child
3. He seeks to develop a relationship with each and every individual of his Torah Community.

References: D'bar chapters 4-8; 10:12-22; 11:1; 29:8; 30:11-20; 32:47; Exodus 33:19; 34:5-7; Numbers 14:17-20; 2Chronicles 7:14-18; 30:9;

Psalms 1:1-2; 19:8-11; 37:28-31; 84:12; 89:31-37; 119:1-176; Proverbs 6:20-23; 7:1-4; YeshiYah 1:10; Malachi 2:10; 3:22(4:4); MattiYah 5:17-20; Ya'akob 2:8-13; 4:6

[Torah-Protection for the Redeemed Community]

The Torah is a divine barrier between Yahweh's domain of the faithful and Ha satans domain of the rebellious. In side the boundaries of YHWH domain is full protection, security and benefits. Ha-Satan has no Authority or power over you. Yet outside the boundaries of YHWH domain Ha-Satan has his legal rights over you, to fight you and oppress you.

Notice the Torah is for an already **Redeemed Community.** The Hebrews of the Torah Community are already redeemed by Yahweh. They(we) don't need another redemption which other religions preach. We are redeemed and Saved by Yahweh "only"! Yishra'ala was already redeemed by Yahweh through Moshe' because of his **Promise** Covenant through Abraham.

As a result of redemption, Yahweh established a house of protection in order for the children of Yishra'ala to Maintain their Redemption and Deliverance status. This is the Torah of Moshe'. Without the Torah there would be no boundaries and "true"Redemption and Salvation would be impossible to maintain, because Ha-Satan would have his legal rights to divide and conquer us as he is doing the world and religions now!

The Torah(which includes the Hebrew writings) teaches us the difference between Holy and Unholy, clean and unclean, life in Yahweh through faithful obedience and death through transgression and rebellion.

(Read whole chapter)D'bar 28: "Now if you obey Yahweh you Father, to observe faithfully all his commandments which I enjoin upon you this day, Yahweh your father will set you on high above all nation of the earth. All these blessings shall come upon you....." verse 15, "but if you do not obey Yahweh

your father to observe faithfully all his commands and laws which I enjoin upon you all this day, all these curses shall come upon you and take effect......"

D'bar 30:14-20, "No the thing Is very close to you, in your mouth and in your heart, to observe it. See I have set before you this day life and prosperity, death and adversity......"

See also Leviticus chapter 26 and Psalm 19:8-12

Spiritual assassination and demonic forces have no power or jurisdiction within Torah boundaries and Community. Many people fail to practice true Torah principles and themselves are constantly under satanic attack. Many have received a counterfeit eastern-religion third person Holy-spirit and operate out of pseudo-manifestations and false faith, simply because they are far away from the Torah Covenant Community of Yahweh. They stand and live on enemies ground and principles(although they may sincerely not know it).

Remember, in YHWH eyes there is only *one* Community, *one* people, *one* faith, and one true Way. That is Yishra'ala. All others are vain unless they have strong roots in Hebrew Israelite Practice and beliefs and they don't contradict or distort Hebrew principles, especially of "Yahweh only"(*if there can be a messianic Judaism, which is Christianity with Israelite roots, then there can be Hebrew Islam, Buddhism, etc....other than that they are false. Selah).

Have you ever wondered why people run to the alter in churches and confess their sins in tears and proclaim themselves, "saved in Christ" and then turn around and backslide? Or why Christianity is mixed/filled with paganism and ungodly practices contrary to true biblical standards? Or why Christians and even Islam have a history of violence and war, thereby creating the demonic atmosphere in the world in which we live today? Or why does racism and discrimination among historically inter-mixed white Jews persist in most of European Judaism?, or even the fact that most so-called Jews influenced by the Ashka'Nazi's can't even define "who truly is a Jew or Hebrew", because they want to exclude Black peoples of America who are descendant of African Hebrew Slaves? Or why did the European Christians, Arab and Jews participate in the African Edenic Hebrew slave trade of America, strip us of our Hebrew identity, rape our mothers, destroy our Hebrew man-hood and now won't take account that they are wrong, and repent(this does not include all Europeans)? And why do many European Jews yell, "anti-Semitism" when some-one points out these wrongs they have done or are doing, and they are not even Shemites? Why are black peoples destroying themselves and their communities, both religious and secular? Why are there so many hypocrites, false prophets…Why is the world?

The answer is all summed up in one sentence. ***"They are outside the boundaries of YHWH Torah, Word and true Community.. The Israelite Torah Covenant Community!***

I don't doubt that there are truly good people living a form of right-eousness outside the Israelite Community, but Yahweh has plans for his people and he wants to include all the peoples of the world in the blessings he has in-store.

Boundaries does not mean limitation to those who are inside the boundaries, it means limitation to those outside the Torah boundaries. Including Ha satans legal rights(except outside).

Ya'akob 1:25; 2:12, "But if a person looks closely into the perfect Torah, which gives **freedom,** *and continues, becoming not a forgetful hearer but a doer of the work it requires, then he will be blessed in what he does.. Keep speaking and acting like people who will be judged by a Torah which gives* **freedom.***"*

[Halacha of Torah Covenant]

The Fullness of the Covenant of Yahweh is a combination of both the Covenant of **Promise or Redemption** through Abraham and the **Torah** Covenant Community or Covenant of **Deliverance** through Moshe'.

Neither deletes of annuls the other. They are interlinked and are received in the order revealed.

The covenant of Redemption is based off of our repentance and trust that Yahweh's grace has bought us from sin to Salvation in him. Redemption is the Hebrew word **p'duth, padah, pidyon, geullah,** which could mean, "to ransom, deliver, redeem, including rights,. to exchange as in to take from one scenario or scene and put in another scenario or scene".

Psalms 130:7-8, "oh Yishra'ala, wait for Yahweh; for with Yahweh is stead-fast love and great power to **Redeem** *. It is he who will redeem Yishra'ala from all their iniquities."*

Psalms 103:2-4, "Bless Yahweh, oh my soul and do not forget all his boun-ties. He forgives all your sins, heals all your diseases. He **Redeems** *your life from the pit, surrounds you with steadfast love and mercy."*

Redemption only occurs after a circumcision of the heart(which if you are uncircumcised or a gentile would lead to a circumcision of flesh), which is repentance towards Yahweh for being disconnected from him. Yahweh uses your repentance as the means for a ransom to "take" away Ha satans legal rights of evil and replaces it with his legal rights of deliverance, guidance and blessings. Your repentance of the heart is the only Atonement/ransom needed for access to receive YHWH grace and mercy. No Sacrifice or blood can do this!

The American heritage dictionary(3rd edition) defines **ransom** as, 1. *"the release of a captive in return for payment of a demanded price."* 2. *"The price demanded or paid for such release."*

Ha-Satan has no Authority to demand anything of Yahweh concerning the releasing of people from bondage. Yet Yahweh only demands that we repent toward him and believe in his sovereign power to redeem us. That is our ransom. Our Atonement! Remember repentance starts in the heart and then manifests in ones life as they are delivered through YHWH Word(Torah).

2Chronicles 7:14, "when my people, who bear my name(Yahweh), humble themselves, pray, and seek my favor and turn(repent) from their evil ways(paganism, heathenism, rebellion, non-Torah observant), I will hear from heaven and forgive their sins and heal their land."

This passage is the pattern for both the Lost or apostate Hebrews and gentiles who seek to be redeemed by Yahweh(read D'bar 10:16) to enter his covenant.

Repentance is the Hebrew word **T'shuwa.** This is not just praying a prayer confessing your Transgression asking for forgiveness because you don't want to be punished or judged, but because you want do what is right and develop a relationship with Yahweh and fulfill his will and purpose in your life. Study Yah'ala(Joel) 3:5(2:32kjv).

Ya'akov 2:14, 19 "what good is it, my brothers, if someone claims to have faith but has no actions to prove it? Is such faith able to save him?(no)...you believe that Yahweh is One? Good for you! The demons believe it too-the thought makes them shudder with fear!"

This passage seems to contradict what I was just saying about faith and redemption. Yet it is not. Most people think that redemption and Salvation or Deliverance is the same. In Hebraic thought it is not. Redemption is instantaneous, but deliverance is not. Faith can redeem you but it takes faithful obedience to Torah and a relationship with Yahweh to deliver you from you former system and pagan/sinful lifestyle. This does not happen over night. faith alone cannot do this. This is what Ya'akov is trying to relay. This kind of deliverance/Salvation is like a rehab deliverance, in which the rehab is the Torah. For example:

There was a man who was on drugs for about 15 years. He was a constant user and his body was accustomed to this lifestyle. Indeed he was addicted to drugs. Although he would think in his mind at times that he was doing wrong, his body being accustomed to drugs constantly demanded for more. Even after his high he would feel miserable and sick. Many people tried to help him and get him into rehab, but he refused. Finally one day this man got fed up with his drug lifestyle and decided to go to the drug rehabilitative center. When he arrived he explained to the rehab director that he was a drug addict and wanted to stop and needed their help(confession, faith and repentance). They admitted the man into the rehab program on the basis that he follow the rules and guidelines of the Center in order to be rehabilitated and maintain that status(redemption). He entered and went through the program, following the rules and guide-lines to be rehabilitated(deliverance). Finally he was rehabilitated(delivered) and clean of drugs and he stayed free and clean of drugs(delivered).

If you got the revelation of this story then you have the revelation of redemption and repentance. The drug addict had to humble himself and admit his drug problem and then ask for help and trust that the help would come through. But his trust or faith after that had to turn into actions and obedience to guidelines for his deliverance.

Do you think that this drug addicts faith alone would have got him delivered? Absolutely not! The Torah is our spiritual Rehab from our former way of life that was contrary to Yahweh. Our admission(redemption) into the Covenant is by the grace and mercy of Yahweh. And if we don't go by the guide-lines(Torah teachings) of Yahweh we can indeed lose our redemption status(admission into the covenant) and our Deliverance/Salvation Status. Therefore it takes our faith and faithful obedience to Yahweh and his Torah covenant, or Covenant of provision, in order to be declared "Saved" and delivered. As a Hebrew "I" now ask the missionary Christian, "are you SAVED?"Selah! That is, think about it!

Shaul in his seemingly guilt on Breaking Torah recants and say,

Romans 7:7, "What are we to say? That the Torah is sinful? Heaven forbid! Rather, the function of the Torah was that without it, I would not have known

what sin is. For example, I would not have become conscious of what greed is if the Torah had not said, 'thou shalt not covet'......"

Rabbi Tony Mccraw version, "without the Torah, one is ignorant of the Jew truths, answers and warnings it contain. For example, "one must not know Torah if one calls Yahweh a trinity, when Torah specifically says, 'hear or Yishra'ala, Yahweh your father, Yahweh is one'. And 'I am Yahweh, that is my name; and my glory I will not give to another(YeshiYah 42:8kjv)'. Perhaps one is merely a transgressor. For when Torah springs to life in someone, indeed deliverance is made known in the transgression that was made"

Remember, "Our faithful obedience to YHWH Torah, is dependant on our Trust and relationship with Yahweh!"

Section 3 Torah, Yishra'ala culture, the way of life for the Hebrew Community

The Torah/Israel is a religious culture and way of life as we worship Yahweh. It teaches us the proper and right way to live and think. Torah teaches us how to build successful communities, governments and educational resources. It teaches us the proper way to establish healthy families, eat and live a healthy life. Ultimately it teaches us how to build civilization and cultures that worship Yahweh and build the earth. Everything this world needs to progress in righteousness and Authority is found in the Torah.

When YHWH Word gets into our hearts, where our wills, intellect and emotions dwell, we began to subconsciously act and live according to that Word!

The Torah teacher Yahshua said,

MattiYah 12:33-34, "if you make a tree good(Symbolic of Torah), its fruit will be good(Torah observers), and if you make a tree bad(Man's teaching contrary to Torah), its fruit will be bad(Torah transgressors)...For the mouth speaks what overflows the heart."

His brother Ya'akov further says,

Ya'akob 1:22-25, "don't deceive yourself by only hearing what the Torah says, but do it!...but if a person looks closely into the perfect Torah, which gives freedom and continues, becoming not a forgetful hearer but a doer of the work it requires, then he will be blessed in what he does."

D'bar 32:45-47, "take to heart all the words(Torot) with which I have warned you this day...it is your very life!"

[The Torah-for both Hebrew and Gentile(goyim)]

D'var 29:9-14, "you stand this day, all of you, before Yahweh Almighty...all the men of Yishra'ala. Even the stranger(non Hebrew/gentile convert)...I will make this covenant, with its sanctions, not with you(Hebrews) alone, but both with those who are standing here this day(see also chapter 31:12).

The Covenant of Promise and Torah Covenant(Provision/protection) is for both Hebrews and goyim(gentiles). Those gentiles who desire to enter the Covenant will receive the same blessing and benefits that the Hebrews receive from Yahweh.

Study the text of YeshiYah chapter 56:1-8. This is the requirements and picture, for those who are not Hebrew, to enter YHWH Covenant. Indeed repentance and accepting Yahweh as your Eternal Master/LORD and deliverer is required. No other god or deity should be in your life and worship afterwards!

YeshiYah 59, "....(vs 12-14) for our many sins are before you, our guilt testifies against us. We are aware of our sins, and we know well our iniquities: rebellion, faithlessness to Yahweh and turning away from our Almighty, planning fraud and treachery, conceiving lies and uttering(confessing) them with the throat. And so redness is turned back and vindication stays afar, because honesty stumbles in the public square and uprightness cannot enter."

2Chronicles 7:14, "when my people, who bear my NAME, humble themselves, pray, and seek my favor and turn from their wicked ways, I will hear in my heavenly abode and forgive their sins and heal there land."

Joma 86a, "great is repentance, for it makes the redemption to come near. Great is repentance, for it lengthens the years of a mans life."

[Goyim-Grafted in/proselytism]

Bereshit 12:3, "I will bless those who bless you and curse those who curse you; and all the families of the earth shall bless themselves by you".

I would like to point out several things in this passage that will help you better understand the verse. According to Strongs concordance, the Hebrew words for **curse** is

arar *which means, "to execrate or bitterly curse(Hebrew #779)" and the word* **qalal** *which means, "to take lightly, to hold in low-esteem or contempt(Hebrew #7043)".*

This mean that all who hold the Hebrews in contempt, or does not esteem them will receive a bitter curse! This could result from stripping the Hebrews of their culture, not accepting the true Hebrews as whom they say they are and ignoring them. This is the case with the Black/Cushite Hebrews of Both America, the islands, Africa and Yishra'ala. They have been either overlooked or taught a white-washed Euro-Religion or disconnected from their roots altogether. As result of this demonic action, the world is being bitterly cursed by Yahweh as he **promised** for breaking the covenant of the Hebrews and acting against them. Until all the true Hebrews(the lost tribes) are restored this bitter curse of Yahweh will continue across the earth, resulting is religious wars(both physically and verbally), race wars, wars, pestilence, lawlessness, poverty and sickness, family break down and etc....

Another word I would like to point out is the phrase, *"bless themselves by you".* **Bless** is from the Hebrew word *barak* which means, *"to kneel before".* Bless is also represented by the word *v'niverecha* which according an analytical explanatory to the Talmud called the *Ba'alei tosafot* is a derivative of the Hebrew infinitive *Mavrich,* which means, *"ingrafted in".* Therefore the text should read, *"and all the families of the earth shall kneel and ingraft themselves into you".*

This makes plenty of sense In the light of YeshiYah 45:23-25,

"by myself(Yahweh) have I sworn, from my mouth has issued truth, a word that shall not turn back: to me(Yahweh) every knee shall bend, every tongue swear loyalty. They shall say: 'only through(being ingrafted into) Yahweh can I find victory and might. When people trust(lit. 'come to') in him, all their adversaries are put to shame. It is through(being ingrafted into) Yahweh that all the offspring of Yishra'ala have vindication and glory."

In order to be a worshiper of Yahweh you must kneel, which is an act of submission, before Yahweh and accept and ingraft or enter into his Covenant through Abraham and his offspring. Indeed this is the season when all the families of the earth will submit to the will and promise of Yahweh and ingraft themselves into the Hebrew Covenant. Remember Yahweh promised that this will happen! Only in Yahweh is the enemy called Ha-Satan defeated and cast out of your lives. Indeed this is the Fear of Yahweh.

[Ger Tzadik-Ger Toshav]

Ger is the Hebrew word for *proselyte/stranger.* there are two types of Gerim; a **Ger Tzadik** and a **Ger Toshav**. A *Ger Tzadik* is a gentile non Israelite Descendant, who has fully ingrafted himself into the Israelite culture and community, in the observance of the Torah of Moshe'. When one becomes a Ger Tzadik they are full spiritual Hebrew Israelite Citizens/members as the regular Hebrews. They have received a mikveh or complete water immersion(male and female) and are circumcised/B'rith Milah(male only). A *Ger Toshav*, also known as the stranger/settler, is one who is redeemed but has not entered the fulness of the Torah of Moshe'. They are still babe's in Yahweh who are learning to become Hebrew or

Hebrew like. They are Yahweh fearers. Another name to call them is *Hebrew/YaHudaim believers* (The European Jews are examples Ger Toshavs and Ger Tzadiks). They accept the basic laws of YaHudaism known as the seven Noachide Laws:

1. Don't commit idolatry 2. Don't curse Yahweh in any way 3. Don't commit sexual immorality 4.don't eat the limb of a living animal 5. Don't murder 6. Don't steal 7. Respect the establishments of court of justice

They also accept the Ten Commandments. Remember these basic requirements are for the foundation to grow and build upon into full Torah Covenant obedience. In other words Walking in the Word of Yahweh.

Ya'akob, the brother of the priest and Torah teacher Yahshua of Nazareth, and leader of the YaHudaim Community(around 40C.E) after settling a dispute against Shaul about Gentiles entering the Hebrew faith said,

Acts 15:19-21, "Therefore, my opinion is that we should not put obstacles in the way of the Goyim(gentiles) who are turning to Yahweh. Instead we should write them a letter telling them to abstain from things polluted by idols, from fornication, from what is strangled by blood. For from the earliest times, Moshe has had in every city those who proclaim him, with his words(Torah) being read in the synagogues every Shabbat."

Contrary to the erroneous teaching of the church today, this is a picture of a Ger Toshav or redeemed gentile who is entering the fullness of the covenant to become a Ger Tzadik or Full Hebrew proselyte. This ruling was actually against Shaul's view that a gentile should not have to Convert to YaHudaism. This ruling indicates that he didn't have to immediately convert, but eventually as he studied in the Synagogues/Temple about the Torah of Moshe, he would be fully ingrafted.

Ya'akob the Just knew that it would take time for Gentiles to study and observe Torah, especially for those the Torah was totally foreign to. This doesn't happen over night. Yet Ya'akov the Just also knew that there were certain guidelines that had to be followed to enter the Hebrew community such as, forbidding idolatry, sexual sins, and things strangled with blood. These are all roots of the Torah, including the dietary laws. As they learned about these basic laws, whether the Ten Commandment or Noachide laws, they learned to walk in the Complete Torah of Moshe'. They learned to become Zealous for the Torah(Acts 21:20)! This is the point of Acts 15:21.

In order for there to be a communication between the Hebrew community and the Gentiles, the gentiles have to accept the basic requirements, which are subsequent to repentance and Accepting Yahweh as the LORD and Deliverer and believing and Living in the his kingdom.

The only body of religious literature the Hebrews had was the Tanakh and the Oral Torah!

[Prophetic Warning to the European Jews]

Much of the European Jewish Community live by a very deceptive demonic practice. Their form of Oral Torah and Talmud teaches and makes a lot of derogatory and racist comments about Gentile and Non Jewish YHWH fearers. This Same Talmud is one of the main causes of the rise of the Hebrew Transatlantic Slave trade, due to the Hamitic Myth, *that Ham was cursed and that all black peoples who are descendant of Ham are therefore under that curse.*

The Europeans Cause many non-Hebrews or Gentiles to Stumble over the Torah and break many commands of the Torah, especially on Shabbat. In Orthodox Communities especially, they will get a Gentile to turn on and off the lights in their Shul or at their homes, because they think that this is a transgression against the command not to kindle a fire on Shabbat, as found in their Talmud. Although this is not a transgression, in their heart they wickedly think that the Gentile is doing this kind of work so that they(the gentile) will transgress for them (The Jew).

Also Most of the Synagogues have Shabbat oneg (Shabbat meal) after their Shabbat service, yet they have Gentile Caterers making and delivering the meals, therefore assisting in helping Gentiles Transgress the Shabbat law of non working(i.e cooking, lighting fires etc).

How sick and deceptive these people who do this are. They should be ashamed of themselves! Not only are they causing Stumbling blocks, but they themselves are breaking the Torah! As long as they continue to do this YHWH Shekinah will never befall them. His Spirit will never guide them and they will always live in greed, sin and persecution and hatred from other peoples. Not because they are chosen but because they are sinful Hebrew speaking Gentiles. That is why their synagogues are filled with a dead, gloomy atmosphere with no life. The Shekinah of YHWH isn't there(speaking to those who transgress). Much of Current Judaism is a circumvention of the Hebrew Torah. They have changed many of the Teachings and introduced their own teachings which are in direct contradiction to the Torah. This has deceived millions of people the world over because of ignorance.

Therefore this is a Prophetic warning to all those Hebrew speaking Gentile Jews and their converts, respectively. If you do not stop this nonsense demonic foolishness of causing and encouraging Gentiles to break the Hebrew Torah, and you yourselves don't stop the Torah transgressions of your forefathers then,

"May YHWH curse you and reject you, may YHWH Shine his wrath upon you and be judgmental toward you. May YHWH take his countenance from you and never give you peace"

Examine your Hearts and Study the Torah for yourselves, seek YHWH's forgiveness as you perform true Teshuvah and return to the true Hebrew Torah of YHWH that his Shekinah may finally rest upon you as he is once again upon the African Edenic Hebrew Israelites.

"Shemot 12:49, "there shall be ONE Law(TORAH) for the Citizen and for the Stranger who dwells among you."

[Hearing YHWH's Voice-bath kol]

In order for anyone to truly walk righteously in obedience to the Word of Yahweh, one must began to hear his bath kol, that is YHWH divine voice. Sure enough he has spoken to us in his Torah and Word, yet he desires to speak to us personally on a daily basis. Therefore we must set aside time on a daily basis to meditate and let Yahweh speak to our hearts through his Ruakh(spirit) that leads us into all truth! This is called prayer.

We must let Yahweh give us the revelation and true understanding in applying his Word and Way in our lives. When we fail to receive the **Bath kol et Wisdom** and the **Bath kol et Knowledge**, we fail to walk and know Yahweh and his true Way. *"Hear oh Yishra'ala"*.....

Chapter 3

Section 1

One of the most controversial subjects today is that of Yahshua being the Messiah of Yishra'ala. Is he really the Son of Yahweh(physically), Yahweh manifested in the flesh, the perfect Yahweh-man? What about the validity of a New Covenant theology? Is this biblical? Countless numbers of Christians and Churches teach that they are the new Yishra'ala, that the church has superseded the Torah Community of Moshe'? Is this really true? Since after the destruction of the Hebrew Temple in 70c.e. until this day, the truth has been suppressed, rewritten and even ignored, by Church officials. For almost two millennia Pastors and Clergy men have been preaching a gospel and looking forward to a mythological unbiblical Messiah-god! This they say is confirmed, as they believe, through signs, wonders, miracles and healings of **the Holy-spirit**, which is a third person(god) of a divine trinity. The Church focus is totally on the **second person(god-man) of their trinity**. Although they say that they believe in the Father, the **first person(god-father) of their trinity,** He doesn't compare to Jesus their savior of mankind, according to their teachings. For to them there is no other name in heaven and earth greater than this *"Jesus"(* *greater than the name Yahweh? what blasphemy!*)! Instead of the pure message taught by Yahshua(vs Jesus) known as **The Kingdom of Yahweh,** it is now being taught by Christians as **the gospel of Jesus Christ!**

Even those who call themselves ***Messianic Jews/Israelites*** have fallen short of Yahweh with such deception as the Christians, by compromising the one true Creator of Yishra'ala for a Tri-Unitarian god(which is still the Trinity) of Christianity and adopting Fundamental Evangelical doctrines. If anyone asks the typical Christian or Messianic Jew, "which one do you worship, the Father, Jesus(Yeshua) or the Holy-spirit"? They will tell you that they worship all three. Yet maintain that all three is one god. They will even go so far as to say something like, " *I can't explain it, but I believe it. You can't explain a big infinite god with a little finite mind. God can be anything he wants to be. Who are we to tell the Creator who or who he cannot be?"* Yet they will turn around and try to explain their god using the ***ice, water, and vapor*** concept, or the ***spirit soul and body*** concept! They actually try to compare Yahweh with these foolish things. But I thought you couldn't explain him?! Cunningness and Deception! Perhaps these words should expose their lies:

Debar 6:4, "Hear oh Yishra'ala, Yahweh our Strength, Yahweh is One(alone)."
ZachariYah 14:9, "and Yahweh shall be king over all the earth; in that day there shall be One Yahweh and his name One!"
Debar 30:14-20, "No, the thing(Word of Yahweh) is very close to you, in your mouth and in your heart... but if your heart turns away and you give no heed, and are lured into worship and service of other gods, I declare to you this day that you shall surely perish...choose life-if you and your offspring would live-by loving YAHWEH, heeding his commands, and holding fast to HIM."(see also vs 11-13)
YeshiYah 42:8, "I am Yahweh, that is my name; I will not yield my glory to another..."
Debar 4:2, "You shall not add 'anything' to what I command you or take anything away from it, but keep the commandments of Yahweh that I enjoin upon you."

Was Jesus a Christian? In fact, was that this mans real name? What is the biblical concept of **Messiah**, and did the Hebrew scriptures speak of a **New Covenant** that would replace an Old Mosaic Covenant and Yishra'ala?

These questions will be answered in this section with proper biblical application. This is not intended to destroy ones faith, discourage anyone, but to correct ones faith and encourage one to Worship Yahweh our Father in…truth contrary to Mythological worship which constitutes idolatry.

May the Ruakh HaKodesh(Spirit of Holy-One) lead you and guide you into all truth as you continue to study the Word.

((Re)New(ed) Covenant analysis]

YirmeYah 31:27-34, "..see a time is coming-declares Yahweh-when I will make a new covenant with the house of Yishra'ala and the house of Yahudah. It will not be like the covenant I made with their fathers, when I took them by the hand to lead them our of the land of Egypt, I covenant that they broke, so I rejected them-declares Yahweh. But such is the covenant I will make with the house of Yishra'ala after those these days-declares Yahweh: I will put my teaching (Torah/Law) into their inmost being and inscribe it upon their hearts. Then I will be their Strength and they shall be my people….."

This prophetic Word was given to YirmeYah by Yahweh around 586b.c.e when the Hebrews were exiled and the Temple was destroyed by the Babylonians. This was YHWH Judgement for the Hebrew/YaHudaim's Stubbornness toward Yahweh. This was a time of much sorrow and weeping(YirmeYah gets his title the weeping prophet to symbolize this), that when the exiled YaHudaim passed by Rackayl(Ya'akobs wife) tomb, the prophet YirmeYah proclaimed, *"thus says Yahweh: a cry is heard in Ramah-wailing, bitter weeping - Rackayl weeping for her children. She refuses to be comforted for her children, who are gone(YirmeYah 31:15)."*

Yet Yahweh's Love and everlasting mercy of the Israelites stilled availed much. The YaHudaim lamented and repented and Yahweh heard their cry. Even after punishing them Yahweh still had a plan for Yishra'ala's future of being a *Priest unto the Nations.* YHWH heart always had Yishra'ala on it, even though they broke their Covenant with him and angered him. So therefore Yahweh, Father and Spiritual husband of Yishra'ala, through his Covenant, decided he would restore Yishra'ala as a nation and renew his covenant with them. (?)

[Scriptural mistranslations]

Most biblical translations of YirmeYah 31:31 renders that Yahweh will make a *New Covenant*...this gives rise to the doctrine that there is an *Old Covenant.* This is how careless Christian teachings and Modern translations of the so-called New Testament has been propagated for almost 2000 years. To them *New* means a *New Yishra'ala(church)* replacing old Yishra'ala(YaHudaim and YaHudaism), and a *New Dispensation*, no longer being *under the Law(Torah).* They base their doctrines off of the self proclaimed Authority of the New testament writings. The New testament authors, such as Paul(Shaul) and the gospels in turn use the Hebrew Writings(Tanakh) for their teachings, yet they are taken totally out of the context of the Hebrew setting. This is not only deceptive, but unfair to both the reader and the Hebrew scripture itself. This is constantly done throughout the New Testament writings(at least in the forms we currently have them)

The proper Hebrew word for **New Covenant(Testament)** is *B'rith Chadasha(kah-dash).* This is derived from the Hebrew word *Chodesh.* Chodesh is the term used to determine the first day of each month on the

Hebrew calendar. The determining factor was the **New Moon**. Each month had a new moon on the first day.

Now in truth and reality there is so such thing as a new moon(Chodesh). Through the monthly cycle, the moon actually *renews* itself. It is the 'same' moon, yet its **renewed**. This is what the words *Chodesh* and *Chadasha* means.

B'rith means "Covenant" (testament /agreement). Therefore the proper scriptural meaning of B'rith Chadasha is, *"Covenant Renewal"* or *"Renewed Covenant"*. This means that the original Covenant still exists. Its just renewed(with possible better benefits). For example, the renewed covenant is no more newer than a marriage where two people renew their vows. Selah!

Another example is when I had gotten car insurance a couple of years ago. I had purchased auto insurance for six months according to the insurance agreement or contract. One of the six months I defaulted on my financial obligation. My insurance got canceled. Yet when I went to go fulfill my obligation for that month, by insurance was renewed. At the end of the six months, I renewed my insurance for another six months. Yet although I had to renew my insurance twice, once being because of breach of financial obligation, I still had the same Insurance policy!

Now while I was in breach of my insurance contract, I was not covered under that policy. if an injury, accident or property damage occurred. I was on my own! It is the same thing with the Torah. Outside or breach of its Policies and Instruction leaves you out in the dark with no protection, Spiritually or Eternally! Yet when you return to Torah, YHWH automatically renews his Covenant policy with you and you receive all the same benefits you had before. And remember unlike auto insurance, YHWH's Love and Mercy Covers your whole life and everything you are and are called to be and do. Daily, Monthly and Yearly(Yom Kippur) YHWH renews his Covenant with his people.

Therefore in proper biblical interpretation, Christianity/Messianic Judaism has been in error and there is no New Yishra'ala, but a renewed

Hebrew Yishra'ala, there is no new replaced, chosen Church, but the same Synagogue/House of Worship of YaHudaism and the YaHudaim., and there is no New covenant, but the same Torah Covenant of Moshe' renewed 'constantly' with the "**House of Yishra'ala** and the **house of Yahudah, the Hebrews!**

Take note! If there was a New Covenant, then it is still with the YaHudaim(YirmeYah 31:31). Gentiles would have to ingraft themselves into the Hebrew Torah Covenant Community to partake of this (RE) New(ed) Covenant(see prev. section & Roman 11:18). YirmeYah's prophecy has **not** been fulfilled yet.

The Renewed Covenant of YirmeYah 31:31-34 is connected to 32:40, Yechizchi'ala 16:60-63, 37:26-27 and YeshiYah 59:20-21. This is an ever-lasting covenant.

The terms of the Covenant as found in the above scriptures are:

1.Yahweh will put his Torah on Yishra'ala inmost being and inscribe it on their hearts

2.Yahweh will maintain a special relationship with Yishra'ala

3.All Yishra'ala shall know Yahweh

4.Yishra'ala Transgression will be forgiven

5.All of Yishra'ala will be restored to all of the promise land

6.Yahweh will multiply Yishra'ala(this indicates an ingrafting in of the Gentiles)

7.Yahweh Holy Temple will be rebuilt and will stand forever in Yishra'ala

8.The Earth shall be filled with the knowledge of the glory of Yahweh, as the waters covers the sea(YeshiYah 11:9)!

9.All of Yishra'ala will be filled with Yahweh Spirit of Holiness

All of these conditions have not been fulfilled. All of Yishra'ala doesn't know Yahweh. Many of my brothers and sisters are trying to suppress and hide Yahweh, and worship Allah'im or adonay! The Temple isn't rebuilt to stand forever yet! The earth definitely isn't filled with the knowledge of the glory and devotion of Yahweh! Its being pumped with the lie of *Jesus is Lord,* and other vain doctrines by the religious world!

Now of course we know that Yahweh constantly renews his covenant with his people, because we all sin and transgress his Torah at times. We are all human beings subject to human error(but we don't have to be overcome by error). Therefore when we repent of our carnality and transgression against Yahweh, he renews his Covenant with us(speaking to those under the Covenant). But there is an everlasting renewal that's coming when there won't be transgressions and sin will be done away with. This will happen in the Renewed World to Come, also known as the Day and rule of Yahweh and his people(reign of the Messiah).

Yahweh is already preparing to Establish his everlasting covenant upon the earth by pouring out his Ruakh (spirit) upon those who are being restored to the Torah covenant. This is a more powerful and real spirit out-pouring that is against the counterfeit anti-Torah charismatic spirit of Christianity. The world will began to see the difference in the two out-pourings and will be able to see the true spirit of Yahweh from the false Anti-torah spirit! The Christians will either then repent and turn to Yahweh 'only' and enter the Torah covenant and receive the True Spirit or be done away with as the Church(and other religions) continues to self destruct with its corrupt Ministers and laymen who are Torah less(Lawless)! Indeed this is a prophetic Word from Yahweh!

Section 2 Origins of the Renewed Covenant Movement in 1st Century Israel

Around the first century(B.C.E. and C.E.) Yishra'ala was experiencing numerous Hebrew and Jewish movements in Judea. Most was the result of rebellion against the established Roman rule, others because of the heated post biblical belief that a Messiah(s) was coming to rescue the Hebrews from their foreign oppressors the Romans. One of these movements called themselves by numerous names, such as the (re)New(ed) Covenant. Where did this renewed Covenant begin and who initiated it?

Most Christian Scholar and Clergy teach that Jesus(Yahshua) the Christ initiated and established the New Covenant through his Death, blood Atonement and Resurrection(how many roman and Greek stories tell this about their god-man before Yahshua was born?). They also teach that this is what is meant when Yahshua said he came to fulfill the law(Torah; Matt. 5:17-20). In the King James Version, Shaul is cited as saying,

Romans 10:4, "for Christ is the end of the Law..."

Yet according to authentic biblical history, and even the words of Yahshua of Nazareth, he was not the founder or initiator of the (re)New(ed) covenant, nor Christianity! He was a priest who Taught the Torah and Oral Torah of an already established Community known as a Renewed Covenant Community of the branch(Netzarim) of YaHudaism, also called Essenes and the Way(DSS), which in many ways parallel a Buddhist-Jewish sect.

[Abolish and fulfill]

Based of MattiYah 5:17-20, *abolish and fulfill* are two P'rushim(Pharisee)-terms. Abolish means, "*to misinterpret, misrepresent contradict or to transgress.* However Fulfill means, "*to interpret correctly, obey* and reverence, to live accordingly or give meaning behind". Yahshua was say-ing that he came to obey the Torah and teach the Torah, not do away or change it. It is every Rabbi's and Ministers Job to Fulfill the Torah and Teach it. We are to be led by YHWH Spirit and give the life meaning behind the Torah, knowing that if we don't we will be condemned by Yahweh for abolishing the Torah! Shaul, and other New Testament Writers, in the form we have them today, is Condemned by Yahweh and Yahweh's Torah as transgressors. Leading people to worship another god!

Philippians 2:5b-11(NKJ), "...in Union with the Messiah Yeshua: who being in the form of Yahweh, did not consider it robbery to be equal with Yahweh...(sterns edition) that in the honor of the name given Yeshua-every knee will bow in heaven(does this include Yahweh?),on earth and under the earth and every tongue will acknowledge that Yeshua the Messiah is Yahweh....."(this is a twisted verse from YeshiYah 45:23).

Yahchonan 1:1b,14a(NKJ), "...and the Word was Yahweh..and the Word became flesh and dwelt among us..Chapter 5:18b, "...He (Yeshua) not only broke the Sabbath, but also said that Yahweh was is own father, making him-self equal with Yahweh."(this is either the translators of the text own inter-pretation, who were Christian or Yahchonan's own view about Yeshua.)

D'bar chapter 13, "if there appears among you a prophet or a dream-diviner and he gives you a sign or a portent(miracle), saying, "let us follow and worship another god(besides Yahweh)-whom you have not experienced-even if the sign or potent that he named comes true, do not heed the words of that prophet or dream diviner....."follow none but Yahweh, and revere none but him...as for that prophet or dream diviner, he shall be put to death....if you hear it said, one of the towns that Yahweh is giving you to dwell in, that some scoundrels from among you have gone and subverted their town, saying,"come let us worship other gods.. You shall investigate and inquire and interrogate thoroughly...put the inhabitants of that town to the sword and put its cattle to the sword....."

Worshiping anyone other than Yahweh and Worshiping Yahweh like an Allah'im(or tri-unity) is a major offence against the Torah! Shaul, although a great miracle worker and Torah scholar taught by Gamaliel, is a Torah transgressor because he deified Yahshua of Nazareth, as well other writers of the New testament such as Yahchonan(religious enemies of Ya'akovs Torah Community at Yerushalem).

Although I don't believe Yahshua taught that he was equal with Yahweh or tried to turn the people away from Yahweh. But. if he did then he deserved to die!

Today its not our duty to slay people, who lead peoples astray from Yahweh, with the physical Sword. There no need for a Holy Jiihad. We are to slay them with the spiritual Sword, that is with the Torah of Yahweh! The Torah of Yahweh is a living Sword that cuts at the roots of the spirit of all things.

When we study to be approved before Yahweh as we are led by his spirit and let Yahweh's glory shine through us, then the world will see the Sword(Torah) we possess and fear Yahweh and repent. As for the apostate false teachers and prophets, when we come face to face with them and Speak the Torah of Yahweh against their words, indeed YHWH power in our lives will slay their lies! And the truth will set them free!

[Dead Sea Sect-Essenes]

In the time of Yahshua of Nazareth up until 70c.e, there were three main sects within YaHudaism(an many sub-sects): The P'rushim, in which Rabbinic Judaism inherited and the *Tz'dukim,* who dominated the Temple and sacrifices. Yet in particular here we want to give a brief history of the *Essenes*.

The Essenes originated as a movement around the middle of 200b.c.e(almost 200yrs before Yahshua was born). They were a protest group against the Hasmonean(Maccabees) rule, who went into exile in the Judean desert(wilderness). Many believe that they were originally apart of the P'rushim. Both sects had much in common. They were an ascetic people who separated themselves from every one and everything else in the world. This group saw themselves as establishing and entering a Renewed Covenant with Yahweh. They were known as the ***New Covenant, The Eternal Yahad(Unity), Eternal Covenant,*** or ***Covenant of Justice.*** They, like the P'rushim, were opposed to blood atonement through animal sacrifice and believed that Atonement for sins was through righteousness, blameless behavior and prayer. They believed in and followed an anointed one(s) called the *Teacher of Righteousness*(Just Teacher), and the Two other future Messiahs(anointed ones), a *Priestly Messiah* or *Messiah of Aaron* and a *Kingly Messiah* or *Messiah of David*(Damascus Document and Charter of a Israelite Sectarian Association, DSS).

They had prophets and they practiced fore-telling. Their Teacher of Righteousness seemed to be more of a Title or office given to an elect person, possibly through priestly inheritance(this can be seen of Yahshua and his Brother Ya'akob later on). Their documents about the Teacher(s) seem at one time to be instruction for the current teacher and at later times seems to be a foreshadow or prediction of a future teacher(Damascus Document 20:1, 13-14,28-32; A1: 3-11; 14:6-12; 1Qhab 2:2-10; 9:9-10). Then again, some scholars say that because of the imagery and allusions found in some of the documents, they are actually 1st century documents, possibly contemporary with Yahshua and Ya'akob, while others writings of the Essenes are earlier writings.

Studying the New Testament imagery and DSS imagery myself, I would favor the latter assumption of the scholars(i.e. the lie imagery in DSS against the wicked priest and Paul, a P'rushim priest, defending himself that he is not lying in the NT: 1Qhab 2:1-10; Romans 9:1; 2corithians 11:31; Galatians 1:20; 1Timothy 2:7).

[Essene Practice vs. Hebrew Netzarim practice(non-Pauline)]

Josephus, the Hebrew historian, and other extra biblical history writings, mention the three Main Sects of P'rushim, Tz'dukim and Essenes, but the New Testament gospels and Hebrew-Netzarim writings mention only two, the P'rushim and Tz'dukim. This is because the New Testament writings(the Gospels) could be a distorted picture of the Essenes or an Essene sub-sect, which were creatively rewritten between 70-200c.e.

To the untrained and unlearned eye, one will overlook the many terms and designations that identify the Essenes(Dead sea group) in the Gospels, Acts of the Shaliachs, and other writings.

The following is a comparison between the Dead Sea Group and Distorted New Testament

1.A. The Essenes called themselves(their sect) **"The Way"**(Community Rule 9:17-19; Damascus Document 4Q270 frag 2:17) B. This is the official identification of the followers of Yahshua of Nazareth and Yahchonan the immerser (Acts 9:2; 18:26; 19:9,23; 22:4; 24:14,22; 2Kefa 2:2,21; MattiYah 3:1-6)

2. A. The Essenes(the Way) also called themselves the **Children of Light, Poor in Spirit,** and the **Many(Majority)**(Community Rule 1:8-10,23-24; 5:9,22; 6:19; 1Qphab 12:2-3).

B.This is also the terminology used to refer to Yahshuas followers. When Yahshua began to teach his talmidim the eight blessings, he starts off saying, "how blessed are the **poor in spirit..**" Yahshua here actually spoke of his own people the poor or Essene(the Way-MattiYah 5:3). in Luke 4:18, Yahshua is recorded as referring to the Essenes as apart of his Mission.(see also Ya'akov 2:5; Compare MattiYah 13:16 with Damascus Document 4Q270 frag 9, 13:7-12; 1QpHab 2:1-10; amascus Document B19:33-chapter20:1-remember Yahshua is of Priestly descent and these writings are possibly contemporary with him-see also Mark 2:15; 6:2, 33; 10:31: Yahchonan 1:12; Acts 2:39).

C. Shaul(Paul) also makes reference against the *Many* /Followers of Yahshua lead by his brother Ya'akov in Yerushalem, (as he does many times in other terms such as those who are **weak, Judaizers,** or those of the **Circumcision**) in whom he blames for causing grief among his(Pauls) own followers at Corinth(2Corithians 2:5-6-see also Luke 16:8-note! Luke is Shauls Secretary!-Ephesians 5:8; 1 thesalonians 5:5).

3.A. The Essenes held all *"things in common"*, from knowledge to all possessions. They even ate in common and prayed in common(Comm unity Rule 1:11-15; 6:7-8, 22-23)

B. The followers of Yahshua under Ya'akov practiced holding all things in common, from property to possessions(acts 2:44-47).

C. Acts tell the story of ChananYah and Shappirah who lied about some property they held back and dropped dead. The Community Rule of the (early)Essenes, for such a violation of lying was not as severe. There punishment was a six month penance.

4.A. The Essenian Leadership council consisted of Twelve Laymen(Shaliachs) and three priests or it could be that out of the twelve laymen three were priest.(Community Rule 8:1-4)

B. The Community at Yerushalem Headed by Yahshua's Brother Ya'akob the "Just" consisted of Twelve Shaliachs in which 3 were the pillars, Ya'akob the **Just** being the Top man(Galatians 2:6, 9; Acts 2-26; 15:4; see Josephus).

5.A. Both Qumran and the Not so New testament Community and the P'rushim were messianic oriented. They both believed in the Advent of a new Messiah. The Essenes believed in two types of Messiahs: A messianic Priest, who brought Atonement and Repentance to Yishra'ala; and a messianic King, who brought National and political Deliverance to Yishra'ala and Ushered in the Kingdom of Yahweh.

B. The New Testament(gospels) after distortion however took both offices of the Messiah Priest and King and made it into one office and gave it to Yahshua. To them Yahshua was the Teacher, Messiah priest, and King. When he was killed the Mythological doctrine of the second coming was developed (these are not the doctrines of the original followers of Yahshua, but later followers of Pauline Christianity-Acts 3:14; 7:52; 22:14)

6 A. Both the Essene Teacher, known as Yahudah and Yahshua die a violent death. In fact Yahshua seems to be the very Teacher himself, with the same teachings, practices and purpose, except the Qumran Teacher Yahudah died about 100yrs before Yahshua was born.

B. Shaul seems to be the incarnate wicked priest and liar of the Essenes, at least this is how the original followers of Yahshua and Ya'akob saw him.

There are many more similarities, time will not permit me to tell. Yet as you thoroughly compare the so-called two groups(Paul being a leader of a third apostate "branch") and study their history, you find out that they are either not two groups, but one and the same, or a group that split off from the earlier Essenes to be more liberal in their preaching proselytism. Josephus does mention more than one Type of Essene group(Wars of the Jews book II chapter 8:1-13).

Although Yahshua has been distorted in a lot of the New Testament writings(i.e. Virgin birth. Being equal with Yahweh, his blood atonement, second coming), once you put him and his Teachings back in their proper historical/Essenian/P'rushim Religion and setting, you will see the true picture of Yahshua and his followers headed by his Brother Ya'akob(Yerushalem Torah Community-see also *James the Brother of Jesus* pg 34-Eisenmen)

Section 3 Messiah(s) Concept and the Son of Yahweh

There are two concepts of the word **Messiah** (Greek Christ) in Hebrew history. One concept is the biblical messiah(s) and the other is the non-biblical or post biblical Messiah.

The post-biblical concept of the Messiah meant, "a descendant of the house of Davyid who would come and restore Yishra'ala back to her home-land and usher in world peace and dominion under the rule of Yahweh". This concept was developed in later generations who were under foreign rule and oppression(586 B.C.E.-destruction of the Temple of Shlomo). Because there seemed no hope for Yishra'ala under oppression, they began to look back at the prophetic writings, such as YeshiYah and make reference to a Messiah-King who would restore them "within" their own time(Josephus Wars, Book II chapt. 5:4) .

The Talmud makes mention of the developed concept of the pre-existence of Messiah.

Pes.54a, "Seven things were created before the world was created: **Torah(the Word), Repentance, the Garden of Eden(i.e. paradise), Gehinnom, the Throne of Glory, the Temple** *and the name of the* **Messiah."**

This is where the writer of the book of Yahchonan(John) gets the, "*in the beginning was the Word*" concept. He just went further to make the *Word* concept, not only the Torah(Word), but the Messiah and Yahweh himself, all as one. This is due to heavy influences of Eastern mysticism, Gnosticism and the cult of Memphite theology from Egypt.

This concept was not based on the biblical or post-biblical concept of Messiah.

As a result of this post-biblical messiah theology, many pseudo-messiahs arose(or were created) during the rule of Rome (to the devastation of many Hebrews) and were crucified. Some of the them were *Judas the Galilean, Theudus, Jesus(Zeus/iseous created by Apostle Paul and after splitting with Yahshuas brother Ya'akob [James] Jerusalem Community, later Gentile pagan Christians such as Constantine further defined Christ according to Roman and Greek theology), Simeon bar Kokhba (2nd century C.E.), Moshe of Crete(5th century C.E.) and many others.*

Here false Messiah didn't necessarily mean that they were not anointed-ones in the biblical concept or were wicked people, but that they just didn't fulfill the office of the post-biblical Messiah-King and one who would bring world dominion and the kingdom of Yahweh and restoration of Yishra'ala as a nation.

Modern Nascent Pauline Christianity(also known as Gentile or Hellene Christianity) believes that the biblical and post-biblical concepts are one and the same. As a major influence by Gnosticism and Yahchonan(Johns) Gospel, they believe that the Christ is a supernatural God-man both equal with and is God(Yahweh). This is neither the Biblical nor post-biblical Messiah concept.

The Hebrews did believe how-ever that the messiah(s) would be able to operate in miracles, powers and signs just like any other prophet of Yishra'ala.

[Scriptural Messiah]

The Hebrew word for messiah in the bible is *Mashiakh* which means, *"anointed or anointed one(s)."* This title referred to one who was either a Hebrew Prophet, Priest, or King of Yishra'ala or anyone who was anointed by Yahweh to do a specific task or mission.

Mashiakh is mentioned many times in the Hebrew scriptures, as *anointed* and *messiah* or *anointed leader*, each referring to some-one different. Leviticus 4:3 declares,

"if it is the Messiah Priest who has incurred guilt, so that blame falls upon the people, he shall offer for the sin which he is guilty..."

Shaul and Davyid are called Messiahs (1Shamuayl 12:10; 24:9-11; 2Shamuayl 19:22; Psalms 2:2).

1Chronicles 16:22, "Do not touch my Messiahs(plural); do not harm my prophets."

Yahweh even calls Cyrus king of Persia, his Messiah in YeshiYah 45:1. The book of Dani'ala even gives a calculated time when two messiahs or anointed leaders would be killed(9:25,26). As for a connection with the house of Davyid and a messiah restoring Yishra'ala, then this credit goes to Zerubabel who led the Hebrew people to restoration out of the Babylonian exile(Ezra 2:2; 5:1-2; Chaggai 1:12-15; ZachariYah 4:6-10).

However it goes, messiah was a human being(s) anointed by Yahweh for a specific task or purpose. They were and are in no way Yahweh-incarnate, a 2nd or 3rd part of a trinity or tri-unity or supernatural.

It was regular for the messiah-King to be selected and Anointed by a messiah-Priest and messiah-Prophet who was selected by Yahweh and then trained in a school of Prophets

[The Messiah/Servant Text of YeshiYah]

"seven things were created before the world was created: Torah, repentance, the Garden of Eden, Gehinnom, the Throne of Glory, the Temple, and the name of the **Messiah**" (Pesachim. 54a).

"and all of Yishra'ala will be saved, as it is written: ""The Deliverer will come out of Zion, and he will turn away ungodliness from Jacob; for this is my Covenant with them when I take away their sins"(Shauls commentary of YeshiYah 59:20,21; 27:9 in his Epistle Romans 11:26-27;NKJV)

Judaism, Islam and Christianity all have one thing in common, they all look forward to the coming of a Messiah as they believe to be prophesied by the Hebrew scriptures. All have separate and distinct beliefs and concepts of who and what the Messiah will be. As for Christianity their main concepts come from what they believe to be prophecies of Jesus as found in the book of YeshiYah.

Examples are: the **Suffering Servant**, the **Anointed One** and the **Chosen of the Lord.**

YeshiYah is the main text used by the Church to try to prove that Jesus is the Messiah, suffering servant, the anointed one and chosen of the Lord. At the same time Judaism uses YeshiYah to refer to the future Messiah of Yishra'ala. Many of the times the Hebrew scriptures are taken out of context by the Christians and their cults, because they refuse to "read" the whole book and text of the Hebrew scriptures.

Here are some of the scriptures that are taken out of context to build erroneous anti-Torah, blasphemous idolatry. I will quote the scriptural error and use the book of YeshiYah as my proof text against Church theology of Jesus;

YeshiYah 42:1-4(Exegeses parallel, Herb Jahn), *"Behold my servant, whom I uphold; my chosen, in whom my soul is pleased: I give my spirit on him; he brings judgements to the goyim: he neither cries, nor lifts, nor has his voice heard in the outway: he neither breaks a crushed stalk nor quenches he a smoking flax; be brings forth judgement to truth: he neither dims nor crushes until he sets judgement in the earth: and the islands await his Torah."*

This is the scripture used by Christians as proof of Jesus being the *Servant* and *Chosen* of God as they believed YeshiYah prophesied. But if you read the whole book of YeshiYah, it will self define and explain itself;

YeshiYah 41:8, *"and you, Yishra'ala-my* **Servant**, *Ya'akov whom I* **Chose**, *the seed of Abraham my beloved, whom I strengthened from the ends of the earth and called you from the nobles, and said to you, you are* **My Servant......"**

Read 43:1-21, "and now thus says Yahweh who created you, oh Ya'akov, and he who formed you, oh Yishra'ala, awe not for I redeemed you;.........you are my witnesses-an oracle of Yahweh and my **Servant** *whom I* **Chose**....."

Read chapter 44; verse 1, "and now hear, oh Ya'akov my **Servant**; *and Yishra'ala whom I* **Chose**....(verse 3) I pour my Spirit(see chapter 42) on your seed and my blessing on your offspring.......(verse 21) Remember these oh Ya'akov and Yishra'ala; for you are my* **Servant**: *Oh Yishra'ala, I forget you not.....(verse 24-25) Thus says Yahweh your redeemer-he who formed you from the belly, I -Yahweh who worked all; who alone spread the heavens; who expanded the earth by myself: who breaks the signs of lies and exposes diviners as mad; who turns the wise backward and follies their knowledge; who raises the* **Word** *of his* **Servant** *and Shalams the counsel of his Malakim........"*

Read Chapter 45; verse 1, "Thus says Yahweh to his **Messiah, to Koresh(Cyrus)**, *whose right I strengthened, to subdue goyim at his face;.....(.verse 4) fore the sake of my* **Servant** *Ya'akov and Yishra'ala my* **Chosen**, *I even call you by your name......"*

Read chapter 49; verse1(YeshiYah speaking), "Hearken, oh islands to me: and hearken, you nations, from afar; Yahweh called me from the belly; from the inwards of my mother he mentioned my name....(verse 3) and he says to me, you are my **Servant**, *oh Yishra'ala, in whom I am adorned.....*(verse 5-7) *and now, says Yahweh who formed me(YeshiYah) from the belly to be his* **Servant**, *to return Ya'akov to him, though Yishra'ala is not gathered, yet I(YeshiYah) am honored in the eyes of Yahweh and my Creator is my Strength....and he says, it is trifling that you(YeshiYah) become my* **Servant** *to raise up the scions of Ya'akov; and restore the guarded of Yishra'ala; I (Yahweh) also give you(YeshiYah) for a light to the Goyim, to become my salvation to the end of the earth...thus says Yahweh, the Redeemer of Yishra'ala, his Holy One, to the despised in soul to the abhorrent of the goyim to the servants of sovereigns, sovereigns see and rise; and governors prostrate; because of Yahweh who is trustworthy-the Holy One if Yishra'ala, and he* **Chooses** *you(Yishra'ala)........"*

As you study the Book of YeshiYah and the many passages of his writings for what it really is(literally), you'll have no choice but to come to a conclusion of who the Servant and Chosen one is. It is not one, but several Servants and Messiahs in YeshiYah; Yishra'ala is the ultimate Messiah and Servant, chosen of Yahweh. Then Koresh(Cyrus)the Persian ruler is called Yahweh's Messiah, and the Messianic Nabi(prophet) YeshiYah himself is called a Servant and a Savior of Yahweh. We know that he is a Messiah because he is a Hebrew prophet. Both Yishra'ala and YeshiYah are a light unto the gentiles and Chosen ones. YeshiYah is a single Servant chosen to restore Yishra'ala, YHWH ultimate Servant and Messiah, back to Yahweh. That's the purpose of the prophetic anointing within YaHudaism to keep the Hebrews in tune with Yahweh!

Yahweh also proclaims that it is the YaHudaim's Word whom he raises, as in authority for teaching, theology and paths of righteousness that leads to Yahweh and all his blessings. This is the Tanakh(Hebrew Scriptures) and Oral Torah

As you read YeshiYah's many passages you will see Yahweh as the King, Father, Savior, Redeemer, Healer and everything that Yishra'ala and the world will ever need and that there is no other besides him!

Now that you have proof of the Real Messiah(s), Servant(s) and Chosen one(s), can you discern by Yahweh's spirit and proper biblical interpretation on who is this Suffering Servant of YeshiYah 52:13-Chapter 53:12;

"behold, Servant comprehends; he is exalted and lifted-mightily lifted. As many astonish at you; his visage so ruined by man; and his form by the sons of humanity: thus he sprinkles goyim; the sovereigns shut their mouths at him: for what was not scribed to them, they see; and what they heard not, they discern. Who trusts our report? And to whom is the arm of Yahweh exposed? For he ascends at his face as a sprout-as a root from parched earth: he has neither form nor majesty when we see him. Nor visage when we desire him. He is despised and abandoned of men; a man of sorrows, and knowing sickness: as one from whom we hide our face; he was despised, and we machinated him not. Surely

he bore our sickness and bore our sorrows: yet we machinated him plagued smitten of the Creator and abased. And he is pierced for our rebellions; crushed for our perversities: the chastisement of our shalom is on him; and with his lashes we are healed. We all strayed as a flock; every man faced to his own way; and on him, Yahweh met all our perversity. Of him they exact, and him they abase; yet he opens not his mouth: taken by restraint and by judgement: and who mediates his generation? For he is cut off from he land of the living: plagued for the rebellion of my people. And he gives his tomb with the wicked and with the rich in his death; because he neither worked violence nor is deceit in his mouth. Yet Yahweh delights to crush him; he strokes him: when you set his soul for the guilt, he sees his seed; he prolongs his days: and the delight of Yahweh prospers in his hand. He sees the toil of his soul, and satisfies; by his knowledge my just servant justifies many; for he bears their perversities. So I allot him with the great, and he allots the spoil with the mighty; because he pours his soul to death: numbered with the rebels; and he bears the sin of many, and intercedes for the rebels."

To help you out, read YeshiYah 50:4-Chapter 53. YeshiYah is speaking throughout the whole passage. Notice that YeshiYah speaks with the authority as if he were Yahweh/Yahweh was present speaking himself, instead of the norm of speaking for Yahweh or of what Yahweh has inspired him to say(i.e. Thus says Yahweh). YeshiYah also speaks of himself and the tragedies he experiences for carrying out the ministry and mission Yahweh has commissioned him. These are not prophesies of a future person or messiah who will atone for sins through his blood therefore reviving Molech worship!

When YeshiYah writes the passage of chapter 53, he uses his life experience and suffering as a teaching and analogy to refer to Yishra'ala and their(our) mission of being a light, a Priest and Servant of Yahweh to the nations. He reveals the consequences of being chosen of Yahweh, because many will hate us for being a light against darkness. When the gentiles and pagans persecute us, hate us and hold us in contempt, they are showing their blindness and ignorance to the fact that through us, the Hebrews, their salvation in Yahweh awaits them and by our sufferings and bruises to be YHWH's light and examples of righteousness in the midst of wickedness they, the world, are healed and sustained by Yahs Word!!

When Egypt and the America's oppressed and enslaved the Hebrews, Yahweh had already planned to abolish physical, emotional, financial and spiritual oppression and slavery and bring Salvation and prosperity to the whole world. When Yishra'ala Temples were being destroyed, Yahweh had already planned to restore and dedicate all peoples to him as living Temples in which he could input his Spirit and Words of Torah. When Yishra'ala sinned and fell short of YHWH Shekinah, Yahweh had already planned to forgive and ingraft all who would be willing come into his Torah Covenant Community. And when Yishra'ala is obedient to YHWH and becomes the light that they are to the nations, then Yahweh will bring the Great Revival promised from ancient times and the Gentiles, pagans and Christians will be able to receive true Redemption and Salvation in Yahweh and Ha-Satan system will be destroyed!!!

Indeed through Prophetic YaHudaism, with Humble Repentance, this is the time for the Great Salvation!!

[The Virgin births a Mighty god with us, everlasting Father, Prince of Peace?]

As you study the other erroneous teachings of the Church and its cults using YeshiYah and other Hebrew scriptures you will see how teachings have been taken out of context! Remember the Hebrew scriptures are your final authority. They are your proof texts. Read the whole passage and let the Hebrew scripture interpret itself. I will be writing a future book on Correction theology for the So called New Testament, revealing its many misinterpretations and erroneous theology that is supposedly based off of the Hebrew Scriptures which constitutes the YaHudaim Bible.

Other Concepts that have been erroneously developed by the Church is the Virgin birth and the God-man;

*YeshiYah 7:14, "So Adonai himself gives you a sign: behold, a **Virgin** conceives and births a son and calls his name Immanuayl"*

YeshiYah 9:6, "for a child is birth to us; a son is given to us-and the dominion is on his shoulder: and he calls his name Marvelous, Counselor, Mighty El, Eternal Father, Governor of Shalom. Of the increase of his dominion and Shalom there is no end, on the throne of Davyid and on his sovereigndom; to establish and to support with judgement and with justness from henceforth-even eternally the Zeal of Yahweh Tzava'ot works this"

(It should be known that the above quotes taken from *Herb Jahn Exegesis Parallel* are the Exegesis of the King James Version and follows the Christian Format of the translation of Scripture. The purpose of using Herb Jahns Exegesis throughout this book is for Clarification of Transliterated Names, Such as Yahweh(Yahveh), and places, and some verses. The Jewish Publication Society However is our Proof text on Scriptural accuracy. However learning Hebrew and using lexicons and Hebrew Concordances can enhance our understanding of certain mistranslated words or inaccurate sentence/phrases as found in many translations of the Scripture, (both Christian and Jewish.)

Out of a whole Text of writings, the above two verses were taken and created into a whole Theology. This theology (of Christianity) is that YeshiYah was prophesying of a Divine Messiah who would be born of a future Hebrew Virgin, that is a woman who never had sexual intercourse with a man, and this Messiah would be "GOD-Incarnate" in the person of Jesus, who is to be the Lawless Reigning King of Yishra'ala, after he has been the suffering Servant(second coming theology).

The problem with these theologies is that it is based of off scripture taken out of context. In order to understand YeshiYah 7:14, we must go back at least to verse 1 of chapter 7. YeshiYah is himself speaking to Achaz, the King of Yahudah, according to the inspiration of Yahweh. The subject is the sign of a child being born. The way the verse has been translated in the Christian Tradition, "a *virgin conceives and births a son*", gives the implication that any woman would conceive this child, which gives rise to Christological prophesy of the Virgin Mary. Then we have the problem of the word translated *Virgin*. The Hebrew word for *Virgin* according to the *Strongs Exhaustive Concordance is #5959, Almah,* which literally means, "*young woman, maiden, lass or damsel(who could be betrothed/married)."* The actual Hebrew word for Virgin is, *Bethulah.*

YeshiYah 7:14 should properly read,

"The young woman(Not "a Virgin") conceives and births a son".

YeshiYah 7:14(JPS), "Assuredly, my Lord will give you a sign of his own accord! Look, the young Woman is with Child and about to give birth to a son. Let her name him Immanuel."

This means that YeshiYah is referring to a young Woman that was known by him or Achaz. Probably Achaz's wife the queen would conceive, considering that Achaz Sacrificed all of his other Children to Molech(2Chronicles 28:1-6). The Queen does later birth YechizqiYah(HezekiYah).

There is also another possible indication that the sign of the young woman conceiving is the Prophetess that has a Son by YeshiYah ;

YeshiYah 8:3(JPS), "I (YeshiYah) was intimate with the prophetess, and she conceived and bore a son"

YeshiYah goes on to say in verse 18,

"Here stand I and the children Yahweh has given me as signs and portents in Yishra'ala from Yahweh of Hosts, who dwells in Tzion."

Compare also the conceived son of Chapter 7:16 and the conceived son of Chapter 8:4 using Chapter 7:3-9; 2Chronicles 28:1-8

[YeshiYah 9:6(5jps)]

As for the passage surrounding YeshiYahs comment in Verse 9:6(9:5JPS), it is obvious that he is speaking of himself and his wife the prophetess who conceives a son for him in chapter 8.

Even if the passage were speaking of the future, it would still be a human being. The translation rendered, *Mighty El* in verse 6, is usually rendered *mighty god* in the KJV. *El* is a Hebrew-Canaanite word which has been translated many times as both *god* and *power or mighty.*

As you have studied the chapter dealing with the Allah'im, you should have learned that *El* means *"mighty, strength or power"*. When using a Hebrew name, *Ayil* should be used which means, *"mighty, strength or Power"*. According to the Strongs Hebrew concordance *Mighty El* (mighty god-KJV) is the Hebrew word *#410 & 1368 El gibbor. Gibbor* means, *"Powerful; warrior; strong or valiant man"* this is the same as #1397 *Geber* which means, *"a valiant man or warrior"*. Therefore it should read,

(using JPS version), "For a child has been born to us, a son has been given us. And authority has settled on his shoulders. He has been named **mighty man of valour**, *Eternal Father, a peaceable ruler....."*

This verse carries the same weight as Judges 6:12, when Gideon is called a *Mighty man of valour.*

Another error that throws people off is the fact that many people do not realize that this Child would have several names. Many scholars and lay peoples mistake this childs names(nicknames) with what they think the passage is saying he will be.

The translators of the scripture translated the meaning of the name(s) instead of giving us the child's name(s). This is unfair. Think about it when Yahshua ben Nun is mentioned in scripture he is not called, *Yahweh's Salvation*. Although that is what his name in general means. YirmeYah, Dani'ala, Moshe, or any other Hebrew in the bible, name is not translated but is written exactly what he should be called.

Yes indeed all Hebrew names have meaning, but that meaning is summed up in the name! Although *mighty man of valour(mighty god-KJV)* is what the name means, the actual name should be *El(in Hebrew case ayil) gibbor*. Instead of *everlasting Father*, the name should be *Av'adah*, and instead of *peaceable ruler(prince of peace KJV)*, the name should be *Tzarshlomo*. Therefore the verse should really have been **transliterated**(not translated),

(using JPS version), "for a child has been born to us, a son has been given us. And authority has settled on his shoulders. He has been named Ayil(El)gibbor Av'adah Tzarshlomo..

As you should notice, YeshiYah says that this child, that is born(present tense), is his child from the prophetess. What is the real name of this child? YeshiYah 8:3 names him *Mahers Halal Hash Baz* What kind of Authority has settled(past tense) on his shoulders (considering he is still a infant or toddler)? Hint. Compare 2Chronicles 20:20,

(JPS) "as they went forth, Yahshaphat(king with authority) stood and said, listen to me, oh Yahudah and inhabitants of Yerushalem: trust firmly in Yahweh Almighty and you will stand firm; trust firmly in his prophets and you will succeed(increase, prosper, rise)

This child is called by Yahweh to continue and carry the Prophetic Mantle of his father YeshiYah. The prophetic authority is given to keep YHWH Leaders(in this case the Kings) who rule his Kingdom, and the people of the kingdom in line with YHWH Torah, will and way, enforcing spiritual and ethical Monotheism. It is the prophetic anointing that carries the Burden of the Kingdom of Yahweh on their spiritual shoulders.

In this case Yishra'ala and Yahudah were in rebellion against Yahweh, and as long as they were in rebellion there would be no peace nor increase in their Kingdom. In fact had the Hebrews listened to the prophetic Authority given them, the Throne of Davyid and the Temple would still be in existence today. In truth the everlasting Throne of Davyid and the Temple will not be restored until the prophetic anointing within YaHudaism is restored. This is why Malachi speaks of AlaYah(Elijah) the prophet returning before the day of Yahweh(or reign of the Messiah King under the Authority of Yahweh). YeshiYah's son was anointed to carry the tradition of the prophetic voice against the sins of Yishra'ala so that there may be a chance that Davyids Eternal throne not come to an end(In which later it did after the prophets were ignored and ceased, but will soon be restored).

[Conclusion]

As you see there is no Virgin birth of a future divine Messiah who is part man and part Yahweh that atones for sins through his blood and does away with Yahweh's Torah. Yahshua(Jesus) of Nazareth is never mentioned in the Hebrew scriptures nor does he fulfill any prophecies.

The new Testament stories of Jesus name being powerful and above every name, virgin birth, death and resurrection(good Friday-Easter), blood atonement and deity, and son of God theology and the Christian teaching of his birthday being on December 25th is nothing more than Worship of Zeus(Jesus), Mithras and Osiris, their real trinity and Molech their God which constitutes an Allah'im(the revival of a mystical Cana'anite/Eastern Hellenist anti-Torah Religion!!!) .

[Hebrew Encouragement]

I know by now that many of you who are studying this book feel confused, somewhat discouraged, disappointed or have many questions because you were not taught this sooner and many are even furious because to you this is foreign theology and you are getting defensive. Yet many more are being filled with joy and finding light and their place in Yahweh. However I want to encourage you and let you know that you are called by Yahweh. That's why you are reading this book.

However your response to this calling is going to determine whether you are chosen by Yahweh to enter his covenant. Because many are called but it is the few(or many) who respond and submit to the calling of Yahweh who are Chosen. Chosen to Enter into the Hebrew Torah Covenant Community given through Moshe at Sinai.

Yahweh does not want you to feel like the rug has been pulled from under you or that he's out to get you because you were not believing in him. This book is a result of his grace and mercy and his awesome love for you so that you may know his will for your life and enter through the Proper Way(Halacha) of his Kingdom.

So I encourage you and bless you and declare that you lift up your eyes to hills around Yerushalem, to Yahweh, the Creator of all the earth, the Eternal helper, the Lord of the heavens who will deliver you and raise you like a Shepherd raises his sheep!!! Now read on.

Chapter 4

Section 1 PaRDes The Four Levels of Biblical Interpretation & Understanding

In order to properly study the Hebrew scriptures without adding or subtracting the value meaning and purpose of the Texts, and to keep from profaning the holiness of the Word, we must began to use the proper method of interpretation and understanding. In YaHudaism we use the ancient interpretation called PaRDeS, which is the Notarikon or acronym of,

Pashat, Hebrew for simple
Remez, Hebrew for Hint
Drash, Hebrew for Search
Sod, Hebrew for Hidden
Each layer above goes deeper into the scriptures than the last.

[Pashat]

Pashat is the literal understanding of the text of Scripture for what it is and actually says. It is the simple meaning. All you have to do is read it for what it Is. The main exegetical rule of the Talmud states that, *"No passage loses it Pashat"*(b.Shab. 63a; b.Yeb.24a).

Although the Hebrew scriptures may have hidden meanings, symbolism, allegory or figurative language in the texts, the literal meaning must be sought and understood. The literal meaning of the scripture is where we get our actual understanding and foundation of truth. Without the Pashat we will not have an accurate understanding of scripture, thereby allowing our imaginations and opinions to manipulate the Scriptures to our own deceit(Christian interpretation of Hebrew Scriptures lack Pashat in the utmost). As a result Cults and heretical groups pop up and lead many astray of the Hebrew Scriptures.

Some examples of a Pashat is,

Duet 4:1-2, "And now, oh Yishra'ala, give heed to the laws and rules that I am instructing you to observe, so that you may live to enter and occupy the land that the LORD(YHWH), the God of your fathers, is giving you. You shall not add anything to what I command you or take anything away from it, but keep the commandments of the LORD(YHWH) your God that I enjoin upon you."

This passage like every other Hebrew passage is meant to be taken literally. Nothing is supposed to change the value or meaning of this text. This text speaks specifically to Yishra'ala, physical Yishra'ala. They are to give heed to the rules and laws Moshe is instruction them. Any teaching relating to this passage must build upon this passage. As this is the same principle with the whole of Torah. The literal meaning must be settled in ones heart first, before they can grow spiritually and intellectually to the next level of understanding.

Another example of a literal meaning; study *Exodus 21:12-17.* Once you have the literal understanding that Shabbat is eternal sign between Yishra'ala and YHWH, It is proof of YHWH's consecration of Yishra'ala, It is holy for Yishra'ala, and that it is an eternal Covenant, then you won't become vulnerable to teachings that destroy or twist the meaning, such as Christian Sunday Worship, or a New Testament(covenant) replacing the Covenant of Yishra'ala. Once you get the Pashat of the Hebrew Scriptures into your heart, you'll automatically reject and disregard teachings contrary to it.

When one accepts a Trinitarian doctrine, it because they never understood the Pashat of D'var 6:4 stating that YHWH is one, literally, which is the foundation. Remember, ***No Hebrew Passage looses its Pashat, its Literal meaning!***

There are also several rule of thumb that are to be used in determining whether a Passage of scripture is figurative, even in it Pashat:

1. A statement is figurative when it uses a non animate object to describing a living being(Psalm 18:2).

2. A Statement is figurative when its expression is out of Character with what it described(i.e. Psalms 17:8; 18:8-12).

3. A Statement is figurative when life and action are attributed to a non-animate object(Proverbs 18:10).

[Ramez]

Ramez is the next level of interpreting Hebrew scripture. It is regarded as hinting at a deeper truth or the implied meaning of the Text other than that mentioned by its Pashat.

For example D'var 5:20 say,

"Answer not a vain witness against you friend(neighbor)"

by this passage we know we are not bear false or vain witness against thy friend or neighbor, in this case a Hebrew Israelite. Using the ***Ramez*** we know that we are not to bear a false witness against our enemies or foreigners, parents or children. It is our duty not to bear false witness at all against anyone!

Another example is Exodus 21:12,

"he who smites a man, thus he dies: in deathifying, deathify him(put him to death)"

Using the **Remez** we know that this applies to a woman smiting a man, a man smiting a woman or child, or a teenager smiting a man, woman or another child or a woman smiting a woman. They were to be put to death.

If I told my son not to steal cookies from the jar anymore of else he would get a spanking, that also applies stealing from a store, my coat pocket or stealing period.

Ya'akov the Just, leader of the Yerushalem Hebrew community in 1st century YaHudaism uses the Ramez in his commentary on the Torah:

Ya'akov(James) 2:10(Stern), "for a person who keeps the whole Torah, yet stumbles at one point, has become guilty of breaking them all. For the One who said, 'Don't commit adultery,' also said, 'don't murder.' now if you don't commit adultery but do murder, you have become a transgressor of the Torah."

[Drash]

The next level of Hebrew scripture interpretation is known as the **Drash** which means *"to search."* This is when we use the homiletical, topo-logical and allegorical application of the Texts. We search the text as it relates to the rest of the Hebrew scriptures, life or a personal experience or other literature. This deals with eisegesis, or the reading of the text.

For example, use D'var(Deuteronomy) 6:4 to understand YeshiYah 41:4; 43:10b-12; 44:6; 45:5-7, 18b, 21b-22 .

Use YeshiYah 41:8 to understand 42:1-4; or YeshiYah 44:1, 21; 45:4; 49:3 to understand YeshiYah 52:13-chapter 54:12

Use Numbers 11:29 to understand Yah'ala(Joel) 2:28-29.

Use D'var 4:7 to understand ZachariYah 8:23

There are two rules of thumb we must follow in using the **Drash**:

1. A Drash interpretation cannot in any way be used to strip or contra-dict the text of its Pashat. Nor can it Change the literal meaning of the Hebrew text. **No Passage loses its literal meaning!**

2. Allow scripture to interpret scripture. Search for the Scriptures themselves to define the parts of an allegory.

[Sod]

The last level of interpretation is the *SOD,* meaning, *"Hidden"*. This is the Prophetic revelation given by the Eternal One himself concerning a part of the Hebrew Text. It can be an implied revelation nationalistically or individually. It is a fresh Prophetic Word from Yahweh concerning life, Torah, business, governments or a number of events. It is an illumination of the Torah and will of YHWH. As always it will not change the Torah or any Hebrewm passage in any way.

As you are using these methods of interpretation, you must remember that the Pashat is the most important, Remez is second Drash is third and Sod is fourth important. All understanding and interpretation is built from the Pashat, which is the foundation of biblical understanding.

Chapter 5

Section 1

While Christianity is a religion based on faith(belief) in a man for salvation, The Israelite Practice is a Divine appointed way of life based on Obedience and actions, also known as faithfulness to Yahweh and Living by his divine Torah teaching and instructions given through Moshe. Unlike Christianity, theology and doctrinal statements is not the essence of Israelite ways. Israelite focus is on Ethics and living in this world according to how Yahweh has designed. This is known as Ethical Monotheism.

According to the *American heritage dictionary third edition pp291*, **Ethic** is defined as,

1. A principle of right or good conduct or a body of such principles. 2. A system of moral principles or values. 3. **Ethics.** *The study of the general nature of morals and of specific moral choices. 4.* **Ethics.** *The rules or standards governing the conduct of the members of a profession.*

While the Israelite faith is not a profession, but a divine cultural way of living in reality, it contains principles, rules and teachings in order to be successful in a profession. The teachings of the Torah are the principles that govern and establishes standards of moral living in which we as

Hebrews and Gentile believers must live accordingly in order to succeed as YHWH has designed us.

The Tanakh or Hebrew scriptures teaches us how to live our lives to the fullest and at the same time how to bare the Shekinah of Yahweh in our lives, that is how to become the essence of what he has purposed us to do. Tanakh teaches us how to live Socially, Culturally, healthy(physically), economically, mentally and spiritually. Indeed these are the 6 principles that one must practice in order to live life according to YHWH design. All are necessary for completeness. You can't live prosperous spiritually, when you are in poverty economically or physically and vise verse. Its not healthy mentally to not be able to live a good social life and vise versa. All are interlinked and must be incorporated into everyday living.

As we discuss some of the customs and practices of Yishra'ala we will see the many teachings and principles that help us live rich, healthy spiritual lives in all areas as we build ourselves in relation to Yahweh.

You will be truly blessed as you incorporate the Torah into your every day lives.

[Torah She-be-al-peh & Torah She-Bikhtav]Oral Torah and the written Torah

As we have studied, the written Torah is the history, teachings and instructions as found in the Five Books of Moshe. The Whole of the Hebrew scriptures known as the Tanakh(Torah, Prophets and Writings) is known as the written Torah. The Writings and the Prophets are exhortations, wisdom teachings and commentaries of the written Instructions given to Moshe by YHWH. **The Oral Torah** although is ancient and originally from Hebrew Yishra'alites origin is now however a Jewish legal commentary on the Torah of Moshe(or written Torah). Its attempts to explains how the Torah of Moshe might be interpreted and carried out. This is known as Halacha. The Oral Torah was intended to give the Who, what, when, where and why and "How" to the undetailed and unspecific

Teachings found in the Written Torah. The Oral Torah is known as the "Spirit of the Law". The Written Torah is the Skeleton/Structure and Flesh of YaHudaism, compared to the human body. The Oral Torah is like the soul/Spirit, it is supposed to give life to the Written Torah. For example. Read D'barim(Deuteronomy 12:21),

(JPS), "If the place where the LORD(YHWH) has chosen to establish his name is too far from you, you may slaughter any of the cattle or sheep that the LORD(YHWH) gives you, as I have instructed you; and you may eat to your hearts content in your settlements"

This passage teaches us that it is permissible to eat non-dedicated(consecrated) meat if we live too far from the Yerushalem Temple, as Moshe Instructed us. But this instruction is not found anywhere as a reference in the Written Torah. This passage is a reference to the Oral Instruction according to the Rabbis.

The Oral Torah we have Today is compiled and written down in a form of a commentary by various Rabbis and Hebrew Scholars. This is known as the Mishna and Talmud. Orthodox Jews believes that the majority of the Oral Torah(we have today) originated with Moshe at Mt. Sinai. They believe that when YHWH gave the Written Torah he also gave the details of it as found in the Oral Torah. Prophetic YaHudaism likewise agree in a limited way, and along with Reformed and Conservative Judaism, believe that the Oral Torah is necessary to understand Written Torah to make it work in our lives, But reject the belief that the Talmud dates back to the time of Moshe. Instead they(We) believe that the Talmud is an evolving system which successive generations of Teachers and Rabbis discussed and debated how to make the Torah work in their lives. Because the Talmud contains the opinion of men(which at times goes extreme and circumvents or destroys the Written Torah), prophetic YaHudaism can disagree, disregard, enhance or modify the Oral teachings we have today. Oral Torah teachings must line up and Strengthen the Written Torah, and not cause a burden or stumbling block to the Hebrew peoples to be accepted. Yet most of all we must allow YHWH's spirit to lead us and guide us in different situations and matters. Culturally Modern Oral Torah holds no value to African Hebrew Yishra'alites.

The Written Torah stands as equivalent to a modern day national constitution, as in the constitution of the United States. In governs a whole nation and community. Some laws and teachings apply only to men while others apply only to women, others are instructions specifically for the Levites, priest, prophets, Kings or leaders of Yishra'ala, others are for the common people in general, other laws can only be followed if you live in physical Yishra'ala, while others are universally binding. Furthermore there are instructions for festivals and days of rest, how to transact business and personal relationships, rituals instructions of pure and unpure for sexual relations and sickness, instructions for daily eating habits and regulations for Temple service(which contains the most traditions of inherited paganism…i.e sacrifice). According to the Ancient Teachers of Yishra'ala there are 613 teaching, laws and statutes found in the Torah.

There are three primary categories of YHWH's Torah:

1.Mishpatim-YHWHs moral and ethical teachings also known as judgements-i.e. how to treat your neighbors, prohibitions against murder, robbery, adultery, covetousness, ect….the second half of the Ten Commandments is the summary of Mishpatim

2.Edyot-this is Hebrew for witness. These are the Teachings that testify of YHWH's Torah and purpose; i.e such as instructions for Pesach or Yom Kippur. The instructions of the festivals teach us the revelation of YHWH's plan for mankind through Yishra'ala and remind us of his living Words. As we walk out his Torah we become a light and a living witness of the truth of the ONE true Creator YHWH and his word, to the goyim(Gentiles/Nations).

3.Chokim-these are the teaching in the scripture that have no specific explanation or reason of being taught to us. They are somewhat difficult to understand, yet are in a way designed for us to use our common sense on why we should or should not do certain things. The dietary Laws, water immersion(mikveh), the wearing of Locks(payot) on the side of male Hebrew heads are a good example to this. They are cultural Laws. However we will never know the true meanings of these teachings until the Rule and Day of YHWH(or YHWH reveal it himself to us).

[Babylonian & Palestinian Talmud]

Around the year 200 C.E., when the Yeshivoth and Thousands of Hebrew Teachers and students were devastated and knowledgeable and learned Hebrews peoples declined due to the Roman destructions of the Great revolt(AD. 70) and the Barkokba rebellion, Jews began to rise and Take the Place of the Hebrews and a Rabbi named Yahudah HaNasi began recording and writing the European version of the Hebrew Oral Torah. Through Rabbi HaNasi's writings, Israelite versions of the Torah became systematically codified in the **Mishna**, the name for the 63 tractates HaNasi set the Oral Torah. The Mishna was arranged by Rabbi HaNasi based on topic. The topics ranged from **Moed(Holidays), Zera'im(seeds;Agriculture), Nezikin(Damages; Civil Law), Nashim(Women), kodashim(Sacrifice & Ritual), Taharot(Purity and Impurities).** Each contained different laws and instructions on the subject of topic. Only one of the Mishna Tractates contains no law or instructions. This is called the **Pirket Avot(Ethics of the Fathers)**, which the Rabbis most famous sayings and proverbs are recorded. The **Talmud** is a result of later generations of Rabbis writing commentaries and discussions of the Mishna. The commentary from the Palestinian Rabbis became known as the **Palestinian Talmud(Talmud Yerushalmi)** around 400C.E. More than a century later Babylonian Rabbis compiled another edition of the Talmud, known as the **Babylonian Talmud(Talmud Bavlio)**. This edition became the most Authoritative commentary of the Oral Torah. As for the Israelite Torah Covenant Community Talmud and B'rith Chadasha teachings became Commentary(Talmud more accepted). Prophetic YaHudaism uses the same principle of Agreeing, disagreeing, enhancing, correcting, criticism and disregarding certain teachings of the Brit Chadasha where it contradicts the Written Torah and Traditional Hebrew Teachings(i.e Yahshuas deity, Post-biblical Messiah ship, Equality with YHWH, anti-Torah teachings by Shaul, virgin Birth, blood Atonement, literal Son ship, and any Teachings that is not rooted or taught in the Hebrew Scriptures or Tradition). The only "authoritative" B'rith Chadasha Commentary is the Writings of Ya'akov(James the Just) and Dead Sea Scrolls. The first B'rith Chadasha commentaries began around 200B.C.E(Essene Writings & DSS).

In both the Talmud and B'rith Chadasha's the Rabbis and Teachers engage in two types of discussions, **Halakha(Legal Matters)**, and **Aggadata(Ethical & Folkloristic)** which includes medical advice, historical anecdotes, moral exhortations, folklore, worship and spirituality(See-Jewish Literacy, Telushkin)

[The Moral Life]

From the theory of Torah which underlies the whole of Talmudic doctrine, it inevitably follows that the way to the living of the **Moral life** must be sought and could only be found in the divine revelation(Torah). What the Torah commands and prohibits is the sure guidance and morality consists in compliance with its precepts(Excerpt taken from *Everymans Talmud, Cohen*).

[Imitation of YHWH]

D'var 13:5(JPS), "follow none but the LORD(YHWH) your God(Almighty), and revere none but him; observe his Commandments alone, and heed only his orders; worship none but him, and hold fast to him…"

The Imitation of YHWH is the way for all of mankind to strive. To Imitate means *to do as one would do, act as one would do, and live like another would live.* It means *to do exactly what another would do.* Because

YHWH is Holiness and we are made in his image and likeness, we are to imitate his Holiness in our lifestyles. We are to be whole, unique and complete in ourselves according to YHWH's Torah. YHWH is a Father of Faithfulness, therefore we are to be faithful to him in everything we do in his Torah Covenant Community. Faith creates situations whether positively or negatively. No matter what, we all have faith in something. And according to that faith will we live our daily Ethical(unethical) lives. Even doubt is faith, except it is faith in what is against your total life and achievements. You're either going to believe and work towards the Goal of Torah which is YHWH's holiness or something else(i.e. Paganism and Ha-Satan). Even Atheist believe there is no Creator?...

YHWH is the pattern after which all mankind must strive to imitate. YHWH has supplied us, the Torah Covenant Community peoples with his Ruakh(those who have received it) in order to be led and taught how to properly Imitate him according to his Torah. Mankind is supposed to be executing the Physical manifestation of YHWH's will upon the earth.

The imitation of YHWH can be seen in ones character, which dictates the kind of lifestyle one lives and molds the personality traits. Character Traits is the Hebrew word, *Middah,* which means, *"measure".* The measure of the quality of your life and success is in the refinement of your Character traits, that is, *moving closer to the Shekinah of YHWH's image,* in which we were all created.

Are you a caring person ? Do you deal with others in business, social or personal matters with respect and integrity? Are you patient and longsuffering? do you value yourself or is your esteem well balanced? Are you aiming at Achieving goals and YHWH's purpose for your life? Do you have effective Torah study? Are you gentle with others ? are you diplomatic, in avoiding strife and confusion? Are you a giving and forgiving person? Are your family priorities in order? Are your morals in line with Torah? Do you keep your diet and physical healthy? Is your personal relationship with YHWH in good standing?

These questions are just some of the many character traits we must evaluate in ourselves. The Ten Commandments are the summarization of the relationship between YHWH and man and mankind with each other. This too summarizes and instructs our character and ways of living.

When we live in accordance with the Torah, people will be able to see the true expression of YHWH in us; *Gracious, Loving, Merciful, Patient, faithful, Self-control, and rejoicing. Nothing in the Torah can condemn this.* This sums up the essence of Character. When Mankind imitates YHWH Shekinah, he's actually imitating YHWH's character.

YHWH's graciousness expresses his patience, kindness, goodness, love and longsuffering. His Kingship and dominion-ship expresses his self-control and responsibility. YHWH has everything in control, that's why he is the Creator of Justice and peace. Peace brings unity and eliminates strife and prejudices, which in turn brings about joy. Because YHWH has not broken his Covenant with the Hebrew/YaHudaim peoples and has continually shown his faithfulness, never to forsake his people or his Word, how much more should we as his people of the Torah Covenant imitate him.

If we are to ever reestablish our reputation and calling of being the true light of the World and a priest unto the nations, then we must began to let the Gentiles see YHWH our Father in us. We must become One with YHWH as we are led by his Ruakh in his Torah. When people see us, the Hebrews, they must see the Word of YHWH in us. We must live as a *Nation of the Anointed Ones.* We must live like royal chosen Sons and Daughter, for YHWH our father is King! We are the true Mashiakhim of YeshiYah! Yahweh's Ruakh is upon us to proclaim the message of the Kingdom of YHWH. We are called to administer Ethical Monotheism!!!

When we finally decide to take our places as YHWH's Chosen and imitate YHWH character, then and only then will the earth be filled with the knowledge of the Glory of YHWH as the waters cover the sea! Then and only then will the people know that, " *who ever calls upon the name of*

YHWH will be SAVED!" Truly Saved!!! And they will desire to imitate YHWH as We!

[Brotherly Love]

Wayyicra 19:17-18, " you shall not hate your brother(Kinfolks) in your heart…but you shall love your neighbor as yourself.

These are the fundamentals principles of the Torah. Brotherly love is the standard of Universal love and is the foundation of human relationship. Because the Hebrew scriptures reveals that all life was fashioned and created from one Eternal Creator, Yahweh, and he designed Adamah to be the physical image in which all human life must strive to imitate, then we must understand that we have the responsibility of recognizing that we are all brothers and sisters by ancient Blood ties regardless of our race, color, Ethnic/cultural or religious affiliation, political or moral status. Therefore we must fulfill the royal command of Brotherly love(first among our own peoples of the Hebrews and then among the peoples of the world). This is the true imitation of YHWH.

The famous Hebrew Teacher Hillel responds to a Gentiles request to teach him the whole Torah, while standing on one foot, by saying,

What is Hateful to yourself, do not do to you fellow man." (Shab.31a)

This is the Talmudic golden rule, commentary on Wayyicra 19:17-18. This means that a person with true brotherly love, which is rooted in YHWH's love, will never try to hurt another person spiritually, mentally or physically by gossiping(Talebearing), character assassinations, anger and hatred, oppressions, depressions, racism and prejudices, discrimination, cultural assassinations, division and anything related to such as mentioned in the Torah.

Division's among the Hebrew Israelites and Jewish communities because of Religious denomination and racial/cultural backgrounds and geographical location is the result of the lack of True Torah and brotherly love for one another. Enmity between races is the same result. The modern design of the Euro-gentile Christian Church,as it received from the True Roman culture in which it was born, oppresses Cultures, attack one another's denominations, creates doctrinal statements that divide themselves, disrespects peoples of other Religions and cultures because they don't believe like them or are not like them, and glorify leaders that made comments that gave rise to the 100,000,000Cushite/Hebrew(Black) Slave Trade and the so-called 6,000,000 German Jewish holocaust, because of the lack of true brotherly love. This world's moral standard has drastically decreased because of the lack of brotherly love and the imitation of YHWH.

True Love of YHWH melts all the above. You'll know the love of YHWH in someone based on how he treats his neighbor, family and society, not how he quotes scripture or tries to evangelize in the name of some god. A Religious system apart from YHWH's Torah and Love is just a system of bondage and fanaticism.

The Caucasians and European Jews, who lie and try to erase the rich blackness of Yishra'ala and world history and try to replace a dominate white history to suppress black culture and roots, do not have the Love of YHWH. The holocaust, Black(Cushite /Hebrew) Slave Trade, Native American annihilation, Pro-Zionist Movement and oppressions of other peoples and cultures is Ha-satanic. Cushite(Dark peoples) who respond with just as much hatred and un-forgiveness is just as guilty(although I understand). The Torah, Talmud and Brit Chadasha places hatred on the same level as murder! No matter how religious, gifted and talented, powerful and influential you are, if you don't have the Love of YHWH and brotherly love, your talents and powers mean nothing.

So whatever you don't want others to do to you, don't do to others and visa versa.

[Humbleness]

*A Mans pride will humiliate him, but a humble man will obtain honor(Proverbs 29:23)

*The Greatest among you must be your servant, for whoever promotes himself will be humbled and whoever humbles himself will be promoted(MattiYah 23:11-12)

*But the grace he gives is greater, which is why it says, 'YHWH opposes the Arrogant but to the humble he gives grace'(Ya'akov 4:6; Proverbs 3:34)…Humble yourselves before YHWH and he will lift you up(James 4:10)

*what is the greatest of the ten steps in the ascent of the righteous? Saintliness, as it is said:"then thou spakest in vision to thy saints"(Psalms 89:20). Rabbi Joshua ben Levi said: Humility, for it is said: "The spirit if the Lord(YHWH)God(Almighty) is upon me, to bring good tidings to the humble," whence we learn that humility is the greatest of all virtues. (Abodah Zarah, 20b)

Humility and humbleness means *to be modest, lowly and void of arrogance and vain pride, and meek"*. Humbleness has nothing to do with being a wimp, with having an oppressed/bound mental expression of oneself. It is the ability to recognize that you are not better than someone else because of your knowledge, anointing, financial status or political, religious, business or social business. You are able to recognize that everything is not about you alone and that without YHWH and other human beings you wouldn't be what or who you are. In fact without YHWH you would be nothing.

Humbleness attracts YHWH's kind of Pride, but eliminates arrogant pride or the *holier than thou* attitude. Humbleness and humility teaches us to submit to YHWH's appointed Spiritual Authority. YHWH operates through spiritual authority. Whether you are gifted or not, or even if you seem to be a better Teacher, leader of whatever, if YHWH has not put you in Authority then you are to submit to his appointed Spiritual authority.

Submission can only come through your ability to take control of your life and humble yourselves. The only way you can truly take control and authority over your lives is through the Torah of YHWH. As long as there is vain pride in your life, you'll never be elevated or honored by YHWH.

Humbleness is the ability to recognize YHWH's timing on Honor. In fact a humble person does not selfishly seek honor, they just seek to do YHWH's will and are obedient to his Word by submitting to YHWH's appointed spiritual authority. As a result YHWH honors him. When one is humble, he will have no problem elevating or honoring others, even if he has to make himself lowly, because in his heart he knows his position and who he truly is in YHWH. He is whole, complete and unique in himself(herself), and understands YHWH's purpose for his life.

Pride is the result of insecurity and low self-esteem. That means you're not sure who you are, where you came from or where you're going. You are not sure that YHWH's Authority is in your life and purpose. When you know who you are, being humble isn't a problem.

This in no way saying that you are to allow yourself to be oppressed by another, or to not stand up for what you believe or turn the other cheek when political, social, cultural, mental or spiritual danger is foreseen.

The Talmud Echoes:

"Every man who is filled with an arrogant spirit is as though he had worshiped idols, denied the basic principles of Religion and committed every kind of immorality...who ever is possessed of an arrogant spirit, the Holy One, blessed be he, says, 'I and he cannot dwell in the world to come.'" (Sotah 4b et seq).

[Tzedakah-Righteousness]

D'barim 10:18-19; 24:19-21; 26:12-15; 27:19; YeshiYah 1:17; 7:5-7; 22:3; ZachariYah 7:9-10;

Righteousness falls into two categories in Hebrew teaching, *Tzedakah(righteousness)* and *Bemiluth Chasdim,* the presentation of loving acts. The latter being of greater quality. Ya'akov 2:14-16 says,

> *What good is it, my brothers, if someone claims to have faith, but has no actions to prove it? Is such faith able to save him? Suppose a brother or sister is without clothes or daily food, and someone says to him, Shalom! Keep warm and eat hearty! Without giving him what he needs, what good does it do?*

Charity is born out of righteousness and a love for the well being of mankind. It is summed up in the term "giving". Giving is an act of YHWH. It is a duty to give. For when we give YHWH will give back to you. That is when you give out of love and cheerfulness. Giving out of forced obligation or giving and hating to do it does not constitute blessing from YHWH.

> *"A man may give liberally, and yet because he gives unlovingly and wounds the heart of the poor, his gift is in vain, for it has lost the attribute of charity; a man may give little, but because his heart goes with his deed and himself are blessed."(Baba Batra, 9b)*

Giving is not just about money, although today it is required to accomplish many things. Giving can be in our time to volunteer to serve our communities or outreach events, especially when we set it aside to help build the Kingdom of YHWH. We can give to organizations our clothes or furniture, we can give to food banks, we can give our times to be Youth leaders, mentors and tutors. When we share our different callings and gifts with mankind we are giving.

There are many ways and options in giving and as a result we will be blessed. Yet when we have an evil eye, that is stinginess, we make our whole body darkness. In our local congregations we are to give our financial offerings, and time according to the vision that YHWH has given the leader.

[All things in Common]

One of the best solutions to giving in the local congregations or synagogues is to eliminate prejudice and low self esteem and bring equality by letting everyone have all things in common. This can be done by having a special committee to collect finance, clothes, and food to help those who are of less advantage due to economical situations within the congregation(speaking of members). The clothes and material things would either be new and modern or like new and modern. This way when all come together to worship study, and fellowship, all feel welcome, be worry free and feel confident in YHWH's love, because of the congregations Charity.

Also in order decrease the economical crisis within congregations, there should be resources or training and info on getting proper education or acquiring certain skills to achieve employment and financial independence. Each member should be held accountable for seeking the best well being of his fellow member.

[Homeless people]

When one is on the streets begging for money or food, I feel touched and am apt to give something to them or buy them some food. No righteous Hebrew or Gentile should ignore a homeless person. They should try to give them something, whether food, something to drink or just some of their time to talk with them, or info on getting help. It depends on the situation and whether the person is violent or not.

Before you give, always pray with that person. Treat them like human beings, just as you would want to be treated if you were in a similar situation.

Recently YHWH gave me wisdom to understand that to constantly give to a homeless person(as in the same person) and yet not have any programs of rehabilitation and economical, spiritual, and mental restoration is actually making him or her worse. This is not to say that you shouldn't give because you have no programs. Therefore one of the aims of Prophetic YaHudaism is develop programs and organizations for the economically disadvantage in the future. To teach and train them Principles of Social economics and how to be leaders, so that can in turn help others of the same disadvantage. This I believe is the true charity. Yet I never try to force my help and charity to those who don't want to be helped or don't want to change their lifestyles.

Sometimes when giving to a person on the streets who says they need money for food, it is best to buy the food yourself. The way you know for sure that they are not going to use it for drugs, alcohol or any kind of substance abuse.

This is not only charity, but brotherly love(Malachi 3:8-12).

[Other acts]

Other acts of Love(Gemiluth Chasadim) includes: Pastoral counseling, Mentor ship, visiting the sick and disabled, hospitality and helping orphans, etc......

The Talmud records;

"Act of Charity, accordingly, not only helps the needy but confers spiritual benefit upon the giver." (Lev.Rabbah 34:8)

"Let your home be open wide, and let the poor be the members of your household."(Aboth 1:5)

This is the imitation of YHWH.

[Honesty and Integrity]

The character of a person will determine the fruits of his works, whether it will be honest or not. Webster dictionary defines honesty as, *"not lying, cheating or stealing; having or giving full value or worth."*

Integrity is defined as, *"Uprightness of Character, honesty; the condition, quality or state of being complete or undivided."*

Uprightness of character is determined by ones fruit of YHWH's Shekinah and formal(and informal) discipline in ones life. When one has integrity in YaHudaism they make it a habit of evaluating and Judging themselves daily to make sure that they have quality honesty in every situation; Leadership, finance, teaching, history, business, social or any everyday situation.

Failure to be honest leads to Character flaws and the inability to interpret YHWH's Shekinah and purpose for your life. Not only does it hurts you but its hurts others. Dishonesty and lack of integrity leads to oppression of other peoples by lying to them or taking advantage of them through any means.

One of the main things that has been dishonest today is the true cultural and historical backgrounds of the people of the Hebrew bibles and history. When one is not connected to his or her Spiritual and Cultural roots, they tend to be vulnerable to oppression, spiritual wandering and lack of vision for the future, both individually and as a people-hood. This has happened mainly to the African American in the America's.

Eurocentric American and Jewish dishonesty of valuable history and peoples has been the leading cause/root to much of the Cultural and spiritual Assassinations among many of the so-called Minorities(which this title is another dishonesty), especially in the inner cities and among the lower class peoples.

Dishonesty among the Euro-centric Christian/Jewish nations has led to massive divisions and destructions of other peoples.; both Hebrews and Arabs, Blacks and Native Americans, and distortions of the Eternal Creator himself, which has now become institutionalized.

All you have to do is read history, dialogue and observe ones actions and you will see his/her fruits. dishonesty is the result of insecurity and failure to put value on life and other peoples. This results in Hasatanic Pride, arrogance and Delusional self supremacy.

Dishonesty especially can come when ones business, surroundings, religion or reputation becomes threatened or under the fire of failing. This can be seen in Christian Fundamentalism, such as the New Testament inerrancy and infallibility, and some aspects of ancient YaHudaism, such as the Allah'im rewriting.

Dishonesty like this results in the oppression and hiding of historical facts and writings, and even the Creative rewriting, alterations, omitting, or mis-education of important documents(as in the Koran, New Testament, aspects of YaHudaism, African American History). ***It should be noted that my criticism is within the realm of those who claim or cling to the Hebrew Scriptures.**

Dishonesty is the Sole reason why mankind and civilizations are immoral, degrading, and full of Wickedness. What is the solution?

We must began to incorporate a measure of integrity and YHWH's pride in life, business, religion, peoples, civilizations and cultures, and the Kingdom of Yahweh.. We must all began to recognize that each individual is apart of a whole of a plan of YHWH that is very valuable, and can be maintained as so through integrity and honesty.

[Forgiveness/Reconciliation]

Wayyicra 19:18, "You shall not take vengeance or bear a grudge against your countrymen"

MattiYah 6:12,14-15, "Forgive us what e have done wrong, as we to have forgiven those who have wronged us...for if you forgive others their offenses(against you), your heavenly father will also forgive you; but if you do not forgive others their offenses, your heavenly father will not forgive yours."

Forgiveness is the greatest Imitation of YHWH that one can do, because YHWH is the Ultimate forgiver of Sins against him. There are two categories of offenses; *1. Offenses against man 2. Offenses against YHWH.*

When we commit an offense against man, we are to ask man(the offended) for forgiveness, and when we commit an offense against YHWH, he will forgive us, that is when we ask or petition forgiveness with actual repentance.

Unforgiveness is one of the key hindrances to answered prayer and generational curses being healed. In fact generational curses can develop from an offense that was never pardoned by the offended(victim). This definitely has been the case among the Cushite(black) and Jewish peoples. Many of us are either descendant of the German holocaust or Cushite Slave Holocaust. These oppressions and destructions have had a toll on both the victims and even the descendants of the victims. Both culturally and psychologically.

The main problem of the European Jewish people due to the offenses they endured in the Holocaust, Christian inquisitions and crusades, is that their spirituality and biblical identity has been dimmed somewhat, causing internal conflict among one another. As the denominations battle, especially in Yisrael, the problem arises on the issue of *who is a Jew.* the answers to these problem cannot be found in the Tanakh but in European and Edomite History(the Black peoples of America are the Real Hebrews, the Word Jew is not Hebrew),. They have been so wounded until now it seems that everything that doesn't seem to identify with them is Anti-Semitism(which does exist, even though they are not Shemites). they seem so easily offended in many areas. Their wounds haven't been healed.

In the case of the Cushites/black peoples of America, We suffer even more(as a whole) due to the Slave Trade that Totally ripped us away from our people-hood, identity, Hebrew/African Culture. We suffer the same pains as a victim who has been kidnaped, rapped, degraded to an animal status and psychologically assassinated. We were internationally Kidnaped. Our families were destroyed and broken apart, sold and auctioned like cattle. Violent rapes, beatings and murders frequently happened to us. Even after our release from Slavery, we suffer psychologically from the institutionalized racism and degradation of our people. YHWH was stripped from us and Christianity, a foreign Religion, was forced upon us. We bare the burden of our Slave Masters including their names which could at times have damaging effects on our lives.

Our people today, who are descendants of the Slaves, face genocide, massive inner city violence and poverty, the highest rate of high-school dropouts, drugs, the least of family structure and values, ignorance of our history and great leaders, Black on black crimes, the highest rate of imprisonment, lack of father figures, Church Deceptions etc.....the effects of a Culture and a people assassinated by Hasatanic Supremacy of another People!

All of this is because the generational curses have failed to be broken by both peoples(blacks and Jews). YHWH can heal generational curses, but one must be willing too stand-up and say that they forgive their offenders or their ancestors offenders. As a people we must petition YHWH to break the curses and then we must stand together to rebuild our inner-people, so that they may function as a people and culture as YHWH purposed.

It's the same thing with the offenders, both race and religiously. Generational curses can develop through them also when an offense is not petitioned to be forgiven. This is why racism and White Supremacy, the great Curses of all, still exists.

Pride must be set aside and humility must be reckoned. The offenders or descendant of offenders must go to the offended or descendant of the offended and seek forgiveness and reconciliation. Until then, no general curse can be pardoned or broken.

In both cases of the offender and offended, unforgiveness is one of the main reasons prayers on behalf a nation or people have been hindered. White Americans and European Jews owe black people and Native Americans an apology and should admit to and ask for forgiveness for the participation in the brutal Slavery, Native American holocaust, whitewash of history and African American History, and make efforts to correct the mistakes. Black should in turn forgive. Christians and descendants of the Nazis owe Jews and Hebrews (&Arabs) an apology and should ask forgiveness for the Crusades, Religious Murders, Participation in and silence of the holocaust, expulsions and demonization accusations and blood libel accusations. Israelites should in Turn Forgive. Jews and Arabs and Hebrew Israelites should forgive one another and reconcile. All people should come and reconcile to break the greatest curse of all, the *Destruction of the Human Race!!*

After reconciliation has truly been successful, then each group should work together to rebuild and learn about the different cultures, peoples and histories of one another. That way each can properly contribute to the world what YHWH purposed in the beginning of Time. Yet unity comes when a people first learn how to work among themselves to properly function in society(Culturally and Religiously).

Megillah 28a, "Never did the curse of my fellow man ascend my bed."

[Talmudic Procedures]

"one who has sinned against his fellow-man must say to him, 'I have acted wrongly against you.' if he accept him, well and good; if not he brings persons and conciliates him in their presence. Should the offended person have died, he must conciliate him over his grave and say, 'I have acted wrongly towards you'"(P.Jom 45c, Taken from Everymans Talmud p. 228-229).

"A man should always be soft as a need and not hard like a cedar."(Taan.50b)

"Forgive an insult done to you....if you have done your fellow a little wrong, let it be in your eyes great; if you have done him much good, let it be in your eyes little; if he has done you a little good, let it be in your eyes great; if he has done you a great wrong, let it be in your eyes little(ARN.XLI)

[Forgive and Forget?]

The concepts of *forgive* and *forget* alone is not enough to go by. It needs more explanation; when one truly forgives he is obligated to forget....not in the since that the incident never happened, but in holding a grudge or holding the incident against the offender after the offender has repented and petitioned for forgiveness and it is granted.

Literally forgetting the incident, meaning not making it history(either personally or Nationally)so that you and others can learn from it to avoid it happening again, could lead to another offense happening, even by another offender....all of this resulting because no solution was made to strengthen one self or others from a potential relapse of the same incident. For example; although Israelites And Black peoples should forgive those and their descendants for the Wrong done to them, they should never forget it. The Egyptian Slavery isn't forgotten. The Roman destruction of the Hebrew Nation and Temple isn't forgotten. Antiochus Epiphanes and his evil against the Hebrews isn't forgotten. So why should the Slave trade be forgotten?

Each generation should be educated and taught about these tragedies(inquisitively, not accusingly), so that they may learn from it, make sure it doesn't happen again, and appreciate what their ancestors suffered that they may live the life of freedom and survival that they have today.

An old Negro Spiritual echoes, *"Freedom oh Freedom, and before I become a Slave I'll be buried in my grave and go home to my Lord and be FREE!"*

In Response to the Holocaust, the European Jews echo, *"it will never happen again!"*

Learning from offenses and tragedies strengthen and prepare you to handle, avoid or stop another offense from happening. Therefor forgive, but don't Forget.

Section 2 Biblical HolyDays or Festivals of Yah (the Witnessess)

The biblical Holy Days were ordained by Yahweh to help us understand some aspects of the nature and character of Yahweh and who we are in relationship to him as we are ingrafted into him faithfully. They reveal many of the plans Yahweh has for mankind and it teaches us many truths of how we are to deal with one another as a people and human race. The Holy Days are as follows; *Shabbat(Sabbath), Pesach(Pass-over),Hag HaMatzah(unleavened bread),Shavuot(Pentecost), Yom Teruah Zikrone, Yom Kippur(Day of Atonement), Sukkot(Tabernacles), Shemini Atzeret & Simchat Torah(eight day assembly and rejoicing of the Torah),*

[Shabbat-The Day of Rest]

Bereshit 2:1-3(JPSV), "the heavens and the earth were finished, and all their array. On the seventh day Yahweh finished the work that he had been doing, and he ceased on the seventh day from all the work that he had done. And Yahweh blessed the seventh day and declared it Holy, because on it Yahweh ceased from all the work of creation that he had done."

Wayyicra 23: 1-3, "Yahweh spoke to Moshe, saying: Speak to the Yishra'alites people and say to them: These are my fixed times, the fixed times of Yahweh, which you shall proclaim as sacred occasions. On six days work may be done, but on the seventh day there shall be a **Sabbath** *of complete rest, a sacred occasion. You shall do no work; it is a* **Sabbath of Yahweh** *throughout your settlements."*

Notice that in the above verses are the instructions of Yahweh for the Hebrews to observe what Yahweh calls fixed times or fixed seasons. As you read, these seasons, also known as festivals, will be mentioned and instructions on when to celebrate them will be given. Yet notice that the Shabbat is mentioned with these festivals as the first and foremost *"fixed time".*

Shabbat means *"to Rest"*. The purpose of rest is **Restoration**. Without rest, weariness, fatigue and various sicknesses and mental/spiritual illnesses can occur. In this day and age where capitalism, and free enterprise reign and work is never ceasing, many people overwork themselves and find themselves always on the run, never resting like Yahweh instructed from his infinite Wisdom. As a result angriness, aggravation, and mental fatigue increases, psychological breakdown devastates many peoples, Corporations fall or Business owners file for bankruptcy because they themselves fall out of the competition due to some illness, physical or mental burnout. this is even the cause of many family crisis(i.e devours). This then hurts commerce which then hurts the economics of society which leads to unemployment, which could lead to homelessness, which could lead to crime, moral breakdowns of society, family disintegration and even suicides. Before you know it a whole nation has fallen, all because the root of the problem was that people fail to follow YHWH instruction on when and how to work and when to rest and restore themselves.

This is not to say that this is the only problem that causes corporations and societies to fall etc. etc.. There are many other reasons such as greed, lack of stewardship and planning, fraud, lack of family structure etc...But lack of rest which leads to restoration is one of the main causes of burnouts.

Just take time one day or so(i.e a Monday or Thursday) and observe the way people on the highways or at traffic lights treat each other. Observe the reactions of people on Monday morning contrasted to Friday evening. Look at the Family structure of many and even in your own home. Most people are so busy working or Buying that they don't have time to be Mommy or Daddy in the home. The day care and school takes care of that. In many cases parents work seven days a week.

As long as peoples are doing the opposite of what Yahweh has instructed concerning the Shabbat and restoration, healthy relationships, businesses, even governments, and health itself will fail.

Even certain objects can be used to teach the need for rest. For example: if you continuously ran a remote control car without stopping to recharge

---

and rest the battery, eventually the battery will go dead, yet when you rest and recharge the battery, the power to run the car is restored.

Yahweh was instructing the Hebrews to rest and restore themselves physically, emotionally and spiritually.

Shabbat, 145, " If it is written of YHWH, who never tires, that he rested on the seventh day, how much the more shouldst thou, oh man, rest on the Sabbath from thy weariness."

Betzah, 17, "The Shabbat was given to you, but you were not given to the Shabbat."

[When is Shabbat]

Shabbat is the seventh or last day of the week. In Hebrew, according to Bereshit, a day starts with evening.

Bereshit 1:5, "and there was evening and there was morning, a first day."

Therefore Shabbat actually begins Friday at sundown and ends Saturday at sundown. Many Christians say that the day of rest is Sunday. This is incorrect. Sunday is the first day of the week on the American Calendar is also called the first day of the week in the So-called New Testament. The first day of the week is the first day of work and labor according to Torah. Anyone resting on this day as a Shabbat is seen as someone who really is Lazy in the eyes of Yahweh(speaking in a religious not corporate since); lazy because they are too sorry to study the scripture for themselves and see what Yahweh has ordained as the Shabbat or day of rest. Biblically all days are counted in relation to the Shabbat.

[Prophetic significance to Shabbat]

YeshiYah 40: 27-31, "why do you say, oh Jacob, why declare, oh Yisrael, ""My way is hid from Yahweh, my cause is ignored by my Strength"? Do you not know? Have you not heard? Yahweh is Almighty from of old, Creator of the earth from end to end, he never grows faint or weary, his wisdom cannot be fathomed. He gives strength to the weary, fresh vigor to the spent. Youths may grow faint and weary, and young men stumble and fall; but they who trust in Yahweh shall renew their strength as eagles grow new plumes: they shall run and not be weary, they shall march and not grow faint"

Shabbat was first of all a prophetic picture of a divine ring/sign that there is a relationship or marriage between Yahweh and those who have entered his covenant. Shabbat is proof of YHWH faithfulness to those who hold fast to the Hebrew Covenant. As Yahweh is forever faithful never breaking his vows or Covenant with his people, we(they) are able to find adequate and sufficient Restoration and strength in him. Through our relationship with Yahweh as we worship him with our lifestyles and praise him with our actions and voices lifted up loud resounding in joy and victory in his Torah, we are able to receive the reviving Ruakh of Yahweh that refreshes us spiritually, mentally, physically and economically. YHWH infinite knowledge and wisdom to life issues are connected to our spirits that we may have unlimited access to the answers that we question and seek daily.

With some effort of study, common sense(a.k.a. wisdom), and rational we are able to tap into the fullness of Yahweh and all that he has in store for us as we take proper authority by his Torah to live in this world which belongs to us. When we as the human race take that authority and responsibility over this world then and only then can we experience a restoration and rest of Yahweh in biblical proportions.

Shabbat was created as a gift to mankind. It is the life giving day to all who are weary and faint, whether in their natural marriage, friendships or family members, and even business endeavors. Shabbat is a time of reconciliation, family restoration, healings of broken relationships(between Yahweh and man or man and (wo)man), healings from emotional or physical infirmities, and community fellowship and repair. It is a time of joy and Synagogue(and home) worship of Yahweh as our Father, Creator and Eternal Savior. It is a time of true spiritual satisfaction which is rooted in happiness through Yahweh. Shabbat is the ultimate day in which we build our lives and pattern all other days after.

NechemYah 10:31-32, "and the rest of the people, the priest, the Levites, the gatekeepers, the singers, the Temples servants, and all who separated themselves from the peoples of the lands to follow the Teachings(Torah) of God(Yahweh), their wives, sons and daughters, all who know enough to understand, join with their noble brothers, and take an oath with sanction(consequences) to follow the Teaching(Torah) of God(Yahweh), given through Moshe the servant of Yahweh, and to observe carefully all the commandments of the LORD(Yahweh) our Lord, his rules and laws....(32) the peoples of the land who bring their wares and all sorts of food stuff for sale on the Shabbat day-we will not buy from them on the Shabbat or a holy day."

As the Torah instructs, no work, labor or commerce selling or buying should be performed on Shabbat. Sunday, through Friday before sundown, is given for you to buy, sell and do business.

Shabbat is a sanctified day of Holiness given by Yahweh to you that you may use for your spiritual benefit(Exodus 20:8). For more info contact your Spiritual Hebrew Leader, Kohanim or a Rabbi.

[Pesach/Hag HaMatzah-Passover and unleavened bread]

Shemot 12:22-28, "take a bunch of hyssop(or Marjoram), dip it in the blood that is in the basin, and apply some of the blood that is in the basin to the lintel and to the two doorpost. None of you shall go outside the door of his house until mourning. For when the LORD(YHWH) goes through to smite the Egyptians, he will see the blood on the Lintel and the two doorpost, and the LORD(YHWH) will Pass over the door and not let the Destroyer enter and smite your home. You shall observe this as an institution for all time, for you and your descendants. And when you enter the land which the LORD(YHWH) will give you, as he has promised, you shall observe this rite. And when your children ask you, 'what do you mean by this rite?' you shall say, 'it is the Passover sacrifice (which is eaten) to the LORD(YHWH), because he passed over the houses of the Israelites in Egypt when he smote the Egyptians, but SAVED our houses.'"

Wayyicra 23:5-8, "these are the set times of the LORD(YHWH), the sacred occasions, which you shall celebrate each at its appointed times: in the first month, on the fourteenth day of the month, at twilight, there shall be a Passover offering to the LORD(YHWH), and on the fifteenth day of that month the LORD's(YHWH's) feast of unleavened bread. You shall eat unleavened bread for seven days. The first day shall be for you a sacred occasion: you shall not work at your occupations. Seven days you shall make offerings by fire to the LORD(YHWH). The Seventh day shall be a sacred occasion: you shall not work at your occupations."

Pesach is the Hebrew Yishra'alite celebration of Deliverance or Salvation from Egyptian slavery and bondage. It is a celebration and remembrance that YHWH instructed to be for all eternity as apart of his covenant. This Salvation was for an already redeemed community (through Abraham) although they fell under oppression. This was a physical salvation from political oppression so that YHWH could lead them into spiritual salvation according to his Torah.

The Hebrews had to receive salvation in all areas of there lives. They had to be delivered from their slave mentality, economical and social dependance, practices and rituals that they learned from the Egyptians and other pagan cultures, pagan lifestyles that they were used to living, the Paganism and polytheistic worship that they learned and etc.. They had to learn how to live as a people and nation, they had to learn how to walk and imitate YHWH and his ways of true Holiness, they had to learn even how to treat each other and those who were not apart of their Community. They also had to learn how to fully live as Royal African Edenic Peoples. This was the purpose of YHWH teachings in the Torah to Yishra'ala so that they would not be entrapped again into the Heathenistic spiritual bondage into which they were formally trapped. For the fullness of their Salvation was dependant on their Loyalty, obedience and relationship with YHWH the one who saved them. When the Hebrews showed through the ways of living that they were spiritually delivered by YHWH then the truth of repentance was expressed. They had turned away from their former ways of life towards a lifestyle and Culture of Holiness in YHWH.

[Prophetic Significance]

YeshiYah 45:15, "Yisrael is Saved in Yahweh with an eternal Salvation
YirmeYah 2:3(Exegesis), "Yishra'ala is Holiness to Yahweh and the firstlings of his produce: all who devour his guilt(is guilty); evil comes on them, says Yahweh"
Yah'ala 2:32, "Whoever calls on the name of Yahweh is rescued(Saved)"

The Prophetic Significance is that Yahweh saved Yisrael from physical bondage so that he may spiritually prepare and guide them to bear his Word and Truth so that they(we) may be a light unto the gentiles, as the firstborn of Yahweh, to lead them(the gentiles) into the same salvation that Yahweh graciously bestowed upon us(Yisrael).

Yahweh separated the Hebrews from Mitzraim by deliverance so that we may be holiness in him, that is to be whole, separate, unique and complete in how Yahweh has called and designed us in him. He spiritually adopted us as his firstborn in replacement of Adamah.

As the unblemished lamb's blood, his nephesh or soul/life, was used as a symbolic means of physical Salvation for Yisrael from the Judgement of Yahwehs *Messager of Death* against Mitzraim, so thus is the Israelite Torah Covenant Community a means and life force in which the world can be delivered and perfected under the Rulership of Yahweh. The firstborn of Mitzraim, symbolic to the gentile way of life, was destroyed, yet all those who enter the covenant of Yahweh become the firstborn of Yahweh and by his Grace and mercy, which is his covenant shield, are Saved. Study *YeshiYah 56.* Those who are gentiles that are redeemed by Yahweh, through Teshuvah, and are ingrafted into his covenant through Mikveh, are just as much Jew as the Jew is Jew, and together both are saved in Yahweh, and Yahweh passes over his judgements and curses of D'bar 28 and gives total blessings, prosperity and victory as we live our life in him(see D'bar 28).

YeshiYah 45:19b-25,"I Yahweh word Justness; I tell it straight. Gather and come; draw near together, you escapees of the goyim: they who bear the timber of their scuptile, know not. You tell; bring near; yes, they counsel together. Who had this to be heard from antiquity? Who told it from that time? Was it not I Yahweh? And no Almighty except me; a just Strength and Savior; there is no one final except me. Face me, and be saved, all you finalities of the earth: for I-Almighty; and there is no one else..."

We are Also taught that YHWH hates slavery and those who enforce slavery in turn will bear the Judgement of YHWH. It was never intended for Mankind to enslave one another or for one Culture to Oppress and be the instrument in advocating Genocide of another culture and peoples. The War of YHWH against Mitzraim to Deliver the Hebrews was a lesson for all of Humanity to learn from. Yet European Culture has not really learned anything concerning this issue. The Worst Enslavement of all recorded history was not of the Hebrew Enslavement in Mitzraim but of the African Atlantic Slave Trade here in the very America's and Carribean Islands. No other People enslaved have been known to be stripped of their Culture, heritage religion and Families and downgraded to and treated like mere wild animals that needed to be tamed as the African Prisoners. Europeans Demonically used the Backs of these Cushite Hebrew people to build what has become the most powerful nation in the world. Even after Slavery was abolished after the Civil War, the Cushite peoples were robbed and discredited of thousands of Inventions and Ideas. They have been treated unequally in both educational institutes and Employment opportunities, even until this day. And no doubt about it, many African and European nations suffer today for participation in the Hebrew Israelite Slavery.

It is very hard to even imagine what my forefathers had to suffer here in America to get some kind of Justice and equality for this younger generation, yet for all that many have not learned the history of Nations and peoples that have risen and fallen all in the name of Injustice.

To build a true society is for all regardless or race, culture or religious background to come together and put in their share of the Work it takes to build a nation. To use slaves or other peoples to do your dirty work is laziness, foolishness and wicked. NO nation should be built on the backs of SLAVES, especially Hebrew SLAVES!!!! That is right those Africans who were enslaved in the Americas were Hebrew Israelite SLAVES. This is the explanation and key to why American society is morally and spiritually degrading itself to a very low status. Slowly but surely Self destructing. They have done harm to YHWH's anointed and have touched the apple of YHWH's eye and unless this is recognized and National Repentance is sought, YHWH's judgement as upon Mitzraim will come upon America. Its already happening, especially in other European country's. Until it is recognized that the African Hebrew Israelite community throughout America are the Chosen people, both Gentiles and Jews alike will perish, especially Mentally and Spiritually. To my Jewish brothers and sisters, "notice how you by the thousands are turning to a Charismatic Gentile god through the Messianic Movement, your people are being destroyed spiritually. Notice the deadness of many of your synagogues and lack of worship you have. Notice that rise in Anti-Torah attitudes among you, notice the continued rise in thieves and robbers of society that are found among you, notice the rise in hatred of other peoples of you. Why? Not because you're chosen and are being persecuted or being tested but because you oh Esau have usurped and participated in destroying the heritage of Ya'akob your brother. And until you repent you shall incur the punishment of YHWH as the Europeans who don't repent and reconcile with us Hebrew Yishra'alites!!! Read ObadiYah.

"Yet they did not realize that the Foundation of a Nation will be the only means to keeping that nation in existence."

[Hag HaMatzah]

Hag HaMatzah or the Feast of Unleavened Bread is the continuation of the Pesach celebration. It commemorates the time in Hebrew history when after the Passover of Yahweh upon Mitzraim, Yishra'ala had to flee Mitzraim so quickly that their bread dough did not have time to rise in the ovens(Exodus 12:39). Therefore every year right before the feast of Pesach every Hebrew home eliminates any leaven from their home and diets until after the Feasts. Then preparation for the Pesach Seder meal, which is the order of service on Pesach, occurs. The Seder is performed according to Exodus 12; Yishra'ala is instructed by Yahweh to eat Lamb, unleavened bread and bitter herbs.

Unleavened bread is known as the Bread of Distress(D'var 16:3). When we are in distress, panic or fear, it become like leaven. It can spread to others and cause the fear to swell among others. No matter how courageous or Faith powered a person can be, if another begins to fear or doubt, that faith is going to be replaced with fear. As in the case of Salvation, when one is in distress to be delivered spiritually, their distress can spread among others, as in a mass distress for deliverance, resulting in repentance. In this case we desire to flee our Egypt, that is whatever is holding us in slavery apart from YHWH, and we run towards the Grace and Mercy of YHWH. As we cry out in our leavened distress for Salvation, YHWH then in turns Delivers us and takes away our leavened bondage and oppressions, cleans out our lives through his Word, and then we become spiritually unleavened and Clean. In the case of the African Americans who are descendant of the Hebrew slaves, when we finally decide as a whole to realize who we are in YHWH and allow the leaven of distress in our political, social, economical and spiritual lives to become unleavened, and Decide to cry out to YHWH to deliver us from our Institutionalized European oppressors, then YHWH will deliver us.

[Torah on Pesach]

"The LORD (YHWH) said to Moshe and Aaron: This is the Law of the Passover offering: No Foreigner shall eat of it. But any slave a man has bought may eat of it once he has been circumcised. No bound or hired laborer shall eat of it. It shall be eaten in one house; you shall not eat any of the flesh outside the house; nor shall you break a bone of it. The whole community of Yishra'ala shall offer it. If a stranger who dwells with you would offer the Passover to the LORD(YHWH), all his males must be circumcised; then he shall be admitted to offer it; he shall then be a citizen of the Country. But no uncircumcised person may eat of it. There shall be one law for the citizen and for the Stranger who dwells among you."(Shemot 12:43-49)

".....Consecrate to me every first-born; man and beast, the first issue of every womb among the Israelites is mine. And Moshe said to the people, 'remember this day, on which you went free from Egypt, the house of bondage, how the LORD(YHWH) freed you from it with a mighty hand: no leavened bread shall be eaten. You go free on this day, in the month of Abib. So when the LORD(YHWH) has brought you into the land of the Cana'anites, the Chittites, the Amorites, the Hivites, and the Jebusites, which he swore to your fathers to give you, a land flowing with milk and honey, you shall observe in this month the following practice:

"Seven days you shall eat unleavened bread, and on the seventh day there shall be a festival of the LORD(YHWH). Throughout the seven days unleavened bread shall be eaten; no leavened bread will be found with you, and no leaven shall be found in all your territory. And you shall explain to your son on

that day, 'it is because of What the LORD(YHWH) did for me when I went free from Egypt.' and this shall serve you as a sign on your hand and as a reminder on your forehead(the Mark of YHWH)-in order that the Teaching of the LORD(YHWH) may be in your mouth......you shall keep this institution at its set time from year to year."(Shemot 13:1-9; see also 11-16)

[Shavuot-Pentecost/The Giving of the Torah]

Zman Matan Torateynu

Shemot 34:22, "You shall observe the Feast of Weeks, of the first fruits of the Wheat harvest..."(see also 23:16)

Study Shemot chapter 19 on through Leviticus and Numbers 10:10.

After the Hebrews were delivered from Egypt, Moshe led them to the Wilderness of Sinai. They camped opposite Mt. Sinai. YHWH then instructed Moshe to prepare the people and gather them to receive the Torah.

In Shemot 19:4, Through Moshe, YHWH makes his Torah Covenant proposal, promising that in response to Yisrael faithful obedience to the his Covenant, that he would make them his treasured possession among all peoples and that Yishra'ala would become a Kingdom of Priests and a Nation of Holiness(the light of the World).

In response to the Covenant proposal the Hebrews responded, **"Na'aseh W'Nishmah, We agree to do even before we have listened."** In other words, the Hebrews seem to have wanted the Spiritual Marriage just as much as YHWH wanted it. Selah.

YHWH then instructed Moshe to have the people wash themselves, their clothes and prepare to receive the terms and definitions of the Covenant, that is the Teachings and instructions of the Torah.

Shemot 19:16, "On the third day, as morning dawned, there was thunder(s), and lightning(s), and a dense cloud upon the mountain, and a very loud blast of the horn(shofar).......vs 19, the Blare of the horn(shofar) grew louder and louder. As Moshe spoke God(YHWH the Almighty) answered him in thunder…..”

Shemot 20:15, “all the people witnessed the thunder(ings) and lightning(s), the blare of the horn(Shofar) and the mountain smoking; and when the people saw it, they fell back and stood at a distant.”

After YHWH spoke the Ten teachings(Commandments) to the Hebrew Yishra'alites in Chapter 20:1-14, it says that they actually saw the thunderings(plural) and the blare of the Shofar

A commentary on Exodus reveals that when YHWH gave the Torah he displayed marvels with his voice. When YHWH spoke his voice resounded throughout the world. As it was uttered it split into seventy voices, in seventy languages so that every nation would hear and understand YHWH' Torah. The B'nai Yishra'ala not only saw YHWHs voice but they actually saw the sound waves as it preceded out of YHWH's mouth. They visualized it as a fiery word that came from YHWH mouth and traveled around the entire Hebrew camp and approaching each Hebrew and asking them if they would accept the teachings and culture of the Torah of YHWH upon their lives. Although the other nations who heard either didn't respond or rejected the offer, Yishra'ala accepted them and entered the Covenant responsibility of being a Nation of Priests and Holiness, a light bearer to the world.

[Prophetic Fulfillment]

YeshiYah 44: 3, “for I pour water on him who is thirsty, and flowings on the dry: I pour my spirit on your seed and my blessing on your offspring…”

Yechezki'ala 36:25-27a, “and I sprinkle pure water on you and purify you; from all your foulness and from all your idols I purify you: and I give you a new heart and a new spirit I give within you: and I turn aside the stony heart from your flesh and I give you a heart of flesh: and I give my spirit within you so that you work to walk in my statutes and guard my judgements and work them...."(see also chapter 11:19,20

Yah'ala 2:28,29, "and so be it, afterward, I pour out my spirit on all flesh; and your sons and daughters prophesy; your elders dream dreams and your youth see visions: and also on the servants and on the maids in those days I pour out my spirit. And give omens in the heavens and in the earth-blood fire and columns of smoke: the sun turns to darkness an the moon into blood at the face of the coming the great and awesome day of Yahweh. And so be it whoever calls on the name of YHWH is rescued......3:15, " the sun and the moon darken and the stars gather their brilliance: and Yahweh roars from Tzion and gives his voice from Yerushalem: the heavens quake: and YHWH is the refuge of his people, and the stronghold of the sons of Yishra'ala." (See also 37:14; 39:29).

Just as YHWH has given us his Torah on Mt. Sinai, he has also gave us his Spirit of Holiness, that is his infinite presence that sets us apart to him and restores our earthly authority, and restores our wholeness in him and leads us and guide us in his Torah. As we receive and are led by his spirit, his Shekinah in our lives we will be able to prophetically speak his Torah, live his Torah spiritually and rebuild this world and the nation with his Torah.

Just as the Voice of YHWH reverberated throughout the world with the words of Torah that all peoples may understand, so is YHWH's spirit of Holiness being poured out on all flesh, those who would receive it, so that they(we) may walk in YHWH's image and are led to become Nation(s) of Total righteousness, holiness and Prosperity after the Model of Yishra'ala, YHWH's people.

Notice that in each scripture above, YHWH specifically indicates when he would pour out his spirit upon his people Yishra'ala and other peoples. If you would read the verses before the above, it specifically shows that YHWH would began Immersing people with his Spirit during and after the periods when Yishra'ala is being restored as a People from shame, dispersement and confusion.

This is the season and time when YHWH is restoring True Yishra'ala and his Torah principles throughout the world. The African Americans and other black peoples are once again spreading their hand to YHWH and are reclaiming their true identity as Hebrew Israelites. YHWH is redeeming his people from the mental, spiritual and economical poverty and oppression that they(we) have endured throughout the millenniums. As a result YHWH's grace and mercy is being realized through his Torah among the nations as they see and help the African Edenic Yishra'alites restore themselves to the Biblical heritage to take the front line in leading this world to perfection according to ethical Monotheism in YHWH's Torah.

Those who are filled with the true Spirit of YHWH, are led to walk and live the prophetic Spiritual and Cultural Teachings of Hebrew Torah. Torah is for all nations, as many as those who would receive it.

[Yom Teruah-Day of the Awakening blast]

Wayyicra 23: 24,25 "And Yahweh words to Moshe, saying, 'Word to the sons of Yisrael, saying, in the Seventh month, in the first of the month, have a shabbathism-a memorial of blasting-a holy convocation. Work no service work therein: oblate a firing to Yahweh.

The Seventh month on the Hebrew calendar, Etanim, was the most important and sacred month of the Hebrew year. It contained the most Days of Holiness. According to the Wayyicra 23:24, the first day of the seventh month is a called *Shabbatone Zikrone Teruah* in Hebrew, which means, *"Memorial blasting of the Shofar"*. It is the day of ingathering and awakening. It is a time of joy within the communities and families. It is also a time of Evaluating ones self as to our spiritual and mental condition and the quality of our relationship with YHWH and with our families and fellow-man. The blasting of the Shofar was our alarm awakener. We were to, *"hear oh Yishra'ala"* Selah. We were to begin to prepare ourselves for the coming of Yom Kippur or Day of Atonement.

It is as if we are preparing to go to the great Courts before YHWH, the great judge to be evaluated as to how we have lived our lives in relationship to others, how have we lived according to the standards of Torah and have we allowed ourselves to become what YHWH has purposed us to become, as to his will and Way. We evaluate everything about us. Have we offended anyone?, transgressed any Torah law?, broken any covenants or relationships with others, caused stumbling blocks before others? Have we been good stewards in maintaining the health of Nature, etc....

This is the time of Teshuvah(Repentance), prayer and spiritual preparation for the Day of Atonement. In other words when we hear the sound of the Shofar we know we are being subpoenaed to appear in the spiritual courts. It is mandatory and we are preparing our case. Hasatans is our accuser/Prosecutor, YHWH is the Judge, the Hebrew Yishra'alites are the Jury and Torah of Moshe is our defense Attorney!

The days following Yom Teruah up until Yom Kippur are known as the **Yamim Nora'im (days of Awe).** The Shabbat that falls within these days is known as *Shabbat Shuvah*, the Shabbat of Return

We are to prepare our case to present before YHWH, in total humbleness, as to await to hear YHWH's verdict of guilty or innocence on our spiritual lives on Yom Kippur.

[Yom Kippur-Day of Atonement]

Wayyicra 23:26-32, "and Yahweh words to Moshe, saying, only, on the tenth of this seventh month is Yom Kippurim-a holy convocation to you: humble your souls and oblate a firing to Yahweh: and work no work in that same day: for it is Yom Kippurim, to kaparlatone for you at the face of Yahweh your Allah'im(Almighty). For whatever soul humbles not in that same day, is cut off from among his people. and whatever soul works any work in that same day, I will destroy that same soul from among his people. Work no Work!-an eternal statute throughout your generations in all your settlements. It is a Shabbat of

Shabbathism(rest) to you to humble your souls: In the ninth of the month, at evening, from evening to evening, shabbathize(celebrate) your Shabbat.

On the Tenth day of the Seventh month(Etanim) is the Day of Atonement, the most important day of the Hebrew Calendar. This was the day of the cleansing of the Nation and the Sanctuary. This day alone was the day the High Priest entered the Holy of Holies to atone for the sins of Yishra'ala. This is the day of reconciliation among families, friends, neighbors, and especially YHWH. We openly confess our sins and offenses to one anther and spiritually regenerate ourselves. The section on forgiveness in this book is the ideal pattern for Yom Kippur. This is the day to Renew our spirits in YHWH and recommit ourselves to his Torah. This is a day of uplifting one another, of love, peace-making, sharing and caring. This is also a day of Deliverance from past oppressions and vows we couldn't keep. We make a resolution in our heart to walk even more upright and live as nation of Holiness in YHWH to be a light before all. Most of all we are reminded that it is by the grace and mercy of YHWH that we are victorious from the prosecution of Hasatan and that our fellow Hebrews are there to help encourage us to continue to live in the Torah with faithful obedience, and that we are safe and defended by YHWH as we are in his Torah Covenant Community. All Praise be to YHWH !!!!

[Prophetic Significance]

There will come a day when all the world will hear the sound of the Great Shofar, and every one will have to appear before the great Throne of YHWH. To be either rewarded Atonement to everlasting life or utter destruction. This is known in Malachi as the Great and Terrible Day of YHWH. All will be judged by the Standard of the Hebrew Torah and Yahwehs will to mankind. Moshe will either be your accuser or your defendant as YHWH will give the final verdict of Mercy or Damnation. Also in the Messianic Age or Rule of Yishra'ala under a messianic King

Appointed by the messianic Prophet, all the world will reconcile its differences, and become as one under Ethical monotheism. This is the time when the prophetic word will be fulfilled....*"and the earth shall be filled with the knowledge of the Shekinah of YHWH, just as the Water cover the sea!!!"* So therefore why not atone now and enter the hebrew Torah Covenant Community! Come before the Final Call!

[Sukkot-Feast of Tabernacles]

Wayyicra 23:33-36a, "and YHWH words to Moshe, saying, word to the sons of Yisrael, saying, the fifteenth day of this seventh month is the celebration of Sukkoth/brush arbors for seven days to Yahweh. The first day is a holy convocation: work no service work therein. Seven days oblate a firing to Yahweh..."

Sukkot is the time when the Hebrews lived in temporary booths or shelters in remembrance of their wilderness experience. YHWH also instructed that a Sukkah be built for him in the wilderness. In Hebrew it is called a *Mishkan,* which is usually translated Tabernacle. Shemot 25:8 reveals that YHWH wanted the Mishkan so that he could dwell among his people. YHWH was with Yishra'ala the forty years they were in the wilderness. And today YHWH is still watching over his people of the Hebrew Torah Covenant Community, and desires to Put his indwelling Spirit upon each of us. He even so desires to put his indwelling Spirit upon all Flesh. Sukkot is also known as *Zman simkhatenu,* the time of our rejoicing. We rejoice because YHWH provides for us and his Shekinah inhabits us.

Sukkot was also seen as the time to rejoice because YHWH had extended his grace and mercy upon us during Yom Teruah and Yom Kippur, the time of repentance and redemption. We celebrate because we are redeemed People in YHWH and by his name we are Saved eternally as we are in his Covenant. We are able to Walk with YHWH and build a special relationship with him as we are faithfully obedient to his Torah, will and Way. This isn't a religious celebration, its our way of life in YHWH!

For African Hebrew Israelite in this time of restoration, Sukkot becomes sort of even more special. For thousands of years we have wondered in Spiritual dryness and caous, disconnected from our Torah Community, in the wilderness of Gentile rule and influence. From generation to generation we became weaker and farther away from our roots as Yishra'ala in YHWH, immersing ourselves in the disillusions of Christianity and other gentile religions. Empty and mentally weak, even at times when some of us were financially successful. We became conditioned to believe that we were nothing, cursed to be black, ordained to think, live and act like half human SLAVES, servants and barbarians, A people with no significant past nor a promising future. We had sinned and YHWH allowed us to be punished. He allowed us to experience dryness and un-civilization. He only allowed us because this is what our forefathers chose, and YHWH was not going to go against our freedom of will.

And now that we have experienced the outside world, we cry in anguish and sorrow. We pant for the Waters of Torah to quench our throats and we throw ourselves at the mercy of his feet and throne. And for all that YHWH say to you, "I have always loved you and have oathed to watch over you and deliver you. And now I stretch out my arms against your oppressors and heal you oh Yishra'ala with a healing arm of compassion, for you are my Sons and daughters and I restore you to a pure nation, a pure heart and a pure language. For all who will receive. Spread hands to me as I spread my everlasting arm to you. And when I deliver thee oh Yishra'ala, never forget from where I delivered you. Remember daily and yearly your wilderness experience and how I Saved you!!!

[Shemini Atzeret & Simchat Torah]

Wayyicra 23:36b, "on the eighth day is a holy convocation to you. -oblate a firing to YHWH: an abstinence-work no service work"

Shemini Atzeret is the conclusion or eighth day of the festival of Sukkot. We are instructed to hold a gathering of Holiness in commemoration of the feast of Sukkot. It is interpreted by the Ancient Rabbinical teachers that YHWH requests all who made pilgrimage for Sukkot to tarry with him an additional day(Atzeret comes from the Hebrew root which means, *"to hold".*)

Section 3 *S'mikhah The Practice of Laying on of Hands*

The Practice of S'mikhah in Hebrew Faith is used for several different functions; Spiritual equipping, transfer of anointings, ordination, promotions and exaltation, Exorcism, healing, Spiritual Deliverance and prophetic blessings.

Barmidbar(Numbers) 27:18-20, "and Yahweh says to Moshe, take Yahshua the son of Nun, a man in whom the Spirit is and prop your hands on him; and stand him at the face of El Azar the Priest and at the face of all the witness; and mitzvah him in their eyes; and give of your majesty on him..."

Through the Laying on of hand Yahshua ben Nun was Separated and promoted into leadership. As he was being promoted by Yahweh through Moshe before the Priest and witnesses he was being instructed on his Position. He Was a man who was Torah observant and YHWH Spirit was upon him already.

Yahweh operates through Authority, his three main Authoritative figures are the Offices of the *Prophet(Nabi)*, *Priest(kohan)* and *King(Malek)*. While the offices of the Prophet is promoted by Yahweh himself and is recognized by the existing Hebrew leadership, the priest and Kings must be promoted and anointed either by another Priest, King or Prophet. The Prophet is usually the one who anoints the King. In the case of Moshe Promoting Yahshua, we see Prophet-Priest(Moshe was a Levitical Prophet) promoting a Priestly leader. The Prophet stands before the people representing the Word of Yahweh to keep the people in tune with the Torah and will of Yahweh, while the Priest is a Minister standing before Yahweh representing the People. The King is the Overseer and ruler(like an administrator) to lead and keep the Nation together, politically. All three are known as Messiahs.

When Yahweh restores the Kingdom of Yishra'ala in the Messianic era, a Messianic Hebrew Prophet(s) will anoint and restore the Messianic/Prophetic Hebrew King to the Throne of Yishra'ala as the Messianic/Prophetic Hebrew Priests will prepare the Hebrew peoples for the Kingdom.

Through the restoration of these offices, the Nation of Yishra'ala will lead the world to perfection under Ethical Monotheism, therefore bringing about the Rule and day of Yahweh. The Priests today are known as Rabbi-Kohanim. They are leaders of the individual Hebrew Synagogues or Houses of Worship. Other offices that are being instituted from ancient times are the offices of the *Shaliach*, or Ambassodors, the *Maggid or Hebrew Proselytist/wise man* and *Hebrew Exorters* such as singers, Dancers, musicians and worship leaders. These will be discussed my next volume, **"Restoration of YHWH Hebrew Prophetic Movement"**

D'barim 34:9, "and Yahshua the son of nun is full of the spirit of wisdom; for Moshe had propped his hands on him; and the sons of Yisrael hearkened to him and works as Yahweh misvahed Moshe.

This verse reveals that after Moshe laid hands on Yahshua, Yahshua became full of the Spirit of Wisdom. The Hebrew word for Wisdom here is *Chokmah.* This a skillful wisdom as in wisdom for leadership. Remember when Moshe was laying hands on Yahshua he was also instructing him according to the Word of Yahweh. As a result of the Knowledge imparted to Yahshua, Yahweh gave him the ability to use that knowledge effectively, by giving him the Spirit of Wisdom, a specific kind of wisdom for leadership. Moshe transferred his anointing to Yahshua and Yahshua was ordained, gifted and Spiritually equipped to be the next leader of Yishra'ala This is the Tradition of Hebrew Authority and Promotion to leadership. Before one can be a leader he must first be a respectful student and disciple of Leadership and understand how to properly respond to those in Authority.

[Prophetic Blessings]

Throughout the Hebrew Scriptures we see the Fathers blessing(or cursing) there children and speaking over their lives. Even the naming of the Children came through the Prophetic channel of blessing and laying on of hands. These blessings (or curses) actually stuck with the individual through his life and manifested through his descendants for generations and generations. The blessings and names of the Child actually molded and determined his/her personality traits and destiny. Read Bereshit 27:1-41; 48:8-22; 49:1-33.

In this time and season we as African Edenic Hebrew YaHudaim need to began to speak over our childrens lives with the Blessings of Yahweh. Our Black youth are under Spiritual and mental attack and on the verge of self destruction. The lack of Cultural spiritual roots among the African Americans has led to a complete spiritual and social holocaust among our peoples. Yet if only one just simply try to live by the Torah of Yahweh they would see that this was our heritage all along. That's right, YaHudaism, the Hebrew faith is our long lost heritage stripped from us during Slavery. Yet we are once again arising and now is the time to receive the Spirit and blessings of Yahweh according to his Torah.

Section 4 Torah Instructions on Dietary and Healithness and Briefing of other Customs and Practices

The dietary laws as found in the Torah were given to us as a Way of keeping our bodies in a healthy state. It was specifically for heath consciousness. Think about it. When we are living a healthy Physical life we are also helping ourselves mentally and spiritually. Most of the time when people are living with health problems, especially food related, they tend to have many psychological dysfunctions. Many of the manifestations that occur are, depression, anger, fatigue, anorexia, various mood swings, lack of focus on vision or goals, and low self esteem. These are just brief.

When we are experiencing physical health problems, which many times lead to manifestations of Psychological problems, we also at times are at the brink of affecting our spiritual lives. Many people can't live the quality spiritual life they want because they are either very ill or mentally disturbed, due to a physical illness or infirmity, that Is diet related.

For example. If a person had an unhealthy diet of not eating much or eating once a day, depending on their type of health, they may be affected drastically because they are not getting the proper nutrients that is needed to function normally. As a result, spiritually speaking, when it comes time to Study the Word of YHWH, they may experience fatigue or inability to think or remember. Therefore their quality in Studying the Torah is very low or not at all. This eventually leads to spiritual blowouts, because no spiritual input is able to be acquired.

Ask yourself, how can a person really think about the Word of YHWH and acquire it within their hearts if they are constantly fatigue, or mentally unable to because they are not taking care of themselves physically?

It's the other Way around. If a person has an unhealthy diet of eating the wrong foods, deemed as forbidden by Torah, they too will be affected Physically. America is known for its high volume of High blood pressure, high cholesterol, obesity, over weight-ness, diabetes and other food related illnesses. Many people are proclaiming to become health conscious. Many are trying various diets, diet pills and diet workouts, only to become frustrated and unsuccessful in their weight loss and healthy quest. They try everything, including herbs, surgery, etc. But one thing Most people don't try especially within the Christian World, is the Torah of YHWH.

The Torah of YHWH gives a specific diet plan, in order to live and avoid health problems. It deems that which in considered Kosher or Clean for consumption, and that which is considered Unkosher or Dirty food not fit to be eaten. If you study the Statistics of people with food related health problems, you would see that 99.9% of the problem is found in foods eaten that are forbidden in the Torah to eat.

Below I will name the animals that are Kosher and un-Kosher and give a brief explanation of why they are forbidden.

[Animals of the Earth]

Wayyicra(Leviticus) Chapter11, "and Yahweh words to Moshe and to Aharon, saying to them, word to the sons of Yishra'ala, saying, 'these are the live beings you eat of all the animals on the earth: whatever Splits the hoof and cleaves the cleft of the hoof(cloven footed) and regurgitates the cud, among the animals, that you eat. only these EAT NOT: of them that regurgitate the cud or, or of them that split the hoof: as the Camel, though he regurgitates the cud, yet splits not the hoof; **he is foul to you.** *And the Coney, though he regurgitates the cud, yet splits not the hoof; he is foul to you: and the Hare, though he regurgitates the cud, yet split not the hoof; he is foul to you: and the Hog, though he splits the hoof, and cleaves the cleft of the hoof(Cloven footed), yet regurgitates not the cud; he is foul to you. Neither eat their flesh nor touch their carcase they are foul to you.*

[Animals of the Water]

vs 9-12, "These you eat of all in the waters: whatever has fins and scales in the waters-in the seas and in the Wadies(rivers) them you eat: and all with no fins and scales in the seas and in the Wadies-all that teem in the waters of any living soul in the waters, are an abomination to you: yes, they are an abomination to you: eat not of their flesh and abominate their carcases. Whatever in the waters has neither fins nor scales is an abomination to you.

[Foul of the Air]

vs 13-20, "and of the flyers, abominate these: eat them not-they are an abomination: the eagle and the ossifrage, and the osprey and the kite(vulture) and the hawk in species; every raven in species; and the daughter of the Owl and the night hawk and the cuckow and the hawk in species; and the little owl and the cormorant and the great owl and the swan and the pelican and the gier eagle, and the stork, the heron in species; and the hoopoe(lapwing) and the bat; all teemers that fly, going on all four, are an abomination to you.

[Insects]

vs 21-23, "only these: eat of every teemer going on all four having legs above their feet to leap with on the earth; of them, eat these: the locust in species and the beetle in species and the grasshopper in species. And all teemers that fly, having four feet, are an abomination to you.

[Others]

vs 27-28, "and whatever goes on his paws, among all live beings that go on all four, are foul to you....

vs 29-31, "and these are foul to you among the teemers teeming(creep) on the earth: the weasel and the mouse and the tortoise in species, and the shrieker and the chameleon and the lizard and the snail and the mole; these are foul to you among all teemers....."

vs 42, "whatever goes on the belly and whatever goes on all four or whatever abounds(has more) with feet among all teemers(creeping things) teeming on the earth, eat them not; for they are an abomination."

vs 44, "I -(am) Yahweh your Almighty: hallow yourselves and be holy; I-(am) holy: foul not your souls with any teemer creeping on the earth. I (am)Yahweh who ascended you from the land of Mitzraim, to become your Almighty: so you become holy; I (am) holy.

Kashrut(noun of Kosher) is one of the most distinguishing cultural customs of the Hebrews than any other culture. It is a Teaching of YHWH. When YHWH gave the instructions of Torah he knew the purpose of why it was necessary to follow. Mostly to protect us and help us live happy, healthy prosperous lives upon the earth. Yet if we are to go in the path YHWH has designed for us, we must began to dig deeper into the Torah by understanding the Purpose of the Torah teachings. Without a proper understanding of the *purpose* of the Torah teachings such as the Dietary laws, we will never be able to fully appreciate them and give proper value of them for our lives. We will never be able to live totally in accord with YHWH as far as our health is concerned.

Notice that the Dietary laws has nothing to do with our redemption. It is a teaching for an already redeemed community. The Torah Covenant Community who already knows YHWH.

Wayyicra(Leviticus) chapter 11 is a description of the kosher and non kosher foods we are to eat or disregard for food. It is the most detailed in the Torah.. The qualifications for a mammal to be kosher was that it had to *both* chew the cud and have split hooves(The cow for example). Yet some of the animals mentioned either only chew the cud and not have the split hooves or vise versa. For example, the pig splits the hoof but does not chew the cud.

All animals that split the hoof are known as *herbivores*, they are vegetation eaters. Making them healthier to eat than eating a meat eating animal. It helped the Hebrews to avoid certain bacteria and parasite that many times develop in meat eating animals. The hog or pig however was not only a vegetation eater, it was a meat eater or it ate basically anything of slop. This is called an *omnivore.*

This is why it was also necessary that the animal chew the cud. Animals who chew the cud have two or three stomachs that filter out potentially harmful bacteria and parasites in their food. They have very effective digestive systems. When they chew the cud, that means they vomit their food up several times as it goes through the different digestive tracts, and their stomach acids filter out the food.

The animals that don't chew the cud, eat whatever bacteria and parasites that is in their food which gets into their system and contaminates them. For example, pork was known to carry Trichinosis.

As far as the prohibition against the different fowl, and sea animals(such as shrimp, lobster shark, crabs or catfish), lizards and other rodents. These animals are known to be the scavengers of the earth. They were designed to be the garbage disposals of the earth. Therefore many of them, especially the forbidden sea animals, have high levels of toxin and cholesterol.

Therefore we must began to see their purpose in the whole of creation. We are not to eat the scavengers of the earth. They were not designed by YHWH for food. They are unclean. Without them our world would be full of excess waste and toxins which could be detrimental to our Kosher food, environment and our health.

Study the other dietary laws in D'barim(Deuteronomy) 14:3-21 and also found in Exodus. D'var instructs you specifically on the animals that are Kosher to eat. Pay close attention to Wayyicra and D'barim's instruction on the teachings of Kashrut. study them thoroughly. You may consult your Rabbi, Kohan, or a competent Hebrew leader concerning more indepth info on Kashrut. Under African Hebrew Yishra'ala tradition, it is not necessary to follow the customs of the Jewish Talmud on keeping Kashrut(i.e using separate dishes, separating meat from milk etc....)

[Vegetation/ the original Dietary Law]

Bereshit(Genesis) 1:29, "and the Almighty says, behold I give you every herb seeding seed on the face of all the earth; and every tree wherein is the fruit of a tree seeding seed; to be food to you and to every live being on the earth and to every flyer of the heavens and to every creeper on the earth wherein there is a living soul(I have given) every green herb for food: so be it"

Although YHWH has given instruction on the dietary Laws given through Moshe concerning the consumption of meat, we must understand that they are an inferior or secondary option to his people. Originally YHWH intended for his people to be vegetarians, as seen in Bereshit chapter one. Meat eating came as a result of Adamahs disobedience against YHWH and falling in the Garden of Eden. Adamah's fall therefore cause all mankind to become mortal, having the ability to die.

Notice that before the fall of Adamah, even the animals were vegetarian. That means scavengers and hunters are the results of a fallen man.

In the rule and Day of YHWH, meat eating will cease. We have a choice now whether we want to be vegetarian or meat eaters. It is up to us. The healthiest diet is the vegetarian diet(accompanied with the proper nutrients and supplements of a vegetation source). Yet regardless of which one we choose to follow we must respect one another as Hebrews and we must eat to live and keep ourselves healthy and strong before YHWH.

[Briefing of other Customs]

Study D'barim 6:4-9 for yourself

Israelites believes in the Total family under the Faith of YHWH. Fathers and mothers are to teach and instruct their children in the Way of YHWH. Not only by word of mouth and, but by their Hebrew lifestyle according to Torah. We are to make Torah apart of our daily lives. Everything we ration, everything we say should come from our heart as it is rooted and grounded in the Torah. We must live in such a way as a family and people that others will see us and desire to know the Torah.

As far as verse 8,

"and bind them for a sign on your hand and to become phylacteries between your eyes"

Bind is *Strongs* Hebrew #7194, **qashar**, which means, *"to tie or join together"*

Hand is *Strongs Hebrew #3027,* **Yad,** which means, *"a hand(the open one [indicating power, means and direction etc]...)*

Phylacteries is *Strongs Hebrew #2903,* **TowPhaPhah(tofafa),** which means, *"to go around or bind; a fillet for the forehead:-frontlet*

Between is *Strongs#996,* **beyn,** which mean, *"distinction(understand), among, asunder, at, between*

Eyes is *Strongs#5869,* **ayin,** which means, *"an eye(lit.or fig.):...-affliction, outward appearance..., countenance....,eye[brow]..., face...., presence...., resemblance, sight*

In the light of this the above could read,

And join them together as a sign upon your hand(as in a bracelet), and to become a fillet for your forehead(as in a wrapping) among your appearance(as in your dressing)

Traditional Hebrews understand this command to mean to wear cultural Hebrew ornaments on the hand(i.e the wrist) and wear clothes with Hebrew words of Torah and YHWH on them, especially African Cultural clothes.

This could also be symbolic to having the Torah leading you in the proper direction(hand) and giving you understanding and discernment(between your eyes).

[Doorpost-Zikrone]

Zikrone is a Hebrew word which is rooted in Zakar which means, *to remember.* We as Hebrew believers are commanded to put writings on our doorpost to remind us of YHWH and his Torah. I have realized that

YHWH is big on having us use our Minds and Rational to uphold and follow his Torah. YHWH gave us a brain with a heart(mind) to think and use wisely. He has given us knowledge and has given us the ability to use that knowledge effectively in our lives. Using knowledge effectively is called *Wisdom*. Wisdom and knowledge of the Eternal Creators will, both natural and spiritual, prepares and increases the Authority and Power of YHWH in ones life. Our Home is our Domain and the spiritual quality of that domain is dependant on the quality of Leadership within the home; The Male or Father being the head leader and the female or Mother being the Leader of Help *alongside* the Father. The **Zikrone** is given to be a reminder to follow the Torah instructions of YHWH in order to maintain that spiritual quality within and outside of the home; meaning in our every day lives.

[Fringes/Tzitzits]

*Numbers 15:37-40(JPS)1, The LORD(YHWH) said to Moshe as follows: Speak to the Israelite people and instruct them to make for themselves **Fringes** on the corner s of their garments throughout the ages; let them attach a cord of blue on the fringe at each corner. That shall be your fringe; look at it and recall all the commandments of the LORD(YHWH) and observe them, so that you do not follow your heart and eyes in your lustful urge. Thus you shall be reminded to observe all my commandments and be Holy to your God."*

This Teaches us that when we where the Fringes/Tzitzit, they are to be an agent in helping us from following our own hearts as opposed to YHWH's will. It reminds us to keep discipline and take authority over our lustful urge, also known as the Evil Impulse. We are given a free will. That means we can choose to follow our will to do good according to the Spirit of Holiness or we can follow our will to do wickedness according to the Evil Impulse. It's our choice. Yet though mankind leans more towards the

Evil Impulse because they lack the Spirit of Holiness, YHWH has given those who seek and desire to do right a reminder to wear, as they are led by the Spirit of Holiness. These are the Fringes/Tzitzits.

[Laws of Cleanliness and ritual purity]

Leviticus 10:10; chapters 12,13, 14 and 15; Deut 23:9-11; Yechezki'ala 22:26

Just as there are Laws and Teachings for Character, personality, morality, spirituality and worship, there are also teachings regarding personal physical hygiene, cleanliness and maintaining good health. These teachings are entwined into the concept of living life eternal and preventing unnecessary spreading of germs and disease among the community.

Many of the problems people face today, especially females with there many feminine problems, are the result of unclean and improper sexual and physical practices. As a result venereal disease cancers, and viruses are wide spread and common among euro-gentile society's or nations where Euro-gentiles have stamped their presence.

As a Pastoral Psychologist, I have met and counseled many women who have been diagnosed with various cervical forming cancers and disease(genital warts, herpes, chlamydia). Many of which are the consequences of having promiscuous, improper unclean sexual habits. For example, many women either fail to cease sexual activity on their menstrual cycle or fail to allow their menstrual cycle to complete the full seven days. The former usually have a flow of blood for about 3-4 days and then the flow of blood seems to stop. Yet although the blood has seemed to stop, the cycle is still in motion until a full seven days, with a normally healthy woman. So if a woman still in her cycle has sexual relations, when the blood or blood spots mixes with a man sexual fluid or sperm, it produces an acid like fluid called "pad" which films the female cervic, vagina or uterus(womb), which could eventually turn into a potentially deadly cancer such as H.I.P. P.I.D(Pelvic inflammatory Disease)

Not washing and cleansing the genital areas after sexual activity can spread germs and bacteria, or even produce yeast infections, rashes and dry brittle skin.

Proper bathing, hand washing(a.k.a. mikvahs-water immersions), Hygiene, and eating according to the Eternal Law of Yahweh, would provent virtually all the deathifying spreading of germs, bacteria and disease among people as we speak .

We are commanded to be in Holiness as Yahweh is Holiness, that is we are to be whole, complete and unique in ourselves and our every day practices in our daily lives. If our practices are hurting us as well as others, then regardless of what it is, it is unholy, that is unclean and dirty.

YeshiYah 1:16, "Wash yourself: purify and clean yourself; turn aside the evil of your exploitations

Yechezki'ala 36: 25, And I sprinkle pure water on you to clean and purify you: from all your foulness and filthiness and all your idols I clean and purify you

How we live our physical lives testify of who is associated with our spiritual lives. We are to separate and discern between Holiness and unholiness, clean and unclean as we are a living testimony in Yahweh and his Torah that Spiritually and physically we are clean and holy.

There are many other customs of the Hebrews, that shows forth our culture and Way of YHWH. If you would like to know more about the Hebrew faith, visit your nearest Hebrew Synagogue or House of Worship. Rabbi Tony McCraw(a.k.a. Shalomim HaLevi.)

[Israelite Family Structure]

Family is the Center of Israelite Living, Culture and Worship. Everything must be centered around one's *Family life.*.YHWH has established the proper order and structure of the Most prosperous family with each contributing by fulfilling his/her proper role:

I. YHWH first, for he is the essense of all life, the sustainer of all the elements of the Universe and the Ultimate LORD and Father of all his People Israel

II. YHWH's Anointed-*Ish*(Man of the Covenant relationship), for YHWH made Adamah in his Image after his likeness according to his will to establish and show forth the Light of Yah to the World of Darkness. Ish ben Adamah is the Divine seed giverof truth physically and Spiritually

III. YHWH's anointed's HELPER-*Ishah*(Woman/Women of the Covenant Relationship, For She/they is/are ordained to help, imitate and execute the Will of YHWH as revealed to YHWH's anointed-Ish who is made in the Image of Yah, after his likeness according to YHWH's will to establish and show forth the Light of Yah to the World of Darkness. Ishah is the Divine Seed reciever, bearer, nourisher and birther of Truth both Physically (Children) and Spiritually(the Word of Yah), as she is assistant to Yah's anointed(Ish)

a. When *Ishah* fulfills her proper role as a woman she has an instinctive anointing to bring out the glory/best/awesomeness of *Ish!!*

b. When *Ishah* fails to follow/fulfill the Structure/role placed *within* her by Yah, then she becomes the Chief destroyer and adversary to the Yah-Ish(Her man of Yah), and the plan and will of Yah, thereby side-lining her destiny and transforming her life into that of Satan Worship, possessing the rebellious spirit of Yezeba'al as manifest through the modern *Euro-Woman's rights movement!!!*

IV. The Seed of the Yah's Anointed and Yah's Anointed's Helper-*Na'ar*(Male child of the Covenant family) /*Na'arah*(female child of the Covenant Family.

a. They are to be trained up according to the Yah mind as recieved through Isha and Ishah in YHWH's Torah

b. They must be nurtured and sustained according to the Yah ordained Edenic culture of the Ben Adamahic family, which provides a positive spiritual atmosphere for intellectual, mental, physical and social and cultural growth in Yah's Torah, thus producing the Adamahic divine lineage.

[Patriarchal Family and-Polygany]

Unlike the Western and Euro-gentile cultures and family structures, the Eastern and African cultures was centered around a Patriarchal styled Family. This family as described previously has the Male as the Head of the Household, with the Woman(en) as the Helper or Assistance and polygany was common. Many of the strongest nations in ancient times were nations who were known to practice polygany, that is a household with One man and more than one Woman/Wife/helpmeet.

Even today many of the strongest structured families are polyganist. In Euro-gentile cultures polygany is looked down upon with disdain and is passed on as socially unacceptable. In most countries it is Illegal, as in America, the pseudo-democratic society where family and personal freedom is a chasing after the wind and government controlled.

Yet it has been pointed out that Christians practiced polygamy at least until the 19th century, when it was legally outlawed according to the "Congrssional Act. March 3, 1887; U.S.R.S1. SUPP. 568; and U.S Supreme Court Case, 186 U.S.1.

Euro-Jews practiced polygany up until the ninth century when Ashkenazic Rabbi Gershom gave a degree to ban polygany among Jews because of the German culture. However Saphardim Jews and African Hebrew Israelites disregard Euro-gentile degrees and maintain polygany as Socially and Spiritually acceptable at all times. Why? Because it is apart our Cultural and Spiritual Heritage from the Torah and our fore-fathers of Yishra'ala. In essence it is a Yah ordained practice.

Yosef A.A Ben Yochannan in his book, *We the Black Jews,* volumes 1 and 2, 1993, Black Classic Press, Comments about the polygamous practice of the Ethiopian Beta Yishra'ala, states:

"There is no Law against Polygamy in the Sacred Torah, neither is there any on Monogamy. But there are many directed suggestions in the same Sacred Torah and Holy Scriptures which support Polygamny against Monogamy"

In Light of this there is many examples of the Torah Stressing polygamous relationships whenever a Israelite had more than one wife whether for good or bad. Yet you never hear it mentioned when some-one had one wife.

Many of Yah's anointed personages such as Abraham, Yitzkak and Ya'akob, Gideon, Elqanah, Shemuels Father The High-Priest Yah-Yada, David, Shlomo etc.. had many wives and they were acounted to be righteous men even when they Died(Bereshit 4:23; 26:34; 29:9; Judges 8:30-32; I Shamuel 1:1-2; 25:42-43; 27:3; 2Chronicle 24:3

*2Chronicles 24:2, 15, "And Yah'ash works straight in the eyes of YHWH all the days of Yah'Yada the Priest: and Yah'Yada takes two women and births sons and daughters....and Yah'Yada ages, satisfied of days and he dies; a son of a hundred and thirty years when he dies: and they entomb him among the Kings in the City of Davyid, **Because he Worked good in Yishra'ala both toward Allah'im and Toward his House***

Notice that this High Priest of Yishra'ala is a Highly Honored Man who worked good towards Yahweh and his House hold, that is his two Wives and his Children. This was such an honor that he was buried with the Kings of Yishra'ala, who also practiced polygamy also. Read the Story of this Powerful Priest preceding these verses above.

The Torah itself sanctions polygamy and even give instructions for avoiding abuses in Polygamous relationships.

*D'bar 21:15 "**When a man has two women**, one beloved and one hated, and they birth him sons-both the beloved and the hated; and if the first birth son be hers that was hated: then so be it, the day his sons inherit what he has, that he cannot make the son of the beloved first birth face the son of the hated firstbirth: but he recognizes the son of the hated as the firstbirth..."*

Shemot 21:7-11 gives the instruction on a father sending his daughter out to be a maiden, maid servant or wife to a man or a mans son. It then gives the instruction on how the Man, her Ish or Adoni should deal with her in cases of Misconduct. If he does marry her as his own and then takes another woman to be his wife, then he cannot reduce her sexual and emotional needs, clothing or food. If he does fail to obey these three basic needs, then she is authorized by Torah to Divorce and Leave the Relationship.

Therefore the Torah does stress the concern and provides the protection for proper treatment of women in polygamous relationships in Israelite culture.

YeshiYah 4:1-2, "In that day, seven women take hold of one man, saying, We eat our own bread and enrobe our own apparel: only call us by your name, to gather our reproach. In that day, the sprout of Yahweh is splendid and honorable and the fruit of the earth for pomp and adornment for the escapees of Yisrael"

Remember, that the Chosen people to be a Light unto the World, the Ultimate Messiah and Bearers of Divine Truth, the Israelites would not be in existence had it not been for their four mothers, Leah, Rackayl and their two hand-maidens(Bereshit 29:31-35; 30:1-25). We were born out of polygany

[Polygany vs Monogamy]

The Western Euro-gentile Marriage is a money making Commercial Marriage or licence. In reality it means nothing, except to make sure you pay the right amount of taxes to the government and make sure you don't get as much benefit if you need to get welfare assistance.

The mental thinking of Most American peoples is grossly distorted when it comes to polygany and their commercial marriage has become just like the capitalist industry....Stingy and selfish!! Only concerned with themselves as opposed to what the purpose of true marriage really is.

Thats why adultery, jealousy, rage, and domestic violence and even murder is commonly reaking havoc among Western commercial

Marriages and relationships. This is non-existent in Israelite Polygany and other African Nations because it is the norm of the Communities and strength is found in our families.

However Polygany is left up to the individuals together to choose polygany or monogamy as their relational practice.

The American and Euro-gentile banning of polygany is just another example of the Satanic influence and system trying to prevent the rise of the Life-style of Torah, the Foundation of the Kingdom of Yah. They know the power, unity and strength of a sound Polygamous community, both financially, economically, and family wise.

Also the banning of polygany is a racial/prejudice issue and also a total disrespect of other cultures, predominately african-asian cultures. This basically prevents black peoples of Africa from being able to come to AmeriKKKa to live because they would be denied entrance based on their Religious and cultural/ ethnic background.

What a hypocrite Euro-gentile America is. There is still no equality nor Justice and the Supreme court nor the Senate or the Presidents are concerned with correcting it. Why? Because they don't give a care about African Matters or Black peoples period!!!

In Other words, we are being discriminated against and denied our rights because of our Religious cultural and ethnic background and beliefs, a violation of our constitutional rights.....Or does the constitution apply to blacks, Africans and Israelite Citizens of America? Selah.

Think about it. Gays and lesbians can get married legally in many states. even within much of Judaism, Homosexual Marriages are sanctioned and performed against the commands of Torah, but Righteous loving Torah Practicing polygamist can't practice it on pangs of Bigamy and a Felony that will land you in Jail as a Criminal. Yet polygamy stands as morally correct according to the Torah!!!! Now whats wrong with that picture?

Many will say that Monogamy protects the Woman, but in Truth monogamy protects the man and by Law he is permitted to be irresponsible when it comes to sex and family and not have one ounce of accountability.

He is permitted to practice an unrestrained loose polygamy fulfilling his every fleshly need and then walking away without any thoughts, leaving the woman to suffer.

The male dominated Euro-gentile society, while it allows men to play around, also opens the demonic doors for women to get easy abortions or obtain birth control thereby mentally luring her into the world of sexual promiscuity.

Yet the Woman is the one who usually has to go through the suffering of the pain and physical and mental effects of abortion and the side effects of birth control and the head-aches and body aches of feminine problems and venereal disease. Man continues to enjoy himself and fulfill his perverted fantasies.

Polygany is outlawed by this Euro-gentile male society because it would make men own up to their actions and be held accountable for what they do and make them be responsible Men and Fathers, thereby protecting the "women" and "Children" involved!!!

The Child support enforcement plan they have for men today is just a run around to destroy good men along with the bad ones and let the mothers use the government to get over on the male authority, therefore actually promoting women to be whores and producing bastard children, because they know that they can depend on the Euro-gentile government to go after the father(who may not even be the real father) to pay up and support "them(the mother)" for their hair dues, their weekly crab boils, and their ghetto dressing clothes for the clubs, while their Children live in poverty with nappy hair, dirty nose and filthy clothes.

Then they have the governments authority by natural right to tell the father when he can and cannot see his children and then use it in court against him as being a dead beat father. Then when the mother does get her money, she then prepares to lure the next victim into her chambers to get into his pockets and like a lustful fool he his, he uses his other head and then ends up in the cycle of Euro-Life. Selah

So most of the adult people involved really victimized themselves because they chose to follow the euro-gentile way of life. But the true victims in these scenarios is the Children!!

America allows three types of loose relationships, pseudo-polygamy: 1. *Serial Polygamy*, that is a man or woman marries, divorce, marry again, divorce, marry, divorce. 2. A man married to one woman, but having affairs with one or more mistresses in whom he has not obligation. 3. An unmarried man having numerous mistresses. Also known as a *Player.*

I believe that the whole concept of Freedom and life in America needs to be re-thought...Because it just does not exist for many of us. And yet we sit back and let the government have their way with our lives, without voicing objection or protest!!!! Signs of an enslaved people.

Polygany the choice for the strong generations of families and nations!!!

[Dynamics of Praise and Worship]

Psalms 29:1-2, "Give to Yahweh, oh you sons of El(The Almighty); give to Yahweh honor (glory) and strength; give to Yahweh the honor of his name: prostrate(praise) to Yahweh in the majesty (Beauty) of his Holies(Holiness)"

Psalms 105:1-3, "O Spread hands to Yahweh; call on his name; make known his exploits among the people: sing to him; psalm to him; meditate of all his marvels; Halal in his Holy name; the heart of them who seeks Yahweh cheers."

As Sons and Daughters of Humanity, we must understand our deep spiritual roots in YHWH. We must began to see that we were created to Worship in our every day lives. Worship is built within us as the essence of our whole being. Yet we also have a will to decide of whom will we worship. No matter whether we worship YHWH or not, we end up worshiping, toiling and laboring for something or someone. It is very abnormal for one to cease to worship. Because YHWH's Glory has been hidden for a time from the whole of Humanity, very few people know him, and as a result various deity's and idols are worshiped and given adoration. This is expected of mankind who doesn't know YHWH. The beauty of the various and although paganistic worship styles and religions is that they are reaching out and searching for the real Eternal Creator. They desire to Worship and praise. This is even true of Christianity and their worship of Zeus (or Jesus). They are very sincere and many have strong characteristics of holiness, goodness, and spirituality. Yet millions of peoples have been lead astray of knowing YHWH, from generation to generation. But no matter how much Hasatan has deceived the many from knowing and Worshiping and working for YHWH, he has never been able to succeed in Stopping Worship. The closest he's gotten is setting him self up to be praised and worshiped by people through various means, like idols, mythological god worship(i.e Zeus, Osiris, Nimrod) Nature Worship and Astrology, Mediums, witchcraft, violence, oppression, destruction of the earths natural resources and the working toiling and laboring of people and governments towards tools, weapons and products to destroy one another etc...

Yet in this day YHWH is once again revealing himself. He desires that humanity turn and worship him, the true Eternal Creator. When we recognize the mercy and goodness of YHWH and all of the trials and tribulations he has brought us through to be victorious, we can truly spread our hand to YHWH and give him thanks. When we understand the Power and wonderfulness of his name and what his name has done in our lives, only then can we cheer and dance and rejoice in him.

We can't Praise YHWH correctly unless we are worshiping him how he desires us to Worship him. We worship YHWH with our lifestyle and our obedience to his Torah, Word and will. The fruit of our lives tell who we really worship. Our Spirituality, Ethics, Covenant relationship and knowledge of the Eternal will all make up how we worship. We must began to develop a passion to know YHWH and be like him, through our prayers, meditations, study and purpose fulfillment. As we submit to the guidance of the Shekinah of YHWH and teach others to do so, we enrich ourselves spiritually and YHWH's blessings are bestowed upon us.

Our Praise and adoration of YHWH should be on a continuous and daily bases. Regardless of situation or issues we face, we must lift up the name of YHWH. This is our strength and our song to last and live life to the fullest as we are alive. Without YHWH's praise in our lives we are a dying people headed for utter destruction and misery. Praise and worship of YHWH can bring real change within our Communities, our Nation and the World. As our leaders are influenced by the Praise and Worship of YHWH, they can receive his Shekinah and began to lead our economy to a more prosperous level. When we Praise and Worship YHWH, it continuously reminds us of our relationship and responsibility of being a true light and priest unto the nations and of our perfecting the World according to Ethical monotheism.

Avot 2:13a-c(The Mishna) "Rabbi Simeon says, 'be meticulous in the recitations of the Shema and the Prayer. And when you pray, don't treat your praying as a matter of routine, but let it be a plea for mercy and supplication before the Omnipresent, blessed be he.'"

[Symbols of Praise]

If one would began to observe their surroundings and see the nature of things, they would see that the earth and nature itself testifies of YHWH. Observe the way the grass and trees grow. They grow in such a way that when they are at their peak or glory, they look like they are spreading toward heaven in a "Y" Shape. The branches of a tree even branch out in "Y" shapes. When and eagle or any kind of fowl soars towards the heavens, they too look as if they are spreading hand to form a "Y". Observe other peoples in worship. When they lift their hands up to Worship in a church, synagogue, mosque or whatever, what do they look like? A "Y"! I see this and many other examples as pointing to the Truth of YHWH the Eternal Creator. The Heavens and the earth and all within it declaring the truth his glory.

I see the grass as it is mowed constantly saying, "know matter how much you cut me down, I will grow again to praise YHWH". An that is the real truth! no matter what people say about us or how they treat us or how lowly they try to make us, we as the Torah Covenant Community must shine and show forth the praise and worship of YHWH and live his Torah as living witness

If the Heaven and earth are witnesses to the greatness of YHWH, how much more we as Human beings have the responsibility of being witnesses of his greatness and majesty!!!!

[Finding our purpose in life-Destiny]

Purpose is defined as," *the reason you were created".* Your purpose is your destiny and your destiny is why you were purposed. Without a knowledge of purpose or why Yahweh made us the way he made us, we are on the cutting edge of darkness and lifeless breathing. Purpose and meaning to life is found in the Source of all life, the Eternal Creator Yahweh. And in order to see and receive the guidance of our purpose and Yahwehs will for our lives, we must look within ourselves and find the meeting place of our spirit with Yahwehs spirit. We must become one with the Creator in order to have a sense of destiny and a guide of right direction on this journey in life. We all, regardless of who we are, are apart of a bigger plan Yahweh has for all creation and we must began to tap into that plan, if we are to live a meaningful life in the earth. When we fail to live as we are to be, we fail to leave a smooth pathway of knowledge and learning for the next generation to inherit and likewise grow. Therefore offsetting the plans of Yahwehs authority through mankind to be established effectively, leading to a threat of human destruction. Many peoples face fear, asocial habits, and low esteem in who they are and where they came from. Many are ashamed of themselves and how they are looked upon by society. Why? Because they have failed to search for who they really are in Yahweh. When one taps into their purpose, nothing anyone says or does can affect them negatively or hinder them from reaching their goals. Yet for one to truly seek Yahweh for their destiny and purpose, they must become students of Yahweh. They must be taught. That is why Yahweh has established teachers of his Word; Kohanim, Rabbis and Ministers of Torah. Seek Yahweh's appointed and learn from his anointed who are ordained to help you reach your goals and release your potential and unleash the unlimited power and authority Yahweh has placed in your life. Learn from the examples of Davyid, Ala'sha(Elisha) and other forefathers of the Hebrew Israelites and how they grew to be great in what Yahweh purpose them to be. Yahweh is there for you and he calls out to you, To come, ingraft yourselves and grow in his Torah and teachings so that you too will have what it takes to be a leader of tomorrow by choosing Yahweh and the Israelite faith Today!!!!

B'ruch Hashem YHWH

About the Author

Rabbi Shalomim Yahoshua HaLevi Ph.D(former slave name Anthony McCraw), 10-31-76, a native of Jacksonville Florida, graduated in 94' from Ribault Sr. High and attended Jacksonville Theological Seminary where he received his B.A. in Psychology in Oct 96'. He Received his Ordination and Masters of Hebrew Education from the Institute of Rabbinical and Hebrew Studies of Jerusalem Yisrael in March 98' and received his Doctorate Degree from Universal Life Theological College in August of 2000.

Dr Shalomim is fruitful with Three Sons of Light, HaNasi Mashiakh-Kohane(12-27-97), Meshakh Yahqim-Shalom(6-18-99) and Yishai HaRukhamah-Ammi(5-3-00). HaNasi and Meshakh's Native Emmah, Alef Ishah, Rackayl Yah-Ishah HaLevi and Yishai's Native Emmah, Bet Ishah, Ribekah Bat-Sheba HaLevi, both establishing the Strength of Israelite Family-hood!!

Rabbi is also a praise and worship leader, a Mystical(Charismatic) prophetic Hebrew Moreh, exorter, National Interfaith Lecturer, and Chief Kohane and establisher Beth Kalamath Kazyinuth(Formely Visions of Dreams) Orthodox Cushite Hebrew Int'l inc.

He is a Reseacher, Hebrew Scholar and fan of Ancient Biblical Archaeology. More so, Shalomim is a compassionate Leader and Father who has a love and life-long dedication to Yahweh, establishing and restoring the Yisraelite Community/family to be a light and blessing to ALL peoples!!!

Appendix

Statement of Faith for Israelite Torah Covenant Community

Appendix I

1. We believe in the UNITY of YHWH and monotheism in the strictest degree

2. We believe in the Shema as stated in Deuteronomy 6:4, "Shema Yisrael YHWH Allahenu, YHWH Echad.......*Listen Yishra'ala the Eternal our Strength Yahweh is One"!!!*

3. We believe with perfect faith that besides YHWH there is on other Creator to be worshiped, revered or adoration given to. YHWH "only" is the Savior of man-kind and whoso-ever calls upon his name alone shall be delivered(YeshiYah-Isaiah 44:6; 45:5-6,15,21; 46:9; Yah'ala 2:32)

4. We believe that the Tanakh(Torah and Hebrew scriptures) is the inspired "Word and progressive revelation of YHWH"

5. We believe that the Talmud (Oral Torah) & B'rith Chadasha of Ya'akob(James) and the Dead Sea Scrolls writings "only" are authoritative for the basis of study, doctrine and history as they illuminate and line up with the Hebrew scriptures which brings freedom(Ya'akov 1:25)

6. We believe that Yisrael (the Hebrews), having been 1st to recognize YHWH, hath received a special revelation of his will with the mission of being his chosen Priest among the nations to lead them in truth and deliverance

7.We believe that the nation of Yisrael(the Hebrew Israelites) is the anointed-one (Mashiakh) spoken by YeshiYah and are the sons and daughters of YHWH by adoptionism, and that our purpose and teachings are inspired to turn the nations to YHWH through repentance and bringing them to Torah observance. Both Hebrew and goyim(gentile) are all Sons and Daughters of YHWH in his Torah covenant

8. We believe in the Prophetic renewal and the immersing of Ruakh HaKodesh that leads to Torah Observance (Numbers 11:29:YaHayl[Joel] 2:28,29;)

9. We believe in the communion and fellowship of the African-American, Israelites and Jewish communities.

10.We Believe in Equipping the Total person-hood (soul-spirit, body) with the Torah of YHWH to establish the Kingdom of YHWH according to Israelite Torah Covenant Community.

11.We Believe with perfect faith that the Creator YHWH rewards those that keep his teachings and principles and punishes those who transgress them, yet because of love, grace, and mercy he convicts and gives transgressors time to repent of their iniquities against him

12.We believe with perfect faith in the coming of an individual King Mashiakh ben David who will be anointed by a Priestly-Prophet Mashiakh and though he/They tarry we will daily wait for his/their coming. Whom-ever Mashiakh is, YHWH will reveal it to his chosen ones of Yisrael without deceit. Ha Mashiakhim will be born of two African-Edenic Hebrew Israelites.

13.We believe with perfect faith that there will be a resurrection of the dead at a time when it will please YHWH; some to everlasting life and reward and some to punishment and utter destruction

14. We believe that Torah Covenant Community is the"true" Ultimate and Universal Faith and Spiritaul Culture of YHWH the one true Creator of Abraham, Yitz'kak, and Ya'akob.

Guiding Principles for "Israelite Torah Covenant Community"

Appendix II

ITCC and its foundations

I. NATURE OF ITCC

ITCC is the biblical/historical/spiritual &religious experience of the Hebrew people. As an unbroken chain of living tradition, it links all the generations of Yisrael, giving them aim and direction.....The message of ITCC is "Universal", aiming at the perfection of all mankind under the sovereignty of YHWH

II. Israelite Torah Covenant Community

The primary object of Israelite Torah Covenant Community is to first restore the true name of our Creator(YHWH) and correct unproper titles and pronunciations of his Holy name (such as Hashem, Adonai, The LORD, and God, Allah'im) so that people may know whom they worship without ignorance, and that a spiritual revival will come and YHWH will pour out his Ruakh HaKodesh and cause a world repentance and a return to his TORAH and WORD. Secondly is to restore the Africaness to Torah and Torah to the Black peoples (and other peoples) by reviving the true Cushite-Shemite(African) history and cultures within the Hebrew scriptures through teaching and education.

III. YHWH (Eternal Creator)

The heart of the Israelite Torah Covenant Community is its doctrine of Ethical Monotheism, affirming that in the living Eternal Creator(YHWH) all existence has its creative source and unity, and all mankind its inspiring ideal and pattern of conduct.

IV. MAN (Adamah)

Israelite Torah Covenant Community regards man as created in the image of YHWH and endowed with moral freedom and responsibility, and that the purpose, Image and lineage of Adamah in its fullness through the Israelite Community is the pattern that Yahweh has designed for all gentiles to adopt

V. IMMORTALITY

The divine in man is the "spirit-soul". As the source of our life YHWH is the ground of our immortality. Union with him bridges for us the chasm of death

VI. Israelite Torah Covenant Community is the Culture and Community of TORAH;

With its message of revealed instruction and teaching. Torah for the ITCC represents the "Progressive Word of YHWH"and the whole body of progressive religious/Cultural values (accompanied with Tanakh, Oral Torah, and Ya'akov writings). It preserves the historical norms, precedents and sanctions of Hebrew behavior and seeks to guide and to mold Jew life In the pattern of Holiness and of good-ness, yet for one to truly understand the true spirit of the Torah and its revelation, one must seek the Ruakh-HaKodesh of YHWH which is the Essence of Hebrewness of Israelite Torah Covenant Community with power behind YHWH's Torah.

VII. Torah is the Soul of which Yisrael is the body; Living in all parts of the world many European and "other intermarried" Jews have been held together by ties of inherited/Converted historical association and by Judaism's(a Form of YaHudaism-the worship of Yahweh) faith and ethical monotheism. "America's Black peoples" however, and although cut off due to oppressions, false teachings and deceit, will be fully restored to their rightful biblical heritage as received through Abraham, Yitz'kak, Ya'akov, Solomon and the Queen of Sheba, Yahudah(Judah), Yosef, Benyamin, as the Lost but restored tribe and children of Yisrael. Just as the inter-married Jew has become apart of the house-hold of The Hebrew faith, so does "any" non-Hebrew (Gentile) who accepts our faith and ethical idealism (Isa 56).

Ethical Torah Covenant Community

I. ITCC emphasizes the sanctity and worth of human personality and the right of the individual to life, freedom of conscience and to the pursuit of his calling and vocation within the moral sphere. Justice to all, irrespective of racial, sectarian or class difference, represents the inalienable right and the inescapable obligation of all

II. ITCC seeks to advance the perfection of humanity by applying the Prophetic principles for Torah, Justice, Love, and brotherhood to social as well as personal relationships, to social order, to industry and commerce and to international affairs. It aims at the total elimination of misery and suffering, of poverty and degradation, of tyranny and slavery, of prejudices, ill-will and ware-fare and economical disadvantages within the inner-cities

III. The vitality of Israelite Torah Covenant Community depends on the preservation of: the Tanakh (Hebrew scriptures), Oral Torah and Ya'akovs B'rith Chadasha observance, of the Ruakh HaKodesh of YHWH in ones life, the religious year, the Shabbat and the Holy-days, upon The education of the black Hebrew peoples and upon the unbuilding of the black and Israelite homes by the hollowing power of religious observance and Spirit of YHWH

IV. PRAYER is the life breath of Spirituality and faith, the concrete expression and aspiration. The exercise of prayer brings YHWH nearer to our lives in fellowship and relationship

YHWH's Israelite Torah Covenant Community

Printed in the United States
23838LVS00005B/92